T0301248

Globalization and the Small Open Economy

NEW HORIZONS IN INTERNATIONAL BUSINESS

General Editor: Peter J. Buckley
Centre for International Business,
University of Leeds (CIBUL), UK

The New Horizons in International Business series has established itself as the world's leading forum for the presentation of new ideas in international business research. It offers pre-eminent contributions in the areas of multinational enterprise – including foreign direct investment, business strategy and corporate alliances, global competitive strategies, and entrepreneurship. In short, this series constitutes essential reading for academics, business strategists and policy makers alike.

Titles in the series include:

Multinationals, Technology and National Competitiveness
Marina Papanastassiou and Robert Pearce

Globalizing America
The USA in World Integration
Edited by Thomas L. Brewer and Gavin Boyd

Information Technology in Multinational Enterprises
Edited by Edward Mozley Roche and Michael James Blaine

A Yen for Real Estate
Japanese Real Estate Investment Abroad – From Boom to Bust
Roger Simon Farrell

Corporate Governance and Globalization
Long Range Planning Issues
Edited by Stephen S. Cohen and Gavin Boyd

The European Union and Globalisation
Towards Global Democratic Governance
Edited by Brigid Gavin

Globalization and the Small Open Economy
Edited by Daniel Van Den Bulcke and Alain Verbeke

Entrepreneurship and the Internationalisation of Asian Firms
An Institutional Perspective
Henry Wai-chung Yeung

The World Trade Organization in the New Global Economy
Trade and Investment Issues in the Millennium Round
Edited by Alan M. Rugman and Gavin Boyd

Japanese Subsidiaries in the New Global Economy
Edited by Paul W. Beamish, Andrew Delios and Shige Makino

China and its Regions
Economic Growth and Reform in Chinese Provinces
Edited by Mary-Françoise Renard

Emerging Issues in International Business Research
Edited by Masaaki Kotabe and Preet S. Aulakh

Globalization and the Small Open Economy

Edited by

Daniel Van Den Bulcke

*Professor of International Management and Development,
Institute of Development Policy and Management,
University of Antwerp, Ghent University and Catholic
University at Leuven (KUL), Belgium*

and

Alain Verbeke

*Professor of International Business and Public Policy,
Solvay Business School, University of Brussels (VUB),
Belgium and Associate Fellow, Templeton College,
University of Oxford, UK and McCaig Chair in
Management, University of Calgary, Canada*

NEW HORIZONS IN INTERNATIONAL BUSINESS

Edward Elgar
Cheltenham, UK • Northampton, MA, USA

Published by
Edward Elgar Publishing Limited
Glensanda House
Montpellier Parade
Cheltenham
Glos GL50 1UA
UK

Edward Elgar Publishing, Inc.
136 West Street
Suite 202
Northampton
Massachusetts 01060
USA

A catalogue record for this book
is available from the British Library

Library of Congress Cataloguing in Publication Data

Globalization and the small open economy / edited by Daniel Van Den Bulcke and
Alain Verbeke.
    p. cm. — (New horizons in international business)
  "This research volume results from a conference at the University of Antwerp,
Belgium ... to honour Professor John H. Dunning"—Pref.
  Includes index.
    1. International economic integration. 2. States, Small—Economic
integration—Congresses. 3. States, Small—Economic policy—Congresses. 4.
International business enterprises—Congresses. 5. Globalization—Congresses.
I. Bulcke, D. Van Den. II. Verbeke, Alain. III. Dunning, John H. IV. Series.

HF1418.5 .G58186 2001
337—dc21
                                                                    2001023779

ISBN 1 84064 729 9

Printed and bound in Great Britain by MPG Books Ltd, Bodmin, Cornwall

This book is the result of a conference organized to honour the immense contribution of John Dunning to the field of international business

Contents

Figures

Tables

Contributors

Buysse, Kristel, Economic Advisor, Research Department, National Bank of Belgium, Belgium.

Campbell, Alexandra, Associate Professor, Schullich School of Business, York University, Canada.

Coeck, Chris, Professor of Public Policy, University of Antwerp, Belgium.

De Beule, Filip, Research Assistant, Institute of Development Policy and Management, University of Antwerp, Belgium.

Dunning, John H., State of New Jersey Professor of International Business, Rutgers University, USA and Emeritus Professor, University of Reading, UK.

Duysters, Geert, Professor, Faculty of Technology Management, Technical University Eindhoven, The Netherlands.

Hagedoorn, John, Professor, Faculty of Economics and Business Administration, MERIT, Maastricht University, The Netherlands.

Hens, Luc, Professor, Free University of Brussels and University of Antwerp, Belgium.

Moon, Hwy-Chang, Assistant Professor, SIAS, Seoul National University, Korea.

Rugman, Alan M., Thames Water Fellow, Templeton College, University of Oxford, England.

S'Jegers, Rosette, Professor, Director Centre for Business Economics and Strategic Management, Free University of Brussels, Belgium.

Scheerlinck, Ilse, Professor, Centre for Business Economics and Strategic Management, Free University of Brussels, Belgium.

Sleuwaegen, Leo, Professor, Faculty of Applied Economics, University of Leuven and Vlerick Leuven Ghent Management School, Belgium.

Van Den Bulcke, Daniel, Professor of International Management and Development, Institute of Development Policy and Management, University of Antwerp, Ghent University and Catholic University at Leuven (KUL), Belgium van Wegberg, Marc, Assistant Professor, Faculty of Economics and Business Studies, Maastricht University, The Netherlands.

van Witteloostuijn, Arjen, Professor, Faculty of Economics, Department of International Economics and Business, University of Groningen, The Netherlands.

Verbeke, Alain, Professor of International Business and Public Policy, Solvay Business School, Free University of Brussels, University of Antwerp, University of Louvain la Neuve, Belgium, Associate Fellow, Templeton College, University of Oxford, UK, McCaig Chair in Management, University of Calgary, Canada (as of Fall 2001).

Veugelers, Reinhilde, Professor, Faculty of Applied Economics, University of Leuven, Belgium.

Zhang, Haiyan, Research Assistant, Institute of Development Policy and Management, University of Antwerp, Belgium.

Preface

This research volume results from a conference at the University of Antwerp, Belgium that had two goals. First, it honoured Professor John H. Dunning on the occasion of his receiving an honorary degree from the University of Antwerp in recognition of outstanding academic work on how multinational enterprises function. Second, the conference aimed to investigate the specific role of small open countries in the globalizing economic system by bringing together some of the principal researchers on international business studies in Belgium, the Netherlands and Luxembourg.

Since 1958, John Dunning has been a leader in the field of international business. That year marked the publication of his book, *American Investment in British Manufacturing Industry*, a detailed empirical analysis in an area of applied economics characterized by extremely scarce data. This important work established the basis for a number of studies about American and other foreign direct investment in host countries. What is more, the book preceded by almost ten years the influential and (from the host country's perspective) alarming bestseller of Jean Jacques Servan Schreiber about the challenge of American investment in Europe.

Today, almost sixty monographs and two hundred and fifty articles and book chapters later, John Dunning has become the world's most prominent figure in the academic discipline of international business and international management. His research in the 1960s was mainly of an empirical nature, but by the 1970s, it became more conceptually oriented. His theoretical writing was instrumental to diffusing the now widely accepted view that international trade and foreign direct investment should be regarded as alternative forms of international corporate activities. As early as 1973, Professor Dunning analyzed the determinants of international production, that is multinational enterprises (MNEs). In an influential contribution of 1976, presented at the Nobel Symposium in honor of Bertil Ohlin, John Dunning combined several theories on foreign direct investment and multinational enterprises in a systemic approach which he called the 'eclectic theory' or the OLI paradigm because it is based on the presence of three types of advantages: ownership, location and internalization.

Since 1987, Professor Dunning has continuously refined the eclectic theory, and adapted it to new developments in international business such as the rise of strategic asset-seeking activities of MNEs, alliance capitalism and network formation.

In addition to his many contributions to theory development, John Dunning has had a substantive impact on economic policy, more particularly on the ways policy makers in national governments and international organizations interact with multinational enterprises in an era of rapidly expanding multinational business activities. As long ago as the early 1970s, he was a member of the group of eminent persons established by the United Nations to formulate measures to cope with the vacuum in international regulations with regard to foreign direct investment. With a few others he was instrumental in creating the Centre on Transnational Corporations (CTC) in 1974, and is still active as Senior Economic Advisor to UNCTAD, an organization that has adopted the objectives and assumed the activities of the CTC.

John Dunning's enormous academic influence extends far beyond his writing and lectures. Over the years he has greatly assisted a very large number of doctoral students by participating in doctoral tutorials and providing direct advice. This contribution to the establishment of countless careers cannot be overestimated.

The editors and authors are proud to dedicate this book to Professor John Dunning. This research volume's focus on comparative institutional thinking, the cornerstone of most excellent international business research today, owes a great deal to the work John H. Dunning conducted during a period that spans more than 40 years. His rigorous thinking and sustained scientific output have established Professor Dunning as the world's leading scholar in the field of international business.

The editors are grateful to the authors who have contributed to the successful completion of this project and to Patricia Franck who prepared the final manuscript and the camera ready copy. The editors also acknowledge Elsevier's permission to publish the article by Hwy Chang Moon, Alan Rugman and Alain Verbeke which appeared in *International Business Review*, Volume 7, 1998, (2), pp. 135-150.

Antwerp, December 2000.

1. Globalization and the Small Open Economy: An Introduction

Daniel Van Den Bulcke and Alain Verbeke

This research volume results from a conference at the University of Antwerp, Belgium. This conference had two goals. First, to honor Professor John H. Dunning for his lifetime academic work on the functioning of multinational enterprises through the award of an honorary doctorate. Second, to investigate the specific role of small open countries in a globalizing economic system, through bringing together some of the main researchers on international business studies in the Benelux.

Conventionally, two key differences have often been identified between, on the one hand, large nations such as the United States, Germany and Japan and, on the other hand, smaller open economies. This is shown in Figure 1.1. Here, the vertical axis investigates the reliance of home governments on domestic policies, to foster national economic development. This reliance can be weak or strong. On the horizontal axis, the reliance of firms on their domestic base to achieve global competitiveness is visualized: this reliance can again be weak or strong. It has often been observed in the academic literature that governments of large economic systems tend to rely primarily on domestic policies to foster national economic development and have firms which largely build upon their domestic home base to achieve global competitiveness. This would position both large nations and their multinational enterprises in quadrant 4 of Figure 1.1. In contrast, it has also often been argued that smaller economic systems are characterized by governments which rely much more on international economic policy to foster national economic development and that firms from small open economies rely to a much larger extent on host countries as a source of competitive advantage. This would position small nations and their multinational enterprises in quadrant 1 of Figure 1.1. One of the main contributions of several chapters in this research volume is that increasingly all actors operating in global environments, including large nations' governments and multinational enterprises are being forced to shift from quadrant 4 towards quadrant 1. Indeed, sole reliance on a domestic home base and domestic policies to guarantee competitiveness are no longer sufficient.

If the single home base approach increasingly loses relevance, even for firms from large nations, the important question arises how multinational enterprises (MNEs) should, at the micro-level, use the concept of 'location advantages' in their strategy formation, especially in this era of knowledge-seeking foreign entry. Recent work in economic geography suggests that, even within a single country, whether small or large, economic activities are characterized by a specific level of geographic dispersion/concentration. Krugman (1991a, 1991b, 1998) has argued that three forces exist which foster concentration and three forces which stimulate dispersion.

Figure 1.1   *Conventional perspectives of large and small nations on the sources of international competitiveness*

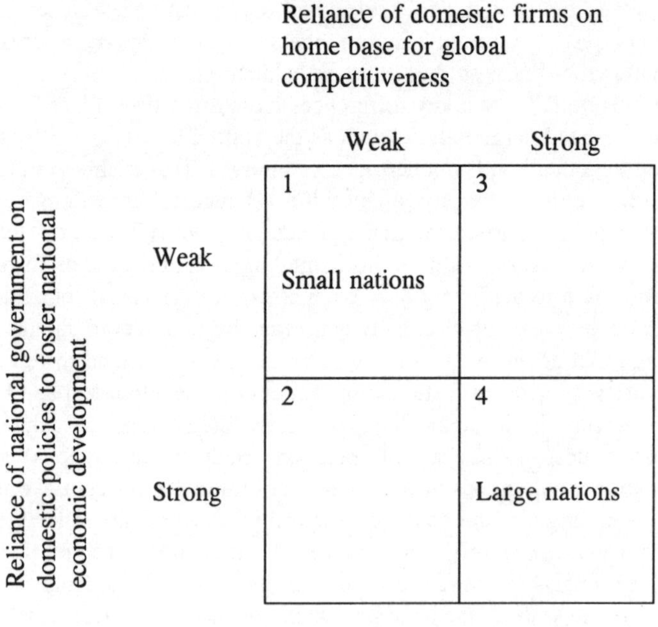

The former forces include: (1) the presence of large markets that allow economies of scale in local production, a reduction in logistics costs, and agglomeration economies with related and supporting industries (backward and forward linkages); (2) abundant markets for specialized knowledge inputs (for example highly skilled labor); (3) knowledge spill-overs that lead to geographically localized positive externalities. The latter forces consist of:

(1) dispersed, immobile production factors such as land, natural resources and some types of labor, as well as immobile demand requiring localized service production; (2) scarcity rents, when an initial concentration of economic activity pushes up prices of scarce production factors in a particular location; and (3) negative externalities such as congestion and technological 'lock-in'.

Apart from the above factors, a localized culture of independence and exchange and institutions such as universities, specialized services and service organizations supporting this culture, may greatly aid superior innovation performance (Audretsch, 1998; Saxenian, 1990).

Two types of knowledge spill-overs exist (Audretsch, 1998). The first type reflects intra-industry knowledge spill-overs that benefit all firms located within a region, but limited to a single industry. The reason for this sectoral limitation of spill-overs is that firms within a specific industry may be very similar in terms of the type of individuals they attract, the way these individuals develop, absorb and communicate knowledge and the networking institutions they build, contribute to and draw upon in the region. The second type, consisting of inter-industry spill-overs in contrast, reflects the exchange of complementary knowledge among firms in different industries. Here, it is the diversity of geographically concentrated knowledge transfers that leads to new richness.

The main contribution of international business scholars has been to analyze geographical concentration/dispersion of foreign direct investment not mainly as the result of exogenous forces but to a large extent as the outcome of MNE behavior. For example, the existence of an economic center, close to a large market, may attract foreign entry, which in turn makes this center even more attractive to other firms. The presence of such path dependencies explains why the international expansion of MNEs is usually restricted to a limited number of locations, because agglomeration economies and spill-over effects only arise over time and are created through a process of cumulative causation. It is a self-reinforcing set of firm level actions that largely contributes to the spatial concentration of industries and the creation of specialized geographic areas.

More specifically, the creation of 'sticky places' fundamentally depends upon the synergies between strong mobile or non-location-bound firm-specific advantages and immobile country-specific advantages. Here, not all synergies are internalized by the firms involved. The spatial proximity between firms in a specific industry and, for example, a pool of workers with specialized skills, the non-business infrastructure, and so on leads to technological and organizational spill-over effects benefiting the entire, localized industrial district.

It is important to note that clustering benefits in the form of, for example, agglomeration economies, access to 'thick' markets for knowledge inputs and technological spill-over effects are not equally important for all MNE value added activities. Porter (1986) has argued that, within the firm, the determinants favoring a specific geographic configuration may be very different for each value chain activity. For example, corporate and regional MNE headquarters typically require a 'strategic location', with easy access to an international communications and transport network, high quality external services and knowledge inputs (for example information processing workers), strong agglomeration potential which allows for frequent personal interactions with top executives of other key organizations, and an environment rich in social and cultural amenities. These elements must obviously be weighted against the cost of scarce inputs such as land, negative externalities associated with large, dense economic centers and so on (Dicken, 1998). In contrast, R&D facilities may require very different location characteristics, depending upon the precise role of the R&D facility in the firm. This role may be either to exploit existing knowledge or to create new knowledge (Kuemmerle, 1999).

As regards activities such as production and marketing, two MNEs facing broadly similar external 'location pulls' may still make their location decisions largely dependent on their administrative heritage (for example a tradition of centralized production building upon home nation location advantages and leading to scale economies versus decentralized operations building upon host nation location advantages and leading to benefits of national responsiveness). It is precisely the distinct administrative heritage of working with multiple home bases that provides firms from small open economies with a potentially very powerful knowledge absorption capability, when operating in foreign clusters.

Apart from this introductory chapter this research volume consists of five parts, each consisting of two chapters. The first part's chapters bring new conceptual perspectives on the interaction between country size and the need to rely on foreign sources of knowledge to gain international competitiveness. The book's second part investigates the role of business-government linkages in the area of international competitiveness. The third part then focuses on inter-firm linkages, with an emphasis on mergers, acquisitions and alliances. The fourth part's chapters discuss the characteristics and the challenges faced by multinational enterprises when engaged in outward foreign direct investment or confronted with inward foreign direct investment by foreign rivals. Finally, the book's fifth part includes two chapters which make a number of conceptual observations on the challenges faced by managers of firms when operating in multiple markets.

In the book's second chapter, John Dunning argues that small open economies have traditionally been characterized by a higher degree of multinationality of their multinational enterprises. These multinational enterprises have also shown a higher propensity to engage in innovative activities outside of the home base. Dunning observes that at this point in time, global alliance capitalism is forcing firms to increasingly rely on networks in the international sphere to be successful globally. Similarly governments increasingly need to engage in international cooperation to 'regulate' or liberalize trade and investment flows. This dual trend towards cooperation, however, appears to be accompanied by increasing market competition. Dunning then suggests that small open economies may have an important advantage in terms of being 'masters of the global paradox', that is he suggests that they have an advantage in reconciling competition and cooperation in the new global economy. In any case, for both firms and governments one of the key strategy challenges is to participate in - and benefit from - the development of 'sticky places found in slippery space'. This conclusion is fully consistent with the third chapter by Chang Moon, Alan Rugman and Alain Verbeke who propose a generalized double diamond model to analyze the competitive advantage of nations. From a conceptual perspective they demonstrate that Porter's single diamond model is inconsistent with present economic reality, whereby especially for small open economies, linkages with other nations are critical to competitiveness. They suggest, in accordance with Dunning's chapter, that Singapore is much more competitive globally than Korea, precisely because of its international linkages through both inward and outward foreign direct investment. The application of a single diamond model led Michael Porter to the mistaken conclusion that Korea should be viewed as more 'competitive' than Singapore, which is obviously in sharp contrast with all common knowledge on these two economic systems. At a more general level, Moon, Rugman and Verbeke suggest that small countries in general may be extremely successful in terms of economic wealth creation precisely because of foreign elements in their economic system.

The fourth chapter, by Kristel Buysse, Alain Verbeke and Chris Coeck, investigates a relatively new area of business-government relations, namely the interactions between environmental policy and corporate strategy. They demonstrate that multinational enterprises usually attempt to transfer the most stringent environmental standards worldwide throughout their network of subsidiaries. The chapter suggests that the 'pollution haven'-seeking behavior by MNEs often alleged in the academic literature and the media does not hold in practice. It also demonstrates that multinational enterprises are characterized by greener strategies than their domestic counterparts. Greening does not appear to result from regulatory pressures, however, but from the identification of market opportunities associated with green strategic management. The chapter argues, again in contrast with Porter's view, that government should not attempt to implement a 'strategic environmental policy' as this is unlikely to have a positive impact on the greening strategies of firms.

The fifth chapter by Ilse Scheerlinck, Luc Hens and Rosette S'Jegers investigates the reaction of firms in four industries (textiles and clothing, road haulage, banking and the pharmaceutical industry) in a small open economy to the forces of globalization. One of the key conclusions is that even within a single industry substantial differences may exist among firms regarding their public policy preferences, for example in the area of trade liberalization. Another interesting conclusion is that virtuous cycles of liberalization may occur when firms engaged in cross-border alliances face incentives to push for trade liberalization. Similarly, governments which pursue internationalization policies also appear to have preferences favoring trade liberalization.

The sixth chapter by Leo Sleuwaegen and Reinhilde Veugelers presents an innovative methodology to simultaneously study the competitive and comparative advantages of firms in a global context. They demonstrate that an in-depth knowledge of the firm-specific advantages and the country-specific advantages facing firms in specific industries may go a long way to understand patterns of international mergers and acquisitions. For example, they demonstrate that Belgian firms with strong footloose firm-specific advantages may prefer acquisitions to alliances to protect their proprietary firm-specific advantages. They also show that a lack of firm-specific advantages in a domestic industry may open the road to acquisitions by foreign multinational enterprises.

Geert Duysters and John Hagedoorn demonstrate, in the seventh chapter, that in spite of the often made suggestion that technology globalization is now very widespread, in fact firms engage only to a limited degree in technological activity outside their home country. One exception to this observation appears to be the case of the Netherlands. The authors show that there has indeed been a growth of international strategic technology partnering, but that this growth is not necessarily faster than that of domestic technology partnering. As regards the Netherlands, they suggest that the strong internationalization of Dutch research and development may prevent the Dutch economy from fully benefiting from spill-over effects. Hence, they suggest that the Dutch government should encourage domestic R&D, both by Dutch and foreign multinational enterprises. In their view, government should try to increase the attractiveness of the Netherlands by improving the Dutch technological infrastructure and providing high quality education. These suggestions, which are fully in line with modern international business thinking on this issue, obviously reject the case of shelter driven strategic trade and industrial policy to increase R&D levels.

In the eighth chapter, Haiyan Zhang and Daniel Van Den Bulcke examine the ownership structure of Belgian-based companies and describe their inward, outward and platform FDI operations. Their extensive analysis of a large Belgian corporate database presents detailed information about the patterns and extent of the Belgian globalizing economy, with special focus on the cross-sectoral analysis. Their findings show that the dynamic interaction between inward, outward and platform FDI in capital- and technology-intensive industries provides Belgium with global competitiveness and the development of clusters of manufacturing activities. However, the role of foreign enterprises in the restructuring process of Belgium's traditional industries is quite limited as a result of low attractiveness of these industries to (foreign) investors. It is in these sectors that local firms have engaged into a so-called 'delocalization' process.

In Chapter 9, Filip De Beule and Daniel Van Den Bulcke take up the paradox of space, which is particularly relevant for small open economies such as Belgium. The authors analyze the importance of industrial clustering with regard to inward investment, specifically Japanese direct investment in the Belgian manufacturing industry. Initially, Japanese firms invested in transplanted industries in which they possessed competitive advantages, such as electronics, mainly setting up greenfield screwdriver plants that were weakly embedded in the local economy. These assembly subsidiaries typically imported supplies either from the parent company or other affiliates, or from keiretsu network suppliers, and allowed only restricted decision-making autonomy and engaged in limited value-adding activities. On the other hand, Japanese multinationals have tapped into industries in which their European counterparts possess strong competitive advantages, such as chemicals, acquiring existing companies. Indeed, there is a significant sectoral difference in Belgium with regard to the entry mode of Japanese investors. Acquisitions appear a far more acceptable practice in the competitive industry clusters, such as chemicals and non-metallic minerals, than in the transplanted sectors, such as the electrical and electronic equipment industry. The ownership structure is similarly skewed towards complete ownership for the more 'Japanese' sectors in comparison with the more 'Belgian' sectors. However, the Japanese corporations apparently no longer concentrate their higher value adding activities, such as R&D, as strongly in Japan as before. The satellite industries are catching up to the industry clusters, although the activities remain more extensive on average in the indigenous industries. They are also granting more local decision-making authority to their subsidiaries in Belgium. The subsidiaries that are active in the industries where Japan had distinctive competitive advantages have gained credibility within the group, leading to an increase in decision autonomy towards shared decision-making. Subsidiaries in the industries where Japan had less competitive advantages are now being integrated within the group, also leading to a shift towards more shared decision-making.

Alexandra Campbell and Alain Verbeke in the tenth chapter provide a managerial framework for the multinational management of multiple external networks. This framework should allow firms to more effectively manage their linkages with economic actors in foreign systems. In particular the dynamic tension between a strategy of isomorphic flexibility and institutionalization is important here.

Finally, in the eleventh chapter, Mark van Wegberg and Arjen van Witteloostuyn develop a resource-based view on multi-market competition, which is particularly useful for firms from small open economies faced with globalization. Their thinking is fully consistent with the double diamond thinking described earlier in Chapter 3 by Moon, Rugman and Verbeke. One of the chapter's main conclusions is that firms from small open economies, which are intrinsically more vulnerable when faced with problems of 'connectedness' and 'feedback' in foreign markets, may simultaneously be better equipped to effectively anticipate and manage unintended dynamic effects of multi-market competition.

The editors hope that this volume may contribute to a better appreciation of the challenges, but also the opportunities, faced by MNE managers and public policy makers in small open economies. Their high vulnerability to globalization pressures may be associated with more flexibility when dealing with foreign actors. In a 'network based' economy, the benefits of the latter may largely outweigh the costs of the former.

REFERENCES

Audretsch, D.B. (1998), 'Agglomeration and the location of innovative activity', *Oxford Review of Economic Policy*, **14** (2), Oxford: Oxford University Press.
Dicken, P. (1998), *Global Shift: Transforming the World Economy*, London: Paul Chapman Publishing Ltd.
Krugman, P.R. (1991a), 'Increasing returns and economic geography', *Journal of Political Economy*, **99**, 483-99.
Krugman, P.R. (1991b), *Geography and Trade*, Cambridge, Mass.: MIT Press.
Krugman, P.R. (1998), 'What's new about the new economic geography?', *Oxford Review of Economic Policy*, **14** (52), Oxford: Oxford University Press.
Kuemmerle, W. (1999), 'The drivers of foreign direct investment into research and development: An empirical investigation', *Journal of International Business*, **30** (1), 1-24.
Porter, M.E. (ed.) (1986), *Competition in Global Industries*, Boston: Harvard Business School Press.

Saxenian, A. (1990), 'Regional networks and the resurgence of Silicon Valley', *California Management Review*, **33**, 89-111.

PART I

New Conceptual Perspectives

2. Resolving some Paradoxes of the Emerging Global Economy: Small Nations as Trailblazers

John H. Dunning

2.1 INTRODUCTION

At the beginning of the twenty-first century, one cannot fail to be struck by both the similarities and differences of circumstances to those faced by our forefathers one hundred years ago. Then, as now, was an era of dramatic and widespread technology change.[1] Then, as now, a new generation of telecommunication advances was shrinking the boundaries of economic activity. Then, as now, the organizational structures of firms and the socio-institutional framework of countries were in a state of flux. Then, as now, the cartography of political space was being reconfigured. Then, as now, the jurisdiction of national governments was being questioned, and the locus and composition of civic responsibilities were being redefined. Then, as now, new relationships and alliances were being forged between, and within, private and public institutions, and among different ethnic, religious and social groups.

But, to a more discerning observer, the differences between the two ages are more marked than the similarities. Key among these is that while, for the most part, the events of the late nineteenth century occurred within a well established and widely accepted social and political order,[2] those now occurring seem to be challenging long-cherished ideologies and values - and, in some cases, the very cohesiveness of society. At the same time, contemporary events are moulding a very unpredictable future - both for individuals and for institutions - and, more often than not, they are as divisive as they are unifying in their consequences. Our contemporary world is in a state of transition and turmoil. Some may view this as a form of creative destruction - of ideas, of technologies, of institutions and of cultures. Others fear that it is the beginning of an era of social and political unrest, the like of which we have not seen for many generations. The order of hierarchical capitalism which, as a wealth-creating system, has served much of the world so well over the past century, is being increasingly questioned;

but no one is quite sure what is going to replace it - or indeed what should replace it.

Part of our increasing sense of bewilderment and insecurity, I suggest, arises because many of the events now occurring are paradoxical, if not antithetical, in both their characteristics and implications. Indeed, we may well be moving out of Eric Hobsbawm's 'Age of Extremes'[3] into an 'Age of Paradoxes'. Nowhere is this more clearly seen than in the globalization of economic activity. Few can surely deny that alongside an impressive array of opportunities and benefits offered by deep cross-border economic interdependence, it is demanding enormous and, often painful adjustments, not only of corporations and governments but of the working lives, leisure pursuits and mind sets of ordinary men and women. One political scientist, in a book published in 1996,[4] avers that our planet is simultaneously 'falling apart and coming together'; while William Greiber (1997), in a new polemic with the intriguing title 'One World, Ready or Not' writes about 'new technologies enabling nations to take sudden leaps into modernity, while at the same time promoting the renewal of economic barbarisms' (p. 12).

In this chapter, I shall identify just four paradoxes[5] or contradictions of our emerging global economy - or what the Chinese might prefer to call the 'yin' and 'yang' of globalization. I believe that the ways in which these paradoxes are approached and reconciled - if, indeed, they are reconciled - will determine the shape of our planet's political and economic future; and the social well-being of each and every one of us. I further believe that hints of how the paradoxes may best be tackled by the larger nation states are already contained in the ways in which smaller states have, over the last century, successfully tuned their domestic economic structures and policies to the changing needs of the international marketplace. At the same time, they have fiercely guarded their political independence, social mores and cultural heritages.

2.2 SOME DISTINGUISHING FEATURES OF SMALL STATES

Before reviewing these paradoxes, let me briefly set out some of the main economic characteristics of small states compared with their larger counterparts. I will, if I may, concentrate my attention on the 45 upper-middle and high-income countries, with a per capita income in 1995 of $3,000 or more, identified by the World Development Report (World Bank, 1997). For the purposes of my arguments, I shall also define (quite arbitrarily) small (or smaller) states as those with a 1995 population of 10 million or less. Using the data set out in Table 2.1, I will focus my attention first on the overall economic prosperity of the 45 countries; second, on their degree of exposure to the global economy; third, the extent and form of their knowledge-based assets; and fourth, on their infrastructural provisions.

First, there are nearly as many small states in high and upper-middle groups as there are of mediumtolarge states.[6] There is no correlation between size and gross domestic product (GDP) per head. Of the wealthiest 20 nations in the world in 1995, 11 had a population of less than 10 million and 7 had a population of 5.5 million or less.[7] Within these two main income groups, the average GDP per head is broadly the same for the small, and medium-to-large countries; however, the smaller countries recorded a somewhat faster rate of gross national product (GNP) per capita growth in the first half of the 1990s.

Second, the critical distinguishing feature between the two groups of countries is the extent to which they engage in international business transactions. In 1995, the (unweighed) average of trade in goods and services as a percentage of GDP for the 22 small countries was 111.2 percent compared with 60.0 percent for the 23 medium-to-large countries. The corresponding (unweighed) averages of inward plus outward foreign direct investment (FDI) stock as a percentage of GDP for that same year were 34.5 percent and 28.5 percent. Other data set out in Dunning (1996), UNCTAD (1997) and Cantwell and Harding (1997) have demonstrated that both the degree of multinationality of firms and the propensity of MNEs to engage in innovatory activity outside their national boundaries are considerably more marked in the case of firms from small countries than those from medium and large countries. Small countries record around double the minutes spent per person on international telephone calls than their larger counterparts (see Column 5 of Table 2.1); they also make more use of the internet (see Column 6 of Table 2.1).

Third, the significance of knowledge-based assets in the wealth-creating process is broadly the same for both small and medium-to-large nation states. Both groups of countries, for example, allocate a similar proportion of their resources to education and to innovatory activities. There is, however, a slight suggestion (see Column 10 of Table 2.1) that economic activity - including industrial clustering - is less concentrated in large conurbations in small countries, particularly in small upper-middle-income countries.

Fourth, the average share of the GDP accounted for by central government expenditure is rather higher in the case of smaller countries, and particularly so in the case of small upper-middle-income countries. These averages, however, conceal wide differences within the two groups of countries.

Table 2.1   Some economic characteristics of small and medium-to-large economies in the mid-1990s

Type of Economies	(a) GNP (1)		(b) Internationalization (2)				(c) Created Assets (3)					(d) Infrastructure (4)
	1995	Growth 1990-95	Trade/ GDP	FDI stock/ GDP	Int'l Tele-phone Calls 1994	Internet 1994	Education Exp./GNP 1992-94	Education Exp./ Gov.Exp. 1993-94	R&D/ 1000 people 1988/95	Urbani-zation Index 1995	Central Gov. Exp./ GDP 1994	Roads Railroads Ports Airports
Upper-middle-income countries (19)												
Small	4,388	2.93	90.8	27.6	27.5	22.2	5.46	13.5	1.17	52.8	35.5	n.a.
Medium-to-large	4,769	2.52	62.0	26.0	14.3	19.0	5.52	20.3	0.50	72.6	32.0	4.59
High-income countries (26)												
Small*(14)	22,300	2.71	122.9	39.5	119.1	288.6	4.66	37.7	2.36	76.0	40.5	7.32
Medium-to-large (12)	22,244	2.13	58.6	30.6	44.1	210.2	4.53	50.0	2.67	81.3	38.4	6.62
Both groups of countries (45)												
Small (22)	15,787	2.78	111.2	34.5	88.6	238.6	5.18	27.9	1.94	67.5	39.3	n.a.
Medium-to-large (23)	13,886	2.33	62.0	28.5	30.5	123.3	5.07	36.7	1.68	77.2	35.8	n.a.

Source: (1) World Bank (1997).
(2) International Telephone Calls (minutes per person), Internet users (per 100,000 population), Education Expenditure as a proportion of GNP, Education Expenditure as a proportion of Total Government Expenditure, R&D Scientists and Technicians per 1000 people, Central Government Expenditure as a proportion of GDP (UNDP, 1997).
(3) FDI stock/GDP (UNCTAD, 1997).
(4) Transportation infrastructure (World Economic Forum, 1994). Ranking on adequacy of transportation network 0-10, 10=meets business requirements the best.

Expenditure per head on transportation infrastructure is consistently higher in smaller countries - particularly in small high-income countries.

The conclusion of this snapshot review is that size per se need not be a significant variable affecting the economic wellbeing or the wealth-creating capacity of a country;[8] but that, almost inevitably, it does affect the extent to which that prosperity and wealth creating capacity is dependent on the volume and structure of its commercial transactions with the rest of the world.

In the following four sections of this chapter, we turn to examine the four paradoxes of the global economy referred to earlier. In each case we shall give special attention to the past and contemporary experiences of small countries and the possible lessons which medium and larger countries can learn from these as they seek to get to grips with the two-edged sword of globalization.

2.3 COOPERATION AND COMPETITION: THE PARADOX OF RELATIONSHIPS

At the end of the nineteenth century, the main form of interface between firms was competition. Most transactions between buyers and sellers were at spot or arm's length prices, and adversarial in nature. Apart from the conclusion of mergers, combines and other business agreements to restrict competition, rival firms perceived little need to cooperate with each other. In most advanced industrial nations, free enterprise was perceived 'to rule OK'; and where markets failed, either firms or non-market entities intervened by internalizing these markets - namely by an 'exit', rather than a 'voice', response. Governments, like private corporations were at best suspicious of, and at worst downright hostile to, each other. To the 'yin' of competition there was no counterbalancing 'yang' of cooperation.

By contrast, yet at the same time, the economic policies of national administrations were predicated on the belief that unimpeded international trade was beneficial because it enabled each country to produce goods and services which were complementary, rather than substitutable, to each other's needs. This, after all, is what the principle of comparative advantage is all about. True, there were some interventionist actions[9] - particularly by governments of later industrializing nations, but the dictum 'Firms compete but countries cooperate - and both obey the dictates of the marketplace' was widely upheld. This was the deeply implanted order of things, which the events of the second industrial revolution of the late nineteenth century did little to disturb.

At the beginning of the new millennium, inter-firm and inter-nation state relationships are taking on more complex, pluralistic and contradictory forms. The last decade, in particular, has witnessed a spectacular increase in collaboration agreements between firms, both to penetrate new markets and to share the costs and speed up the process of innovation. Paradoxically, at a time of increased competition between firms in the factor and final goods markets, there has been a shedding of non-core activities by firms along and between value chains; and a replacement of them by a range of closely monitored inter-firm alliances and networking arrangements. This movement has also led to another paradox - namely the renaissance of small- to medium-size firms at a time when giant MNEs continue to engage in international mergers and acquisitions (M&As), and dominate the markets for technology-intensive and branded goods and services.

The reasons for the emerging 'yin' and 'yang' of the organization of economic activity are many, but most reduce to the emergence of knowledge capital as the main resource for upgrading the competitiveness of firms; an accelerating rate of technological obsolescence, a closer interconnection between many cutting edge technologies; and the growing integration between different stages of the value added chain (especially between the R&D and the manufacturing departments of firms). Such events, together with the lowering transaction costs of many kinds of inter-firm cooperation, have encouraged multinational and other enterprises to specialize in activities based on their core competencies, while, at the same time, to forge new and on-going relationships with firms - both domestic and foreign - supplying complementary inputs to these activities.

National governments, too, are finding that globalization is leading to new, and incongruous, cross-border relationships. Increasingly, in a world in which trade and FDI are within rather than between industrial sectors, unemployment is unacceptably high, human resource development is at a premium, and firm-specific assets are more easily transplanted across national borders, governments are increasingly and openly competing with each other for similar resources, as well as seeking to advance their own particular social agendas. As the economic structure of countries tends to converge, so institutional and organizational factors are becoming more important location-specific endowments. Foremost among these are the actions of governments, which I will consider in more detail a little later. For the moment, I would simply note that, in contrast to the late nineteenth century scenario, where the policies of national administrations were either independent of, or tended to complement, each other, those of today are a mixture of the yin of competition and the yang of cooperation.

Even the most cursory review of now emerging relationships between firms and governments suggests that, far from being antithetical, cooperation and competition each has its unique and mutually reinforcing role to play in a dynamic market economy. In and of themselves, each is a neutral concept; however, each may be deployed in a market distorting or a market facilitating way. There is an unacceptable face of cooperation and an unacceptable face of competition. One of the challenges of the globalizing economy is to manage and resolve the apparent contradictory nature of these two organizational forms.

In its *World Development Report*, the World Bank (1997) called for a rethinking of the role of the State in economic affairs, so that it can be a more credible and effective partner to the private sector in upgrading the productivity of the resources and the competitiveness of the firms within its jurisdiction. 'Good government,' the report concluded, 'is not a luxury but a vital necessity for economic prosperity' (p. 15). Clearly, the decision of when, with whom, and how to cooperate, and when, with whom, and how to compete is partly determined by firm-, industry- and country-specific characteristics. Because of this, it is difficult to lay down any universal guidelines. But, in the last two decades or so, Western firms and nations have learnt a great deal about the 'yin' and 'yang' of commercial relationships and institutional arrangements practised in East Asia. The knowledge so gained is now being assiduously revamped and adapted to western norms and needs - so much so that the expression 'alliance' capitalism is now being used to describe a new trajectory of market-based socio-economic systems. A feature of this trajectory is that it is reconstituting the concepts of competition and cooperation, from being exclusive alternatives, to being mutually reinforcing organizational forms.

In seeking to manage and reconcile the paradox of relationships, I would like to suggest that larger sovereign states have much to learn from their smaller counterparts. In particular, multinational enterprises (MNEs) from countries like Sweden, Switzerland and the Netherlands are 'masters of the global paradox'. They are well experienced both at translating the horns of dilemma of international economic exchange into virtuous circles of corporate growth and profitability; and of using both competition and cooperation as strategies to advance their long-term objectives (Baden-Fuller and Stopford, 1992). They have also long acknowledged the need to tap into foreign resources and capabilities, and to combine these with their own core competencies. It is surely no coincidence that all of the early binationally owned MNEs were from smaller countries, notably the Netherlands and Belgium, while the more recent merger between Asea (Sweden) and Brown Boveri (Switzerland), and the multiplicity of alliances in the telecommunications, pharmaceutical, car and airline industries, excellently demonstrate both the continued pressure on firms from smaller countries to seek technological, organizational and marketing synergies with those of firms from other countries; and the conditions for such partnerships to be successful. In the period 1988-1996, the value of the cross-border purchases by firms from the smaller economies identified earlier, expressed as a proportion of their GDPs, were twice those of their medium-sized or larger counterparts (UNCTAD, 1997).

In addition, I would suggest that smaller economies are in a particularly favored position to benefit from several of the demands of alliance capitalism. This is so because their limited domestic markets force their firms to seek, and be competitive in, foreign markets, while their institutions have been among the trailblazers engaging in a network of synergistic cross-border coalitions. Domestic competition and M&A policies reflect these imperatives. Such arrangements have been both intra-firm and inter-firm as well as between firms and governments. Here, there is some reason to suppose that the transaction costs of establishing and maintaining trust-based relationships, and capturing dynamic learning economies, are considerably less in the case of closely knit smaller economies than in that of their larger counterparts. This is because of the lower psychic distance between the top decision takers in the private and public sectors of the former economies.

2.4 GLOBALIZATION VERSUS LOCALIZATION: THE PARADOX OF SPACE

The extension of geographical space has not affected all activities to the same extent. While the markets for some goods, for example Coca Cola, fast food, Levi jeans, Gucchi handbags and some kinds of services, for example financial assets, music, television and sports span the globe; others are restricted by the specificity of local supply capabilities, customs, tastes and government regulations. Similarly, while some parts of the value chain, for example those involving the electronic transmission of standardized data, are spatially unanchored; others, in which trust-based relations, personal inter-face and complex, but non-codifiable, knowledge are at a premium, are faced with distance-constrained capabilities and needs. Hence, we have the paradox of what the geographer Ann Markusen (1994) has referred to as 'sticky places within slippery space'. At the same time, the imperatives of much of contemporary product and production technology, and the lowering of natural and artificial barriers to traversing space, have most certainly enabled firms to take a more holistic stance to their foreign and domestic operations.

The liberalization of markets, more software-oriented development policies, and the current attractions of regional economic integration have all helped to push out the territorial boundaries of firms. While FDI is the main route by which this extension is being accomplished, increasingly, as I have already mentioned, cross-border alliances - varying from international subcontracting and 'keiretsu'-type relationships, to R&D consortia among rival firms - have become more significant in the last decade, and seem likely to be a major feature of the capitalism of the twenty-first century.

If we can think of the spatial widening of economic activity as the yin of globalization, the yang is surely the increasing pressure on individuals, firms, nations and localities to reassert their distinctive traits and values. The paradox of regional economic integration - albeit it is often market driven - is that it introduces an economic uniformity or universality into people's lives, which they frequently wish to offset by emphasizing other, and more distinctive, characteristics of their individuality. In some cases - although we would hesitate to suggest this has been caused by the emergence of the global economy, however much it may facilitate it - it leads to ethnic and ideological schisms and to political disintegration and fragmentation. Just as there can be little doubt that the merger movement among corporations is going on alongside a reinvigoration of medium and small businesses, so as countries group together to better advance their common economic aspirations, they, or their peoples, are reasserting their singular cultural and ethnic heritages. As John Naisbitt (1994) has put it 'there is a rising conflict between universalism and tribalism, and between regional unification and fragmentation'.

As the global economy favors the growth of the large MNE, so many of its spatial units are becoming smaller. The same may well be true of 'body politique'. The concept of subsidiarity is gaining widespread acceptance at all levels of governance; and the role of sub-national economic entities is becoming more, rather than less, influential. Certainly, this is the view of Kenichi Ohmae, who, in his book on this topic (Ohmae, 1995), argues persuasively that, in a borderless world, region states may well come to replace nation states as the ports of entry into the global economy and the centerpiece of knowledge-based economic activity.[10] And, certainly, there is accumulating evidence of the benefits of the increasing spatial concentration of the higher order of value added activities, in spite of the tremendous advances in all forms of telematics (Storper, 1997).

Once again, however, I would suggest to you that the contradiction between the globalization and the localization of economic space is more apparent than real, and that this is well demonstrated by the experiences of the more successful MNEs from smaller economies. They know full well the axiom 'think globally but act locally'; and of the need to balance the gains offered by the coordination of scale-related economies, with those stemming from the adaptation of world product mandates, production techniques and work practices to local situations. They also appreciate that the ability to recognize these latter needs, and to efficiently organize and manage them are important competitive advantages in their own right.

At a more macro-level, since, by definition, the spatial governance of small economies is geographically contained, one might expect this particular paradox to be less pronounced than in the case of larger economies. Yet, clearly within such nation states as Finland, Austria, Ireland and Israel, regional issues are not unimportant, particularly where there are distinctive spatially-related economic, social, religious and cultural specificities. And, there is certainly some clustering of particular types of value added activities in such regions or urban areas as Flanders in Belgium, the cork and wine districts of Portugal, the seaport complex at Rotterdam, and the Geneva watch industry, which, like their counterparts in larger countries, often help to generate substantial agglomerative economies. Smaller countries, like smaller firms, also tend to be more experienced in the flexibility now being demanded by the global marketplace of production technologies and organizational structures.

At the same time, I do not see (though I stand to be corrected) that there are major small-country specific issues which arise from the globalization versus localization paradox. In general, I would expect sub-national authorities in small countries to play a less decisive role on the location of mobile investment within their areas of jurisdiction than those in larger countries. What, however, has been clearly demonstrated over the past three or more decades is that investment and other incentives offered by the national governments of small nation states have been just as powerful in affecting the location of MNE activity as those offered by state and district governments of the medium-to-large countries. Yet, again, issues relating intra-national ethnic and cultural distinctiveness, while no less important in the case of some small nation states, seem to have been settled relatively amicably.[11]

In summary, globalization is leading to a spatial reconfiguration of economic activity, and also the governance of such activity. In some cases this is resulting in a harmonization of technical standards, of the functions of firms and a homogenization of consumer tastes the world over. In others, it is increasing the value of close spatial linkages between firms (such as that fostered in business districts and science parks) at a sub-national level, and stimulating individuals and nations to emphasize their discriminating characteristics. The yin of slippery space is then going hand in hand with - indeed some would say giving rise to - the yang - or sticky place; and to a reevaluation of local cultural religious and ethnic mores. As long as these trends of globalization are treated as complementary, rather than substitutable for each other, then I believe there is no real paradox of geographical space. And, as I have suggested, smaller nation states have much to teach their larger counterparts, both about the ways in which spatially-related tensions can be minimized, and on the need for positive attitudes and constructive policies towards structural change and social cohesion.

2.5 THE ROLE OF GOVERNMENTS: THE PARADOX OF 'LESS, YET MORE', AND THAT OF 'CENTRALIZATION VERSUS DECENTRALIZATION'

A century ago, there was comparatively little dispute about the role of national administrations - at least in Western economies.[12] The spiritual heritage of Adam Smith and the founding fathers of the American Revolution was very much alive. In economic matters, at least, the invisible hand of the market was thought superior to that of the visible hand of extra-market planning and government intervention. The duties of government were to defend the realm's territory, to maintain internal law and order, to combat the unacceptable face of capitalism, to provide the legal and commercial framework in which property rights were respected and unfettered markets might flourish, and to alleviate unavoidable social distress.

There was no conflict in performing these tasks; they were not even regarded as competitive with those of other organizational forms. The fact that, in some countries, for example France and Germany, governments pursued more paternalistic policies and were more interventionist than others, for example the UK, was accepted to reflect their particular institutional heritages, or their stages of economic development, rather than any differences in their political philosophies. In any event, because of the immobility of resources and absence of any cross-border structural integration of economic activity, national administrations were able to follow largely independent economic and social strategies. Even what international commerce there was at the time was largely determined by a world order, namely the gold standard; although restrictions on some kinds of trade, and other forms of government intervention, were beginning to emerge.

Today, the optimum or appropriate role of government is hotly debated. In particular, the last twenty years have seen a blurring of the boundaries of the role of the private and public sector in capitalist economies; while globalization has led to an intensification of the yin and yang of government intervention. On the one hand, as markets have become more liberalized and central planning has become discredited, the interventionist role of governments has lessened. On the other, as the economic prosperity of firms and nations has become more dependent on the continual upgrading of indigenous created assets - notably intellectual capital and physical and commercial infrastructure - then, insofar as it has the power to influence, for example by its educational and technology policies, the role of the state has become more critical.

I believe that, for the most part, globalization is not leading to a hollowing out of the responsibilities of national governments. But it is changing their raison d'être, and their content. And it is doing so within the context of deepening structural integration; the growing importance of public goods, for example crime prevention, health care, education and the environment; and the increasing ease by which corporations can avoid unpopular actions by their national or regional authorities by relocating their activities outside their jurisdiction (that is by 'voting with their feet').[13]

Another feature of globalization and economic change is that it is leading to a greater coincidence of interests between governments and the private sector in market economies. The yin of a policing and umpiring, but otherwise non-interventionist, stance of governments is being supplemented by the yang of governments as builders and monitors of economic systems and supportive institutions, as facilitators of efficient markets; as catalysts of dynamic comparative advantage; and as managers of social conflict. Hence, the paradox that a free market needs strong and effective government - a paradox which scholars are only able to resolve by constructing a theory of state involvement which, in the words of the Cambridge economists Ha-Joo Chang and Robert Rowthorn, 'takes full account of uncertainty and innovation, institutions and political economy' (Chang and Rowthorn, 1995, p. 46).

To date, the need for a reconstituted role of governments in the age of alliance capitalism has only been fully acknowledged - and put into practice - by some East Asian governments (Wade, 1995). The competing or adversarial relationship between governments and private enterprise, which was (and is) a feature of hierarchical capitalism, remains strongly embedded in Western - especially US - cultures. But, the phenomenon of the globalizing economy, the growing recognition that a nation's competitiveness rests as much on its ability to supply the location-bound assets necessary to attract or retain firm-specific mobile assets, as those assets themselves; and the acceptance that, de facto, governments do compete with each other for these latter assets, are combining to foster a 'sink or swim together' philosophy among all except the most extreme free market administrations.

Of the three paradoxes so far identified, that of the 'less' or 'more' of governments may be the most difficult to resolve. This is not only because of entrenched ideologies and institutional rigidities, but also because the costs and benefits of non-market intervention are extremely difficult to measure.

So, if and when markets do fail, it cannot necessarily be presumed that government intervention will improve the situation, as the costs of such intervention may be greater than the benefits. Such evidence as we have, for example Bradford (1994) and Wade (1995), suggests that the interaction between national government fiat and markets in countries such as Korea, Taiwan and Malaysia has led to a virtuous circle of growth and efficiency, while that in many parts of Latin America, at least until recently, has led to a vicious circle of low economic growth and social unrest.

Although there has been some research done on the kinds of government action which are most likely to improve economic performance,[14] for the most part our knowledge is woefully inadequate. Once again, however, there are some hints from the responses of governments of small countries to international market failure and to the imperative of globalization. For example, even a cursory review of the contemporary milieu suggests that governments of larger sovereign states - and particularly of those which, in the past, have not been greatly involved in international commerce - are much more concerned about the possible loss of sovereignty than are those of smaller states. Compare, for example, the reactions to globalization of the US and the Canadian governments, those of the German and Swiss governments, and those of the Indian and Singaporean governments. And, it is true that, even before the advent of globalization as we know it today, the economies of Belgium, Austria, New Zealand, Hong Kong, Israel, and so on were all closely interdependent with those of the rest of the world;[15] and much of their domestic economic policies were already constrained by the dictates of the international marketplace.

At the same time, when one talks to government representatives of those small nation states, and especially those which practice the East Asian pattern of State-guided market capitalism, one gets the strong impression that the advent of globalization, far from emasculating their policy making authority, has greatly enhanced their opportunities for capturing a large basket of economic 'goodies' than was earlier available to them.

I think this particular issue - the comparative role of national governments of smaller and larger countries, in response to, or in consequence of, globalization - is worthy of a good deal more scholarly research. But, from their past experiences, national governments of small countries may offer their opposite number from larger countries some grains of comfort, that despite their being carried along with a wave of ever closer economic interdependence, their economies remain vibrant and continue to achieve enviable efficiency and growth performances.

Normalizing for other variables, there is little discernible difference between the share of the GDP accounted for by central government expenditure in smaller, as compared with medium-to-large, countries. In

1994, the respective proportions for the countries in our sample were 39.3 percent and 35.8 percent. Nor is it apparent that the patterns of government expenditures are markedly different from those of their larger counterparts. Clearly, if internationalization or globalization matters at all, it is in respect of the types and quality of economic strategies and policies pursued by governments, rather than the total expenditure incurred by them. And, here, there is a clear suggestion that the fostering of the competitiveness of home-based firms in international markets has played a more explicit role in the macro-organizational (or micro-management) strategies[16] of small countries.

One other aspect of globalization,[17] which might be mentioned, is that it is forcing both private and public institutions to reappraise their organizational structures. Pyramids of hierarchies are being increasingly flattened as more non-hierarchical (and horizontal) relationships are being forged between decision takers and line managers. Nowhere is this being more clearly demonstrated than in the giant Swedish/Swiss MNE - Asea Brown Boveri (ABB) - which, some years ago completely reconfigured its organizational structure.[18] In its contemporary philosophy, the job of top management is less to control and take decisions, and more to orchestrate strategic vision, set performance standards, nurture organizational values and encourage down-the-line entrepreneurship. The yin of a centralized corporate strategy and the setting of targets is being accompanied by the yang of decentralized responsibility for achieving these goals, that is subsidiarity in action. Are there not lessons to be learnt by governments in this respect? And, is it not the case that governments of smaller nation states are showing themselves to be the most resilient and adaptive to the organizational changes demanded of them?

Finally, globalization is leading to a decentralization of some of the traditional tasks of national governments to sub-national, that is regional or district authorities; while others, for example the management of trade, FDI and competition policies, and the variety of technical and environmental standardization of harmonization of norms are increasingly becoming the responsibility of regional or supra-national regimes. One wonders, indeed, whether, in the course of the next decade or more, we shall see, as Charles Handy (1995) has put it, (and I quote his words) 'the disappearing middle of national administration'.

2.6 THE HUMAN CONSEQUENCES OF GLOBALIZATION: THE PARADOX OF BENEFITS AND DISBENEFITS

Perhaps the most perceived, and currently the most hotly debated, effects of globalization - or more accurately the economic forces associated with it - is that on the everyday lives of people the world over. While the yin of closer economic interdependence and the liberalization of markets is undisputedly raising average living standards, offering new job opportunities, popularizing new technologies and skills, widening consumer choice and, in a whole variety of ways, improving the lifestyles of large numbers of people; the yang, or downside, of globalization is no less dramatically portrayed in terms of: disturbingly high levels of unemployment, particularly among the younger unskilled workers; a personal sense of insecurity and foreboding associated with rapid technological change; the division of societies into new islands of conflicting economic interests; the breakdown of traditional social conventions; the resurgence of ethnic conflicts and, not least, the easier cross-border movement of tangible or intangible disbenefits, for example organized crime, drug trafficking, international terrorism and unacceptable patterns of behavior.

It is downsides such as these which Klaus Schwab and Claude Smadja (1996) - two of the most prominent advocates of global trade and integration - had in mind when, at the Davos Forum in 1996, they referred to a 'mounting backlash against globalization, and a rising gap between those able to ride the wave of globalization because they are knowledge and communications oriented, and those left behind'. Jeremy Rifkin, in a fascinating monograph entitled *The End of Work* (Rifkin, 1995) has gone even further. He believes that the effects of the current generation of technological advances on the world's labor force may prove to be the 'Achilles heel' of globalization.[19] Other commentators have gone further by asserting that, unless the less desirable consequences of globalization are tackled and, at least, partially resolved, the Utopian vision - and I paraphrase Aldous Huxley's words - of a 'brave new economic world' could quickly be turned into a cauldron of social unrest, political upheaval, cultural fragmentation and ideological conflict between nations, or even civilizations.[20]

Whether you are an optimist or pessimist on these matters, such a stark paradox, I believe, was much less in evidence at the turn of the last century. True, at that time there was much structural change, brought about, inter alia, by the advent of electricity, the telephone, the internal combustion engine and the introduction of the Fordist system of production. But by and large the pace and direction of economic growth, in both the older and newer capitalist economies of the time, was, in general, able to cope with the less welcome consequences of the new technologies; the jobs created were generally more congenial than those which they replaced; while, for the most part, improvements in education and vocational training were able to keep pace with the needs of the marketplace. Moreover, most of the required social adjustments were contained within domestic economies and it was not until after the First World War, that FDI became a significant allocator of cross-border economic activity and, hence, jobs between countries.

At that time, too, there were far fewer non-economic claims on the resources of countries than there are today. Most social welfare programs were in their infancy, and little attention was paid to environmental issues. In the main, the second industrial revolution of the late nineteenth century was accomplished with considerably more observable benefits and fewer observable costs than those resulting either from the emergence of the factory system of a century earlier, or (so it would appear) its successor a century later. Even the hierarchical system of managerial capitalism, although it had some adverse consequences on the entrepreneurship and fortunes of small family-owned enterprises, generally offered the ordinary worker more benefits and opportunities than it took away from him!

Again, the situation is totally different in the emerging global neighborhood of the 1990s. This is apparent both at the level of the individual firm and that of the nation state. Almost daily, it seems, one reads about huge restructuring and relocation programs of corporations, which frequently have traumatic effects on people's lives and livelihoods - not just in one country, but in several. Often the slogan 'one man's job is another man's dole' is all too true. Often, the gains - as well as the costs - of McWorld are exploited by ethnic or religious fundamentalists to advance the course of jihad.[21] In the short run (and in practice, this can be quite long!) there are both losers and winners in the globalization process and the very pace of economic change often requires major adjustment even in the lives of the winners. Over the last two decades, I would suggest, the international restructuring of economic activity has involved more people-adjustment, both within and between countries, than at any other time since the late eighteenth century.

At the level of the nation state, globalization is requiring one of the basic tenets of comparative advantage - namely the cross-border immobility of resources - to be questioned. Not only are many firm-specific assets mobile across national boundaries, but the demands being made by the owners of these assets on those which are spatially more sticky is changing. Thus, for example, in their choice of investment locations, both between and within countries, MNEs are being increasingly influenced by the presence of sub-national agglomerative economies, and by the quality of human and physical infrastructure.[22] As it is, the latter type of assets and quality is strongly influenced by government policies. If these policies are perceived to be inappropriate, or less congenial in their effects than those offered by other governments, then those assets which have the opportunity to do so, will move elsewhere.[23] In such an event, globalization may result in more - or more abrasive - economic disbenefits than benefits - certainly to the countries and to the immobile assets losing the economic activity. Equally, because of differences in age, structures, social policies and the competence of national administrations, the ability of countries to respond to the yang of globalization will vary considerably.

How can one hope to reconcile the conflicting consequences of globalization - which, in the economic arena at least, are time-related and are mainly distributional? I believe the first essential thing is to recognize that, barring natural or man-made catastrophes or a major reconfiguration of social values, the globalization of economic activity is largely irreversible. This is because it is the result of technological advances which, themselves, cannot easily be reversed. However, the pace and form of globalization can be affected as can the recognition and response of governments to some of its more daunting challenges. And, it is the extent to which countries can successfully devise new ways to minimize these costs by effective 'voice' rather than 'exit' strategies which will determine the net benefits they derive from globalization. In the last few years, among the advanced nations, the US has done rather better than most European countries and, in the developing world, China and Malaysia rather better than Brazil and India, in their structural adjustment programs.

What of the specific experiences and likely future roles of small economies in reconciling the huge restructuring and social problems which we have just identified? Is it, for example, the case that, as with successful firms, smallness may confer certain benefits on nations, notably the ability to more speedily adjust to economic change - which might stand them in good stead in coping with an innovation led and uncertain global economy? Are the closer personal contacts and alliances between the leaders of the public and private sectors in such countries as Austria, Switzerland, Denmark and Singapore likely to facilitate and accelerate the process of structural adjustment, or ameliorate some of its costs? What of the capabilities of legislators and administrators of small, as compared with medium-to-large, countries to design and implement the appropriate economic policies, for example with respect to human resource development, demanded by globalization? What, too, of the social dimensions of globalization? Why is it, for example, that it is not the most powerful nations in the world, but developed small countries like Canada and Sweden which, in the past, have been at the forefront of international diplomacy; which are currently among the most aware of the plight of the less-developed countries; and which are among the trailblazers in the protection of human rights and upgrading environmental and safety standards?

These are all questions which, I believe, social scientists should be addressing. I have no easy or pat answers to any of them; but I do have a strong feeling that the past examples of, and further possibilities open to, smaller economies - with their exceptional strong emphasis on economic diversity and social values - do point to their playing a unique role in helping to resolve the various human challenges and dilemmas being posed by the globalizing economy.

The constituents of small countries have also played an important role in promoting a dialogue between the main stakeholders in global capitalism. In this connection, a special mention may be made of the work of the Commission on Global Governance. The Commission - the brain-child of ex-German Chancellor Willy Brandt - was set up in 1992, under the joint chairmanship of the (then) Prime Minister of Sweden, Ingwar Carlsson, and Shridath Ramphal, the ex-Secretary General of the Commonwealth and comprised 28 distinguished statesmen, businessmen, bankers and presidents of international agencies from throughout the world.[24] In its 'call to action', the report makes many astute recommendations on matters ranging from global security, to managing economic interdependence and fostering a global civic ethic. It also urges the UN to convene a World Conference on Global Governance, to which (it suggests) should be invited not only the political leaders of the world, but those of 'the wider human constituency' who are 'infused with a sense of caring for others and a sense of responsibility to the global neighborhood' (Commission on Global Governance, 1995). Such a gathering of men and women of goodwill would, indeed, be an expression of the yin of international cooperation which, I would argue, is needed to counterbalance the yang of international competition.

2.7 CONCLUSIONS

To conclude: at the beginning of the twenty-first century I feel a mixture of optimism and pessimism, and of hope and trepidation. The future seems both more complex and more daunting than that faced by our forefathers a century ago. This, I have suggested, is for four reasons. The first is the increasing dichotomy between the territorial space open to individuals and corporations, and that under the jurisdiction of governments. This is leading to a number of paradoxes and dilemmas - particularly as far as the inter-country distribution of the gains and losses of globalization is concerned. The second is the erosion of the boundaries of the leading institutions for organizing economic activities - and particularly those of firms, markets and governments. Inter alia, this is resulting in a more intricate and pluralistic network of inter-institutional arrangements, and to a new complementarity between the yin of competition and the yang of cooperation.

Third, improvements in standards of living - especially among wealthier nations - are increasingly taking the form of quality-of-life enhancing goods and services (for example computer software, telecommunications, education, health care, environmental protection and the absence of crime, terrorism, and so on), the supply of which governments, by their actions or non-actions, strongly influence. The consequences of globalization are being increasingly evaluated by their effects on the availability, character and distribution of these 'public' products. Insofar as communication advances and the cross-border integration of economic activity are being accompanied by a renewal of national or sub-national (for example tribal) specific cultures and values, this is creating a range of inter-relational tensions and dilemmas quite different in scale and effect from those arising from the second industrial revolution.

Fourth, while twentieth century hierarchical capitalism has generally been accompanied by an expansion in the economic role of national governments, twenty-first century alliance capitalism and the renaissance of the market economy seem likely not only to demand changes in the nature of that role, and an upgrading in the capabilities of public sector decision makers; but also to increase and deepen the tasks of both sub-national and supra-national authorities.

In seeking to reconcile the paradoxes of globalization, I have further suggested that the ways in which small countries have adapted their economic structures, organizational forms and policies to meet the demands of the international marketplace, while maintaining a high degree of political and cultural autonomy, is worthy of scholarly attention. I have also suggested that, up to now, most of the attention of scholars - and, indeed, of most governments - has been focused on the gains of globalization and that, in the future, at least as much attention needs to be given to overcoming its downsides - both actual and perceived.

At the same time, it is important that governments - of both small and medium-to-large economies - do not attribute to globalization all the woes in the world - most of which I believe would have been a lot worse had the introduction of market-friendly economic policies not been implemented. Moreover, the cross-border activities of firms - noticeably via FDI and strategic alliances - may, themselves, assist national governments not only to upgrade the competitiveness of their own firms and indigenous resources, but to do so in a way which fosters their longer-term economic and social goals.

Of course, the strategies of MNEs, like those of governments, may be protective and result in a vicious circle of market-state interface; and the discouragement of these is as important as any competitive enhancing actions which both firms and governments might pursue.

Looking further ahead into the twenty-first century, as the Yale historian Paul Kennedy did in a BBC broadcast in 1996, one cannot but be sobered by one final paradox which, in many ways, over-arches everything I have written up to now. That is, currently the wealthiest 12 percent of the world's population owns or controls 85 percent of the world's stock of created assets, while the rest, that is 88 percent of the population, owns or controls only 15 percent of these assets. Moreover, virtually all of the 50 percent increase in the world's population over the next 30 to 35 years is likely to occur in the less wealthy parts of the world. Clearly, the geographical imbalance between the current technology revolution and the population revolution - to use Kennedy's (1993) terminology - is a potential social time-bomb. Whether or not the bomb is diffused will, I suggest, largely rest on two factors. The first is the nature and pace of Indian and Chinese economic development as, between them, these two super giants are expected to account for between 25 percent and 30 percent of the world's population by 2015. The second is whether the peoples of the world, and their leaders, can summon up enough determination and emotional intelligence to reconcile the growing threat of ideological and class warfare which is epitomized by the Jihad versus McWorld syndrome. For, I fear, unless this is done, our global dream could so easily turn into a global nightmare!

NOTES

1. Some economists, for example Carlota Perez (1983) would go as far as to argue that both the 1880s and the 1980s heralded in a new Kondratiev cycle of techno-economic and socio-institutional change.
2. Although when combined with those of the first two decades of the twentieth century, they did bring quite climacterical changes to some societies, for example Russia.
3. Eric Hobsbawm is a distinguished historian who has authored several books with titles depicting (what, to him, is) the key characteristic of the period he is writing about. Among these are *The Age of Revolution, 1789-1848, The Age of Capital, 1948-1875, The Age of Empire, 1875-1914 and The Age of Extremes 1914-1991* (1995).
4. Namely *Jihad vs. McWorld* (Barber, 1995). Jihad refers to an ideology of parochial ethnicity, which is often portrayed as extreme ethnic or religious fundamentalism. McWorld is the ideology of the global corporation, which is primarily interested in economic gain and would like to ignore all national or political boundaries.
5. Put more accurately, perceived paradoxes; we believe the paradoxes described are more 'imaginary' than they are 'real'.
6. We accept, of course, that the size of nation states may, itself reflect the number of such states; compared with, for example, the size of the erstwhile USSR with the number of countries now making up the Russian Federation.

7. Taking another measure of wellbeing, the UN's human development index (HDI) of the 30 countries with the highest HDI value, 17 were small countries.
8. Of course, what the data do not show is whether, if a particular country was larger or smaller, it would be better or worse off!
9. And more than is commonly realized. For a contemporary account of the interventionist - albeit catalytic - role of the US government in the development of US industry and agriculture in the nineteenth century, see Kozul-Wright (1995).
10. See also a perceptive article on a related theme by Richard Florida (1995).
11. The extent to which small countries are more homogenous than medium-to-large countries in their ethnic, social and cultural mores is, itself, open to question.
12. The same might well be true of most Eastern economies, but here the functions of government were viewed in a very different light from those in the West.
13. An expression first coined at the time of the American Revolution to reflect the extent to which firms and/or individuals could escape (through emigration) unacceptable taxes and other fiscal duties imposed by national governments.
14. As is reviewed, for example, in Dunning (1994) and Panic (1995).
15. And, of course, with some countries and regions more than others.
16. Which include, *inter alia*, industrial, competition, technology, education, trade, and regional policies; and also the provision of efficient infrastructure to attract (and retain) mobile investment (compared with, for example, the expenditure *per capita* on roads, railroad, airport and telecommunication facilities of small and medium-to-large countries.
17. And the technological advances which have accompanied it.
18. As documented, for example, by Bartlett and Ghoshal (1994).
19. He points to similar, but less dramatic, consequences (as they tended to be confined within national borders) of the technological advances, coupled with the mass advertising of the 1920s and 1930s, and migration of unskilled jobs from the Northern to the Southern US in the 1950s.
20. See Barber (1995) and Huntington (1993).
21. Barber (1995) gives some fascinating examples of how practical application of the two starkly opposing ideologies often aid and abet each other; and that neither is complete without the other. For example, he points out that modern transportation technologies, and the export of Jihad ideologies and practices often lead to non-Jihad nations or regimes becoming more dependent on Jihad nations or regions for their economic well-being.
22. For a review of the literature, see Dunning (1993), Braunerhjelm and Svensson (1995) and Mariottti and Piscitello (1995).
23. For an excellent review of the role of investment incentives, offered by governments, on the location of mobile investment, see UNCTAD (1996).
24. Of which eight came from countries with populations of under 12 million.

REFERENCES

Baden-Fuller, C.W.F. and J.M. Stopford (1992), *Rejuvenating the Mature Business*, London and New York: Routledge.

Barber, B.R. (1995), *Jihad vs. MacWorld*, New York: Times Books.

Bartlett, C.G. and S. Ghoshal (1994), *Beyond the M-Form: Towards a Managerial Theory of the Firm*, Working Paper No. 94-6, Pittsburgh: Carnegie Bosch Institute for Applied Studies on International Management.

Bradford, C.L. (1994), *The New Paradigm of Systemic Competitiveness: Toward More Integrated Policies in Latin America*, Paris: OECD.

Braunerhjelm, P. and R. Svensson (1995), *Host Country Characteristics and Agglomeration in Foreign Direct Investment*, Stockholm: Industrial Institute for Economic and Social Research (mimeo).

Cantwell, J. and R. Harding (1997), *The Internationalization of German Companies' R&D*, Discussion Papers in International Investment and Management, no. 233, Reading: University of Reading.

Chang, H.-J. and R. Rowthorn (eds) (1995), *The Role of the State in Economic Change*, Oxford: The Clarendon Press.

Commission on Global Governance (1995), *Our Global Neighborhood*, Oxford and New York: Oxford University.

Dunning, J.H. (1993), *Multinational Enterprises and the Global Economy*, Wokingham, UK and Reading, Mass.: Addison Wesley.

Dunning, J.H. (1994), *Globalization: The Challenge for National Economic Regimes*, Dublin: The Economic and Social Research Council.

Dunning, J.H. (1996), 'The geographical sources of competitiveness of firms: some results of a new survey', *Transnational Corporations*, December, **5** (3), 1-30.

Florida, R. (1995), 'Towards the learning region', *Futures,* **27** (5), 527-36.

Greiber, W. (1997), *One World, Ready or Not*, New York: Simon and Schuster.

Handy, C. (1995), *The Empty Raincoat*, London: Arrow Business Books.

Hobsbawn, E. (1995), *Age of Extremes*, London: Abacus.

Huntington, S. (1993), 'The Clash of Civilizations', *Foreign Affairs,* Summer, **72**, 22-49.

Kennedy, P.M. (1993), *Preparing for the Twenty-First Century*, New York: Random House.

Kozul-Wright, R. (1995), 'The Myth of Anglo-Saxon Capitalism: Reconstructing the History of the American State', in H.-J. Chang and R. Rowthorn (eds), *The Role of the State in Economic Change*, Oxford: The Clarendon Press.

Mariotti, S. and L. Piscitello (1995), 'Information costs and location of FDIs within the host country: empirical evidence from Italy', *Journal of International Business Studies*, **26** (4), 815-41.

Markusen, A. (1994), 'Sticky places in slippery spaces: a typology of industrial districts', *Economic Geography*, **72** (3), 293-313.

Naisbitt, J. (1994), *Global Paradox: The Bigger the World Economy, the More Political its Smallest Players*, New York: William Morrow.

Ohmae, K. (1995), *The End of the Nation State: The Rise of Regional Economies*, London: Harper Collins.

Panic, M. (1995), 'International economic integration and the changing role of national governement', in H.-J. Chang and R. Rowthorn (eds), *The Role of the State in Economic Change*, Oxford: The Clarendon Press, pp. 51-78.

Perez, C. (1983), 'Structural changes and the assimilation of new technologies on the economic and social system', *Futures,* **15**, 357-75.

Rifkin, J. (1995), *The End of Work*, New York: G.P. Putman's Sons.

Schwab, K. and C. Smadja (1996), *Start Taking the Backlash Against Globalization Seriously*, Address given to Davos Forum, January.

Storper, M. (1997), *The Regional World*, London: Guilford Press.

UNCTAD (1996), *Incentives and Foreign Direct Investment*, Geneva and New York: UN.

UNCTAD (1997), *World Investment Report 1997, Transnational Corporations, Market Structure and Competition Policy*, Geneva and New York: UN.

UNDP (1997), *Human Development Report 1997*, New York and Oxford: Oxford University Press.

Wade, R. (1995), Resolving the State-market Dilemma in East Asia, in H.-J. Chang and R. Rowthorn (eds) (1995), *The Role of the State in Economic Change*, Oxford: The Clarendon Press.

World Bank (1997), *The World Development Report 1997: The State in a Changing World*, Oxford and New York: Oxford University Press.

World Economic Forum (1994), *The Global Competitiveness Report*, Geneva, WEF.

3.   A Generalized Double Diamond Approach to the Global Competitiveness of Korea and Singapore

Hwy-Chang Moon, Alan M. Rugman and Alain Verbeke

3.1 INTRODUCTION

In his famous book, *The Competitive Advantage of Nations,* Porter (1990) studied eight developed countries and two newly industrialized countries (NICs). The latter two are Korea and Singapore. Porter is quite optimistic about the future of the Korean economy. He argues that Korea may well reach true advanced status in the next decade (p. 383). In contrast, he is less optimistic about Singapore. In his view, Singapore will remain a factor-driven economy (p. 566) which reflects an early stage of economic development. Since the publication of Porter's work, however, Singapore has been more successful than Korea, as will be discussed in this chapter. This difference in performance raises important questions regarding the validity of Porter's diamond model of a nation's competitiveness.

Porter has used the diamond model when consulting with the governments of Canada (Porter and the Monitor Company, 1991) and New Zealand (Crocombe, Enright and Porter, 1991). While the variables of Porter's diamond model are useful terms of reference when analyzing a nation's competitiveness, a weakness of Porter's work is his exclusive focus on the 'home base' concept. In the case of Canada, Porter did not adequately consider the nature of multinational activities (Rugman, 1991). In the case of New Zealand, the Porter model could not explain the success of export-dependent and resource-based industries (Cartwright, 1993). Therefore, applications of Porter's home-based diamond require careful consideration and appropriate modification.

In Porter's single home-based diamond approach, a firm's capabilities to tap into the location advantages of other nations are viewed as very limited. Rugman (1992, p. 59) has demonstrated that a much more relevant concept prevails in small, open economies, namely the 'double diamond' model. For example, in the case of Canada, an integrated North American diamond (including both Canada and the United States), not just a Canadian one, is more relevant. The double diamond model, developed by Rugman and D'Cruz (1993), suggests that managers build upon both domestic and foreign diamonds to become globally competitive in terms of survival, profitability, and growth. While the Rugman and D'Cruz North American diamond framework fits well for Canada and New Zealand, it does not carry over to all other small nations, including Korea and Singapore. Thus, Moon, Rugman and Verbeke (1995) adapted the double diamond framework to a generalized double diamond which works well for analyzing all small economies. The main purpose of the present chapter is to assess the global competitiveness of Korea and Singapore using this new, generalized double diamond framework. It should be emphasized that the comparison between the single diamond approach and the generalized double diamond will be performed at the macro level rather than the level of individual industries. In this context, it should be remembered that Porter himself made statements about Korea and Singapore at the macro level.

This chapter consists of three sections. The Section 3.2. reviews Porter's (1990) original diamond model and contrasts it with a new framework, the generalized double diamond model (Moon, Rugman and Verbeke, 1995). Section 3.3. presents data and analyzes the variables. In the subsequent section, the results are discussed.

3.2 SINGLE OR DOUBLE DIAMONDS?

Porter (1990, p. 1) raises the basic question of international competitiveness: 'Why do some nations succeed and others fail in international competition?' As its title suggests, the book is meant to be a contemporary equivalent of *The Wealth of Nations*, a new-forged version of Adam Smith's opus (Ryan, 1990, p. 46). Porter argues that nations are most likely to succeed in industries or industry segments where the national 'diamond' is the most favorable. The diamond has four interrelated components: (1) factor conditions; (2) demand conditions; (3) related and supporting industries; and (4) firm strategy, structure and rivalry; and two exogenous parameters (1) government and (2) chance, as shown in Figure 3.1.

This model cleverly integrates the important variables determining a nation's competitiveness into one model. Most other models designed for this purpose represent subsets of Porter's comprehensive model. However, substantial ambiguity remains regarding the signs of relationships and the predictive power of the 'model' (Grant, 1991). This is mainly because Porter fails to incorporate the effects of multinational activities in his model. To solve this problem, Dunning (1992), for example, treats multinational activities as a third exogenous variable which should be added to Porter's model. In today's global business, however, multinational activities represent much more than just an exogenous variable. Therefore, Porter's original diamond model has been extended to the generalized double diamond model (Moon, Rugman and Verbeke, 1995) whereby multinational activity is formally incorporated into the model.

Figure 3.1 The home-based single diamond

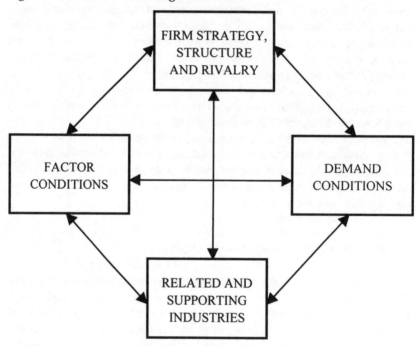

Firms from small countries such as Korea and Singapore target resources and markets not just in a domestic context, but also in a global context.[1] Therefore, a nation's competitiveness depends partly upon the domestic diamond and partly upon the international diamond relevant to its firms. Figure 3.2 shows the generalized double diamond where the outside one represents a global diamond and the inside one a domestic diamond. The size of the global diamond is fixed within a foreseeable period, but the size of the domestic diamond varies according to the country size and its competitiveness. The diamond of dotted lines, between these two diamonds, is an international diamond which represents the nation's competitiveness as determined by both domestic and international parameters. The difference between the international diamond and the domestic diamond thus represents international or multinational activities. The multinational activities include both outbound and inbound foreign direct investment (FDI).

In the generalized double diamond model, national competitiveness is defined as the capability of firms engaged in value added activities in a specific industry in a particular country to sustain this value added over long periods of time in spite of international competition. Theoretically, two methodological differences between Porter and this new model are important. First, sustainable value added in a specific country may result from both domestically owned and foreign owned firms. Porter, however, does not incorporate foreign activities into his model as he makes a distinction between geographic scope of competition and the geographic locus of competitive advantage (Porter and Armstrong, 1992). Second, sustainability may require a geographic configuration spanning many countries, whereby firm-specific and location advantages present in several nations may complement each other. In contrast, Porter (1986, 1990) argues that the most effective global strategy is to concentrate as many activities as possible in one country and to serve the world from this home base. Porter's global firm is just an exporter and his methodology does not take into account the organizational complexities of true global operations by multinational firms (Moon, 1994).

Porter's narrow view on multinational activities has led him to underestimate the potential of Singapore's economy. Porter (1990, p. 566) argues that Singapore is largely a production base for foreign multinationals, attracted by Singapore's relatively low-cost, well-educated workforce and efficient infrastructure including roads, ports, airports and tele-communications. According to Porter, the primary sources of competitive advantage of Singapore are basic factors such as location and unskilled/semi-skilled labor which are not very important to national competitive advantage. In actual fact, Singapore has been the most successful economy among the NICs.

Figure 3.2 The generalized double diamond

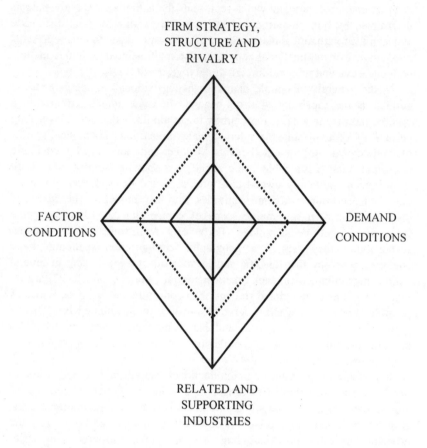

FIRM STRATEGY,
STRUCTURE AND
RIVALRY

FACTOR
CONDITIONS

DEMAND
CONDITIONS

RELATED AND
SUPPORTING
INDUSTRIES

Singapore's success is mainly due to inbound FDI by foreign multinational enterprises in Singapore, as well as outbound FDI by Singapore firms in foreign countries. The inbound FDI brings foreign capital and technology, whereas outbound FDI allows Singapore to gain access to cheap labor and natural resources. It is the combination of domestic and international diamond determinants that leads to a sustainable competitive advantage in many Singaporean industries.

Multinational activities are also important in explaining Korea's competitiveness. The most important comparative advantage of Korea is its human resources which have been inexpensive and well-disciplined. However, Korea has recently experienced severe labor problems. Its labor is no longer cheap and controllable. Major increases in the wages in Korea were awarded to a newly militant labor force in 1987-1990, which lifted average earnings in manufacturing by 11.6 percent in 1987, 19.6 percent in 1988, 25 percent in 1989 and 20.2 percent in 1990 (The Economist Intelligence Unit, 1992). Korea's wage level is now comparable to that of the United Kingdom, but the quality of its products has not kept pace. For the last several years, Korea's wage increases have been significantly higher than those in other NICs and three or four times as high as those in other developed countries (Chungang Daily Newspaper, February 25, 1995). Faced with a deteriorating labor advantage, Korean firms have two choices: (1) go abroad to find cheap labor; (2) enhance their production capabilities by introducing advanced technology from developed countries. In both cases, the implementation of these choices requires the development of multinational activities.

To sum up, multinational activities are very important when analyzing the global competitiveness of Korea and Singapore. In fact the most important difference between the single diamond model (Porter, 1990) and the generalized double diamond model (Moon, Rugman and Verbeke, 1995) is the successful incorporation of multinational activities in the latter. In the next section, we will assess the Porter versus the generalized double diamond models using data for both domestic and international determinants in the cases of Korea and Singapore.

3.3 DIAMOND VARIABLES AND DATA

3.3.1 Dependent Variables

The dependent variable of the diamond model is a nation's competitiveness. Porter (1990) argues that the only meaningful concept of competitiveness at the national level is national productivity (p. 6), although he uses exports and outbound FDI as proxies for competitiveness (p. 25). In our view, the two latter variables should be regarded as explanatory variables and not as proxy for the dependent variable. Table 3.1 lists possible proxy variables for the dependent variable of the diamond model in the cases of Korea and Singapore. Productivity variables include output per capita and output per unit of energy consumption. Managers' perception variables include the strength of the general economy and manufacturing base. While these variables are used for illustrative purposes only, they suggest that Singapore is more competitive than Korea.

Table 3.1 Dependent variables of the diamond model

	Korea	Singapore
Productivity		
GNP per capita ($), 1993	7,660.0	19,850.0
GDP per energy kg (oil equil.) ($), 1993	2.6	3.6
Managers' Perception		
Strong economy as a whole (% agreed), 1992	14.1	58.8
Strong manufacturing base (% agreed), 1992	27.1	57.5

Source: International Monetary Fund (1996); The World Bank (1995); IMD (1992).

Table 3.2 Domestic independent variables of the diamond model

		Korea	Singapore
Factor Conditions			
Basic	Wages in manufacturing (USA = 100), 19940	37.0	37.0
Advanced	Scientists and technicians (1,000 persons), 1986-1991	45.9	22.9
Demand Conditions			
Size	Average annual growth (%), 1980-1993	8.2	6.1
Sophistication	Education index (literacy + schooling), 1992	2.6	2.1
Related & Supporting Industries			
Transportation	Paved roads (km/million persons), 1992	1,090.0	993.0
Communication	Telephones (per 100 persons), 1990-1992	41.4	39.2
Firm Strategy, Structure and Rivalry			
Rivalry	Unequal treatment of foreigners (% agreed), 1992	43.7	37.2

Source: US Department of Commerce (1995); United Nations Development Programme 1994); The World Bank (1995); IMD (1992).

3.3.2 Independent Variables

As discussed, the most important debate over the diamond model is whether the international variables should be incorporated into the model or not. We will assess the model, first with the domestic variables only, and then with both the domestic and international variables. Table 3.2 lists the domestic independent variables and Table 3.3 lists the international independent variables. These variables do not constitute a full set of all relevant parameters but represent acceptable proxies to illustrate the 'value added' of incorporating international elements in the diamond model.

Table 3.3 International independent variables of the diamond model

		Korea	Singapore
Factor Conditions			
Basic	Outbound FDI per capita ($), 1994	56.	743.0
Advanced	Inbound FDI per capita ($), 1994	18.	1,907.2
Demand Conditions			
Size	Export dependency (% of GNP), 1994	25.	140.5
Sophistication	Export diversification (% of export without top 3), 1992	53.	58.6
Related and Supporting Industries			
Transportation	Good air transport system (% agreed), 1992	70.	97.8
Communication	International telex traffic (outgoing traffic in minutes per capita), 1990	0.	7.7
Firm Strategy, Structure and Rivalry			
Rivalry	Openness to foreign products (% agreed), 1992	57.	87.7

Source: International Monetary Fund (1996); Europa Publications Limited (1995); IMD (1992).

3.3.2.1 Factor conditions

Porter distinguishes between basic factors and advanced factors. Basic factors include natural resources, climate, location, unskilled and semiskilled labor, and debt capital. Advanced factors include modern communications infrastructure and highly educated personnel such as engineers and scientists. Porter (1990, p. 77) argues that advanced factors are now the most significant ones for competitive advantage. Since Korea and Singapore are not yet fully developed countries, however, basic factors remain important for their competitiveness. In this study, we choose to measure basic factors by wages in manufacturing and advanced factors are measured by the number of the technical staff per 1,000 persons as shown in Table 3.2 which reports domestic independent variables.[2] Since wages are rapidly increasing in these countries, Korea and Singapore are investing in other countries such as China and the Southeast Asian countries where labor is cheap. Yet Korea and Singapore still need to attract multinational firms from advanced countries, as this may be one way to obtain access to modern technologies. In short, both inbound and outbound FDI are important in enhancing these countries' factor conditions. These international determinants are reported as international independent variables in Table 3.3.

3.3.2.2 Demand conditions

The rate of growth of home demand can be more important to competitive advantage than its absolute size. Rapid domestic growth leads a nation's firms to adopt new technologies faster, with less fear that such technologies would make existing investments redundant, and to build large, efficient facilities with the confidence that they will be utilized (Porter, 1990, p. 94). In addition, a nation's firms gain competitive advantage if domestic buyers are sophisticated and demanding as regards the product or service (Porter, 1990, p. 89). It can be hypothesized that a higher level of education of the consumers increases demand sophistication. The size and sophistication of demand conditions are measured by average annual growth and an education index, respectively in Table 3.2.[3]

For both Korea and Singapore, however, domestic markets are relatively small so global economies of scale cannot be achieved. The most successful firms in these countries target international, rather than domestic markets.[4] The export market measured as a percentage of GNP can serve as a proxy for the relative importance of international demand. If a country's exports depend on just a few foreign countries, however, its export markets are not diversified and are thus not sophisticated. The diversification of export markets serves as a proxy for the sophistication of international demand faced by a nation's firms. It is hypothesized that a high ratio of exports, excluding the top three destination countries, *vis-à-vis* total exports, reflects a more diversified and more sophisticated international demand. These data for proxies for international demand are shown in Table 3.3.

3.3.2.3 Related and supporting industries

Related and supporting industries are those whereby firms coordinate or share activities in the value chain or those which involve products that are complementary to the firms of a given nation. These industries may have strong backward and forward linkages with the firms in a given sector. Since we are testing the competitiveness of manufacturing industries in general in Korea and Singapore, however, the information on general infrastructure such as transportation and communication is important. Transportation is measured by paved roads (km/million persons) and communication is measured by telephone lines (per 100 persons) as shown in Table 3.2. We recognize that modern physical infrastructure could be regarded as an advanced factor, but we did not incorporate it in our earlier section on factor conditions as we believe that it is better to incorporate physical infrastructure as a related and supporting industry.

Again, both Korea and Singapore depend heavily on international business. In today's global business, it is neither efficient nor desirable to rely solely on home-based related and supporting industries.[5] The infrastructure for international business is important. The infrastructure for international transportation is measured by the extent to which international air transport infrastructure meets business requirements. The infrastructure for international communication is measured by the international telex traffic in terms of traffic in minutes per capita. The relevant data reflecting these variables are shown in Table 3.3. We recognize that other proxy variables could be used, such as seaport infrastructure, but we have chosen these proxies for convenience of illustration.

3.3.2.4 Firm strategy, structure and rivalry

The final determinant of a nation's competitiveness reflects the context in which firms are created, organized and managed. National advantage may result from a good match among these variables. However, Porter (1990) finds that no one managerial system is universally appropriate (p. 108). Instead, he expresses a strong preference in favor of vigorous domestic rivalry for creating and sustaining competitive advantage in an industry (p. 117). In this study we attempt to measure whether rivalry, as well as strategy and structure, is domestically oriented or not. This is difficult to do and we choose to measure it by the extent to which foreigners are treated unequally as compared to domestic citizens as shown in Table 3.2. It is hypothesized that a high level of unequal treatment of foreigners is xenophobic and it is correlated with a high domestic orientation of rivalry and firm strategy and structure.

Porter (1990, p. 117) argues that domestic rivalry is superior to rivalry with foreign competitors. This argument may be true in large economies such as the United States, but not in small economies such as Canada (Rugman, 1990), Korea and Singapore. The successful firms in Korea and Singapore are more concerned about international rivalry than about domestic rivalry. International rivalry can be measured by the openness to foreign products which is the extent to which national protectionism does not prevent competitive products from being imported as shown in Table 3.3.

3.4 EMPIRICAL RESULTS OF THE DIAMOND TESTS

The data for domestic independent variables in Table 3.2 and international independent variables in Table 3.3 are transformed into 'competitiveness indices' in Table 3.4. It should again be emphasized that these are used for illustrative purposes only, as indications that Porter's single diamond model lead to wrong conclusions. To calculate the competitiveness index, for each variable, a maximum value 100 is given to the country which has the higher value and a relative ratio in terms of percentage is given to the other country which has the lower value. If a variable is measured by two elements, one half weight is given to each element. For example, in Table 3.2, both of Korea's basic and advanced factor conditions have equal or higher values than those of Singapore so that maximum value 100 is given to each of the two factor conditions of Korea. Thus, the competitive index of Korea's domestic factor conditions is 100/2 + 100/2 = 100.0

Singapore's basic factor condition has the same value (37.0) as that of Korea. The maximum value 100 is given to Singapore for this element. However, Singapore's advanced factor has the value (22.9) which represents 49.9 percent of that (45.9) of Korea's advanced factor. Thus, the competitive index of Singapore's domestic factor conditions is 100/2 + 49.9/2 = 75.0

Table 3.4 Competitiveness index of the diamond model

	Korea	Singapore
Factor Conditions		
Domestic Variables	100.0	75.0
International Variables	4.3	100.0
Demand Conditions		
Domestic Variables	100.0	77.6
International Variables	54.7	100.0
Related and Supporting Industries		
Domestic Variables	100.0	92.9
International Variables	37.4	100.0
Firm Strategy, Structure and Rivalry		
Domestic Variables	100.0	85.1
International Variables	65.6	100.0

Table 3.4 shows that for all four determinants of the diamond model Korea has higher competitive indices for domestic variables, but Singapore has higher competitive indices for international variables. This difference is clearly visualized in Figure 3.3 and Figure 3.4. Korea's domestic diamond consisting of solid lines and its international diamond consisting of dotted lines are shown in Figure 3.3. Similarly, Singapore's domestic and international diamonds are shown in Figure 3.4. The international diamond is constructed by adding the international competitiveness index to the domestic competitiveness index for each variable. In Figure 3.3, for example, domestic competitiveness index (D1d) for factor conditions is 100.0. By adding the international competitiveness index 4.3 to this value, the coordinate D1i represents 104.3. Therefore, the international diamond represents domestic plus international determinants. It can thus be said that the difference between the international diamond and domestic diamond is the international or multinational determinants of the nation's competitiveness.

Three interesting points can be made when comparing the domestic and international diamonds in Figure 3.3 and Figure 3.4. First, Korea has a larger domestic diamond than Singapore, but Singapore has a larger international diamond than Korea.[6] This result implies that Korea is more competitive than

Singapore when considering only domestic determinants, but less competitive than Singapore when considering both domestic and international determinants. As shown in Table 3.1, Korea is less competitive than Singapore according to several parameters. This leads to the conclusion that both domestic and international determinants are important to the competitiveness of Korea and Singapore.

Figure 3.3 The competitiveness of Korea

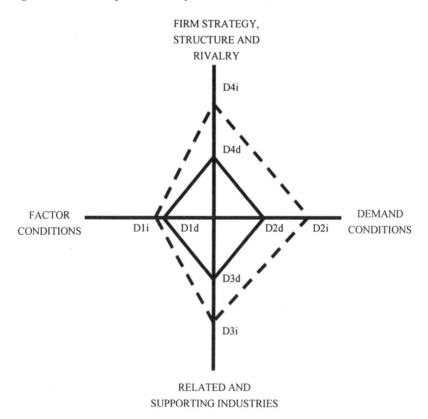

Figure 3.4 The competitiveness of Singapore

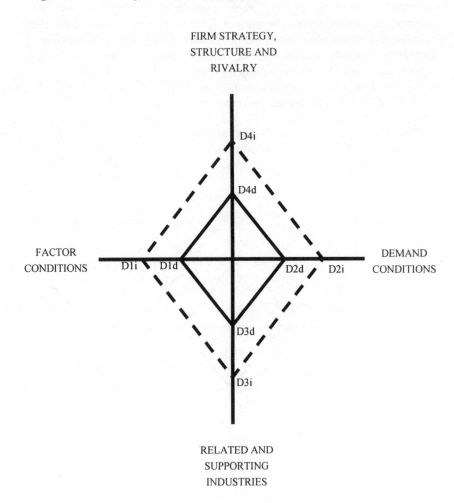

Second, compared with that of Singapore, Korea's international diamond appears to be almost identical to its domestic one with respect to factor conditions. This implies that Korea is relatively weak as regards the international portion of the factor conditions. Singapore has actively pursued outbound FDI to compensate for a shortage of domestic labor and inbound FDI to obtain access to foreign capital and technology. However, Korea has not been as active as Singapore in these multinational activities. In contrast, Porter's work reflects a lack of knowledge of the Korean economy and leads to an incorrect suggestion. Porter (1990) claims that Korea's competitive advantage has thus far rested largely on basic factor conditions (p. 477), but that its future depends upon (domestic) demand conditions, related and supporting industries, and vigorous (domestic) rivalry (p. 479).[7] These variables represent three corners of the diamond, yet neglect one - factor conditions. As can be seen in Figure 3.3, the future of the Korean economy depends more on factor conditions than anything else.

Third, the government factor is very important in influencing a nation's competitive advantage. Governments frequently pursue interventionist trade and industrial strategies (Rugman and Verbeke, 1990). For example, the thirty years of Korea's economic growth have been marked by a number of different phases and in each period government intervention in economic and business affairs has been high (Moon, 1992). Facing a new global environment, the Korean government is now taking various steps to enhance Korea's competitiveness. For related and supporting industries, the government brings together research institutions, universities and private companies in a joint effort to create science parks.[8] As regards demand conditions, Korea pushes global demand because of the relatively small size of its domestic market. The government also emphasizes globalization in the area of firm strategy, structure and rivalry. Korea has unveiled plans to privatize or merge many state-funded companies. Recent efforts to alleviate entry barriers against foreign companies are also examples of public effort to achieve a globalization of industry structure and rivalry.

Yet, as shown in Figure 3.3, the most important determinant of Korea's global competitiveness lies in factor conditions. Korean firms are no longer cost-competitive in overseas markets because the Southeast Asian countries have cheaper sources of labor. On the other hand, Korean firms' technology does not match that of developed countries such as the United States and Japan. The implications for Korea's competitiveness are now clear: to find cheap labor and to increase technological capability. In order to obtain access to cheap labor, Korean firms need to invest in Southeast Asian countries and China. For technological improvement, Korean firms need to invest more in R&D and specialize in the most competitive sectors. However, this is a risky and very long-term strategy. The most practical means of compensating for the country's lack of advanced technology is to import foreign technology. To conclude, both inbound and outbound FDI are important to maintain Korea's competitive edge regarding factor conditions. At the current stage of economic development, the crucial role of the Korean government is to relax various regulations and to provide a favorable environment for both inbound and outbound FDI.

3.5 CONCLUSION

The concept of globalization has become both a buzzword and a crucial long-term goal in many small economies such as Korea and Singapore. Globalization represents both a challenge and an opportunity for these countries. However, this concept is extremely complex and it is not clear how to increase global competitiveness. Porter's diamond model is a good starting paradigm for analyzing important determinants of global competitiveness. However, Porter's original diamond model is incomplete, mainly because he did not adequately incorporate multinational activities.

A new model, the generalized double diamond model, developed and extended in this chapter, has led to three important extensions to Porter's original framework. First, the new model explicitly incorporates multinational activities, whereas Porter's original diamond considers mainly the impact of traditional home-based activities. Second, the new approach easily allows us to operationalize the competitiveness paradigm, whereas Porter's original approach is hard to operationalize. In the generalized double diamond approach, a comparison of the sizes and shapes of the domestic and international diamonds reveals major strategic differences. Third, the new model includes government, not as an exogenous parameter, but as an important variable which influences the four determinants of the diamond model.

All of these three extensions are important when analyzing the global competitiveness of Korea and Singapore. First, as discussed above, both outbound and inbound FDI, that is, multinational activities, are crucial to a nation's competitiveness. Second, by comparing the sizes and shapes of both domestic and international diamonds of Korea and Singapore, the most important variable requiring policy intervention can be identified (that is, factor conditions in the case of Korea). Third, the government factor in small economies such as Korea and Singapore is more important than anything else in affecting the other variables. This does not mean that the government should intervene in every aspect of business affairs, but that the government should be very careful when intervening, considering its potentially large impact on competitiveness.

APPENDIX 1

Table 3.5 Information sources of the variables

Dependent variables		
Productivity		
GNP per capita ($), 1993		WB, pp. 163
GDP per energy kg (oil equil) ($), 1993		WB, pp. 171
Managers' Perception		
Strong economy as a whole (% agreed), 1992		IMD, pp. 1.26
Strong manufacturing base (% agreed), 1992		IMD, pp. 1.28
Independent Variables	*Domestic*	*International*
Factor Conditions		
Basic	USDC, p. 865	IMF, p. 344, 508
Advanced	UNDP, p. 138	IMF, p. 344, 508
Demand Conditions		
Size	WB, p. 163	IMF, p. 344, 508
Sophistication	UNDP, p. 129	EPL, p. 1789, 2697
Related and Supporting Industries		
Transportation	WB, p. 225	IMD, p. 5.20
Communication	UNDP, p. 160	IMD, p. 5.27
Firm Strategy, Structure and Rivalry		
Rivalry	IMD, p. 2.39	IMD, p. 2.37

Source: International Monetary Fund (IMF) (1996); The World Bank (WB) (1995); IMD (1992); US Department of Commerce (USDC) (1995); United Nations Development Programme (UNDP) (1994); Europa Publications Limited (EPL) (1995).

NOTES

1. Global targeting also becomes very important to firms from large economic systems such as the United States.
2. Both Korea and Singapore are natural-resource-poor countries. Therefore, only labor, but not natural resources, is considered as a determinant for the state of the factor conditions.
3. See United Nations Development Programme (1994, p. 108) for the calculation of the education index.
4. For example, Korea's export market at the beginning of internationalization was larger than the domestic market (Cho, Choi and Yi, 1994)
5. Porter (1990, p. 103) argues that foreign suppliers (and related industries) rarely represent a valid substitute for home-based ones. However, when a firm cannot compensate for the disadvantages (for example technology) in the home country, the firm will seek this factor in the foreign country (Moon and Roehl, 1993).
6. Figure 3.3 and Figure 3.4 are drawn on the same scale.
7. In 1994, one of Korea's leading business newspapers, *Mae-il-kyung-jai* (Daily Economic Review), invited several world-famous scholars to express their opinions on Korea's competitiveness. Porter received special attention, thanks to his diamond model. Porter (1994) suggested a similar policy to this, but neglected a possible solution to the problem of factor conditions through multinational activities.
8. For example, Daedok Science town includes 13 government institutes, 3 private research institutes, and 3 universities on its 53 square kilometres. The primary goal of the science parks is to develop their own indigenous technologies. These parks are also playing major

roles in the transfer of technology from the West. For a comparison of science parks of NICs, see Gwynne (1993).

REFERENCES

Cartwright, Wayne R. (1993), 'Multiple linked diamonds: New Zealand's experience', *Management International Review*, **33** (2), 55-70.

Cho, Dong-Sung, Jinah Choi and Youjae Yi (1994), 'International advertising strategies by NIC multinationals: The case of a Korean firm', *International Journal of Advertising*, **13**, 77-92.

Chungang Daily Newspaper (1995), *Wages of Korea and Other Major Countries*, February 25.

Crocombe, F.T., M.J. Enright and M.E. Porter (1991), *Upgrading New Zealand's Competitive Advantage*, Auckland: Oxford University Press.

Dunning, John H. (1992), 'The competitive advantage of countries and the activities of transnational corporations', *Transnational Corporations*, February, **1** (1), 135-68.

The Economist Intelligence Unit (1992), 'South Korea 1992-93: Annual survey of political and economic background', *EIU Country Profile*.

Europa Publications Limited (1995), *The Europa World Year Book 1995*, London, England.

Grant, Robert M. (1991), 'Porter's competitive advantage of nations: An assessment', *Strategic Management Journal*, **12** (7), 535-48.

Gwynne, Peter (1993), 'Directing technology in Asia's dragons', *Research Technology Management*, March/April, **32** (2), 12-15.

IMD (1992), *The World Competitiveness Report*, Lausanne, Switzerland.

International Monetary Fund (1996), *International Financial Statistics*, February.

Moon, H. Chang (1992), 'New Challenges for Korean Conglomerates', in Thomas Chen, Young B. Choi and Sung Lee (eds), *Economic and Political Reforms in Asia*, New York: St. John's University Press.

Moon, H. Chang (1994), 'A revised framework of global strategy: Extending the coordination-configuration framework', *The International Executive*, **36** (5), 557-74.

Moon, H. Chang and Thomas W. Roehl (1993), 'An imbalance theory of foreign direct investment', *Multinational Business Review*, Spring, 56-65.

Moon, H. Chang, Alan M. Rugman and Alain Verbeke (1995), 'The generalized double diamond approach to international competitiveness', in Alan Rugman, Julien Van Den Broeck and Alain Verbeke (eds), *Research in Global Strategic Management: Volume 5: Beyond the Diamond*, Greenwich, CT: JAI Presspp. 97-114.

Porter, Michael E. (1986), 'Competition in Global Industries: A Conceptual Framework', in Michael E. Porter (ed.), *Competition in Global Industries*, Boston: Harvard Business School Press.

Porter, Michael E. (1990), *The Competitive Advantage of Nations*, New York: Free Press.

Porter, Michael E. (1994), 'Competitiveness of the Korean economy', *Mae-il-kyung-jai* (Daily Economic Review), January 4, 5, 6.

Porter, Michael E. and John Armstrong (1992), 'Canada at the crossroads: Dialogue', *Business Quarterly*, Spring, 6-10.

Porter, Michael E. and the Monitor Company (1991), *Canada at the Crossroads: The Reality of a New Competitive Environment,* Ottawa: Business Council on National Issues and Minister of Supply and Services of the Government of Canada.

Rugman, Alan M. (1990), *Multinationals and Canada-United States Free Trade*, Columbia, South Carolina: University of South Carolina Press.

Rugman, Alan M. (1991), 'Diamond in the rough', *Business Quarterly*, Winter, **55** (3), 61-4.

Rugman, Alan M. (1992), 'Porter takes the wrong turn', *Business Quarterly*, Winter, **56** (3), 59-64.

Rugman, Alan M. and Joseph R. D'Cruz (1993), 'The double diamond model of international competitiveness: Canada's experience', *Management International Review*, **33** (2), 17-39.

Rugman, Alan M. and Alain Verbeke (1990), *Global Corporate Strategy and Trade Policy*, London/New York: Croom Helm/Routledge.

Ryan, Richard (1990), 'A grand disunity', *National Review*, July 9, **42** (13), 46-7.

United Nations Development Programme (1994), *Human Development Report 1994.*

United States Department of Commerce (1995), *Statistical Abstract of the United States 1995.*

The World Bank (1995), *World Development Report 1995.*

PART II

The Role of Business-Government Linkages

4. Environmental Policy and Corporate Strategy in a Small Open Economy

Kristel Buysse, Alain Verbeke and Chris Coeck

4.1 INTRODUCTION

A large body of literature on greening strategies has emerged in the recent past. The resource-based view of the firm, as pioneered by Wernerfelt (1984), Peteraf (1993), Barney (1991), Grant (1991) and Prahalad and Hamel (1990, 1994), has provided a useful framework for analyzing the development of 'green' firm-specific advantages (FSAs) and the implications for firm performance (Judge and Douglas, 1998; Russo and Fauts, 1997). One major implication of the resource-based view is that environmental management strategies may actually contribute to the firm's financial and market performance. Greening, that is the introduction of proactive environmental management approaches, building upon firm-level resource allocation, may lead to efficiency gains and new markets to the extent that consumers value products and manufacturing processes with superior environmental performance.

The greening of multinational enterprises (MNEs) merits special attention. MNEs dominate most pollution-intensive industries such as chemicals, petroleum, mineral extraction and heavy manufacturing. In addition, MNEs perform a key role in the international diffusion of technological know-how (Dunning, 1992), including know-how on environmental practices. The question then arises whether MNEs actually develop green FSAs and attempt to diffuse 'best environmental practices' across subsidiaries, even those located in small economies, and to other actors in their business environment. If this is the case, it becomes important to study the determinants of green FSA development, including the impact of environmental regulation prevailing in home and host countries on this greening process. In this chapter, the degree of proactiveness of a firm's environmental strategy (see Section 4.4) is used as a proxy for the existence of green FSAs.

This chapter identifies the variables not critical to the choice of a specific corporate environmental strategy, with a focus on MNEs. An empirical study was conducted in a small open economy (Belgium), covering the most important polluting firms, both domestic ones and subsidiaries of foreign MNEs. The remainder of this chapter is organized as follows. The second and third sections identify the key determinants of a corporate environmental strategy (government regulations, internal and external stakeholders, public opinion and managerial perceptions) and suggest a number of hypotheses to be tested. The fourth section discusses the empirical research methodology. The fifth section presents the main results. Finally, the sixth section discusses the relevance of the various hypotheses tested.

4.2 ENVIRONMENTAL REGULATION AND CORPORATE STRATEGY

Societal concerns about the quality of the natural environment began to emerge in the late 1960s, leading to public demands for environmental regulation in many industrialized countries. Environmental regulation was deemed necessary to internalize the externalities of industrial production and consumption. In many countries, the conventional 'command and control' approach has been increasingly combined with the use of financial instruments, such as environmental taxes (OECD, 1989, 1993).

A typical response by firms faced with environmental regulation consists of adopting 'end-of-pipe' technologies that reduce pollution levels. However, the complex and ever-changing regulatory system has made such a reactive environmental strategy increasingly more expensive and less effective for many firms (Berry and Rondinelli, 1998). Since end-of-pipe installations need to be replaced, modified or supplemented with additional investments with each regulatory change, firms increasingly prefer to prevent pollution 'at the source'. This is especially important for firms operating in several countries, including small economies that represent only a small fraction of the firm's total sales. Some proactive firms have even moved beyond preventing pollution at the source. They have developed green products and adopted so-called sustainable technologies. In this context, it has been suggested that proactive environmental strategies may result from stringent environmental regulation at the sectoral level (Porter and Van der Linde, 1995). Here, firms in specific industry clusters innovate to offset the costs of environmental regulation. Consequently, a positive relationship would be expected between the perceived pressure of environmental regulation and the extent to which an environmental strategy is proactive, that is moves away from end-of-pipe solutions toward developing green FSAs. This perspective leads to the first hypothesis:

Hypothesis 1: Higher perceived regulatory pressures induce firms to adopt more proactive environmental management strategies.

The linkage between environmental regulation and the strategies of MNEs is more complex than suggested by the above hypothesis. MNEs often need to comply with environmental regulation at various institutional levels simultaneously: international, national, sub-national and local. Moreover, at the national level, a further distinction needs to be made between home country regulation and host country regulation. Depending on the perceived pressures of national and international environmental regulation and the configuration of an MNE's FSAs and country-specific advantages (CSAs), several strategic responses to environmental regulation are conceivable (Rugman and Verbeke, 1998a, 1998b, 1998c).

The present chapter focuses on responses whereby an MNE chooses to develop green FSAs. This may occur either as a result of the pressures exerted by international environmental regulation (providing the potential for global scope economies) or when national environmental regulation in either the home country or a host country is perceived as instrumental to obtaining a first mover advantage in 'greening' (Rugman and Verbeke, 1998a, 1998b). One type of MNE strategic response to environmental regulation is suggested implicitly by the mainstream international business literature, on MNE expansion, following Dunning's (1958) and Vernon's (1966) seminal contributions. According to this view, an MNE would develop green FSAs mainly in response to home country (sub)national regulation. These green FSAs would then be replicated in every host country of operation, with minor modifications made only if necessary to comply with host country regulation. Hence, economies of scope would be gained. If home country environmental regulation were relatively stringent,[1] the green FSAs developed at home would also allow the MNE to outperform its local rivals in host countries (Porter and Van der Linde, 1995). In sum, this traditional view of MNE strategic behavior suggests the following hypothesis:

Hypothesis 2: The environmental management strategies chosen by MNEs are responsive to environmental regulation in their home country.

A related hypothesis, building upon Rugman (1995) is that MNEs would be less responsive to host country regulation as compared to domestic firms if the host country is a small open economy, typically representing only a small portion of the MNE's total production and sales.

Hypothesis 3: The regulatory pressures exerted by the national and sub-national governments of a small open economy are more critical to environmental strategy choices by domestic companies than by subsidiaries of foreign MNEs.

Not all MNEs choose to develop green capabilities. Some firms simply aim to comply with environmental regulation in every country of operation. According to Rugman and Verbeke (1998c), this occurs when the perceived pressures exerted by national and international environmental regulation are weak. However, other parameters than environmental regulation may affect strategic choices regarding environmental management in a small open economy. These are discussed in the next section.

4.3 OTHER DETERMINANTS OF GREENING

In the previous section, it was suggested that moving beyond regulatory compliance at the national level may lead to the development of green FSAs. Such FSAs may actually reduce the costs of meeting environmental standards in the different countries of operation (scope economies) and lead to a first mover advantage at the international level. Recent empirical evidence indeed suggests that improvements in environmental performance and industrial performance can be achieved simultaneously (Judge and Douglas, 1998; Russo and Fouts, 1997). However, the development of green FSAs cannot occur in a vacuum, but is related to the technological and organizational know-how already present in the firm (Florida, 1996). Path dependencies explain why some firms may find it easier to allocate resources to the simultaneous achievement of gains in industrial and environmental performance than others in the same industry. For example, firms with strong R&D capabilities or firms with a focus on product differentiation (as measured by advertising expenditures) appear to gain most from proactive environmental management (Florida, 1996; Arora and Cason, 1996). This leads to hypothesis 4.

Hypothesis 4: A stronger perception by managers that gains in environmental and industrial performance can be achieved simultaneously induces more proactive environmental management.

The above hypothesis is also consistent with the 'shareholder-value' approach to strategic management. To the extent that shareholders themselves are convinced that a reputation for good environmental performance is valued positively by financial markets, shareholders are likely to exert pressure on managers to adopt a green strategy in all affiliates. In addition, shareholders may withdraw from companies with a poor environmental management record and which face high compensation claims for environmental damage or risk having their managers under criminal investigation. Shareholder interests may therefore have a considerable influence on corporate environmental strategy (Steadman, Zimmerer and Green, 1995).

However, the shareholder-value approach has been gradually replaced in the strategic management literature by the 'multi-stakeholder' approach, broadening the focus of strategic management from mere profitability seeking to include other corporate goals such as meeting consumer demand, regulatory compliance or maintaining good relationships with the local community (Freeman, 1984; Garrod, 1997; McGee, 1998). In this context, the greening of corporate strategies can also be interpreted as an attempt by firms to align their corporate environmental performance with stakeholder desires and expectations (Gladwin, 1993). In fact, the proliferation of environmental risks and the potentially high costs to society in case of an accident have raised stakeholder demands for greater environmental consciousness by manufacturers (Beck, 1992; Shrivastava, 1995). Employees are directly affected by the environmental risks associated with the production process. Consumers are increasingly willing to pay a premium for environment friendly products. Environmentally conscious suppliers may adopt environmental screening of their customers as part of their environmental strategy and may even exert pressure on customers to improve their environmental performance. This leads to hypothesis 5.

Hypothesis 5: Stronger internal and external stakeholder pressures induce firms to adopt more proactive environmental strategies.

The configuration of economic actors in the firm's external network affects its opportunities to successfully develop green FSAs. Porter (1990) identified the key determinants in the firm's external environment contributing to international competitiveness, namely: (1) demanding consumers and customers, (2) competitive suppliers and related firms, (3) favorable factor conditions and (4) strong industry competition. This framework can also be utilized to explain why the development of green FSAs may constitute a distinct source of competitive advantage. External pressures to adopt a proactive environmental management approach may result from advanced environmental practices within the firm's network of external stakeholders. This leads to hypothesis 6.

Hypothesis 6: Strong simultaneous pressures by various external stakeholders induce firms to adapt a more proactive environmental management strategy.

Finally, a specific hypothesis for MNEs can be formulated. Public demands for greater environmental responsibility have altered the relationship between MNEs and their host communities. Foreign direct investment is increasingly being scrutinized in terms of expected environmental impact, especially if performed by MNEs active in highly polluting and resource-intensive industrial sectors. Given that many MNEs now view the development of good relationships with host countries as important, an increasing number of firms has adopted stringent environmental management practices in every country of operation, exceeding most local environmental standards (Arora and Cason, 1996; Rondinelli and Vastag, 1996; Berry and Rondinelli, 1998). Some of them even sponsor local environment-related events, environmental projects and environmental prizes (Garrod, 1997). Hypothesis 7 therefore suggests the following determinant of proactive environmental management choices by MNEs.

Hypothesis 7: MNEs which place a high value on good relationships with host communities are more likely to adopt proactive environmental management strategies.

4.4 DATA AND METHODOLOGY

The data used in this chapter were gathered through a survey of the most strongly polluting firms in Belgium. The relevant government agencies in Belgium were contacted to obtain the coordinates of all companies contributing significantly to water pollution and waste production. This resulted in a sample of 450 companies, representing 80 percent of water pollution and solid waste production. All companies were first contacted by phone in order to identify which manager was responsible for environmental management issues and to solicit their cooperation with the survey, which was subsequently sent to them. A total of 196 responses were received.

The content of the survey was based on a review of the recent literature on environmental management and corporate social responsibility, with a special emphasis on the greening of MNEs (Henriques and Sadorsky, 1996; Hunt and Auster, 1990; Rugman and Verbeke, 1998a; Judge and Douglas, 1998; Hart, 1995; Levy, 1995; Garrod, 1997; United Nations, 1993). The survey contains four parts and allows to test the hypotheses formulated in the previous sections. The first part aims to decompose the sample into groups according to the firm's environmental management strategy, that is, the level of green FSA development. The second part's main goal is to obtain more information on environmental management practices (reporting, functional coverage, resource commitments) and the factors determining these practices. The third part invites managers to voice their opinion on a number of statements related to the linkages between environmental regulation, environmental management and competitiveness. The last part contains additional questions for MNEs only.

Measurement of proactive environmental management: The difference between reactive and proactive environmental management is by now well understood. A strategy is labeled as reactive when a firm only responds to environmental problems as they occur (TYPE 1) and as proactive when a firm systematically allocates resources to reduce pollution levels. Following the work of Hart (1995), a distinction is made among three types of proactive environmental management strategies each associated with increasing green FSA development: pollution prevention (TYPE 2), product stewardship (TYPE 3) and sustainable development (TYPE 4).

Pollution prevention implies that firms continually adjust their production process in order to reduce pollution levels below what is required by law. As prevention at the source allows firms to achieve regulatory compliance at a lower cost and to reduce liabilities, this environmental strategy may be viewed as a cost reduction approach. Product stewardship can be viewed as a form of product differentiation, whereby products are designed so as to reduce their environmental impact during their entire life cycle (the successive stages of input selection, production, consumption and disposal). Finally, sustainable development refers to the design of new products and processes explicitly aiming to avoid any new burden on the ecosystem.

Environmental management strategies can be ranked on a scale from 1 (TYPE 1) to 4 (TYPE 4), in increasing order of proactiveness. Managers were asked to indicate which of the four types most closely resembled the environmental management system put in place in their firm. The frequency distribution is given in Table 4.1 for all observations together and for subsidiaries of foreign MNEs and local firms separately.

Table 4.1 Distribution of environmental management types in Belgian sample (number of firms)

Management types	Complete sample	Foreign MNEs	Belgian firms
Reactive strategy	36	9	27
Pollution prevention	127	54	73
Product stewardship	20	13	7
Sustainable development	13	10	3
Total number	*196*	*86*	*110*

Pollution prevention at the source (TYPE 2) was clearly the most popular response. There also appeared to be a positive relationship between the proactiveness of environmental strategy and multinationality, with product stewardship and sustainable development more commonly chosen by MNEs and reactive strategies more typically by domestic companies.

Stakeholder pressures: To measure the importance of different pressure sources, the managers were asked to rate on a Likert scale of 1 to 5 the influence of several pressure sources on decisions related to environmental management, with 1 denoting no influence at all and 5 a very strong influence. The list of stakeholder pressures included: domestic (Belgian) and international customers, domestic (Belgian) and international suppliers, the

Belgian national and sub-national governments, environmental regulation of the home country if different from Belgium, shareholders, employees and domestic (Belgian) and international rivals. The pressure exerted by customers (suppliers, rivals) was then defined as the highest of the ratings given to domestic (Belgian) customers (suppliers, rivals) and to international customers (suppliers, rivals).[2]

Linkage with other goals: To learn whether the goal of effective environmental management is complementary to other corporate goals, the managers were asked to express their opinion on a 1 to 5 Likert scale about the following statements (1 means strongly disagree, 3 means no opinion or neutral, 5 means strongly agree) :

(a) Improvements in environmental and industrial performance can be achieved simultaneously.
(b) Good relationships with every host country where a subsidiary of the firm is located are important to the firm. In this context, the company sponsors local educational programs and projects in the area of environmental improvements.

Statement (a) captures the perceived existence of economic opportunities associated with environmental management, and statement (b) measures the MNE's valuation of good relationships with the host community as a corporate goal (for MNEs only).

Control variables: In order to take into account differences in the availability of alternative and cleaner production technologies among industries, differences in industry regulation, and possibly other effects, industry dummy variables were included. Seven broad industry groups were taken into account: (1) food and beverages, (2) textiles, (3) other light industries such as pulp and paper, printing, furniture, wood processing, plastics and other packaging materials, (4) minerals and metals, (5) chemical products also including pharmaceuticals, oils, detergents and cosmetics, (6) heavy manufacturing, and (7) other sectors such as distribution, construction, transportation and utilities.

In addition, possible regional differences were taken into account. In Belgium, the enactment of environmental regulations and the investments in public environmental infrastructure are the responsibility of the regional authorities. Therefore, a dummy (REGION) was also included, which equals 1 when a company is located in Wallonia.

Finally, previous research and preliminary findings (see Table 4.1) suggest that a firm's multinational character contributes positively to the environmental awareness of the firm. Hence, a dummy (MNE) was included which equals one when the firm is a subsidiary of a foreign MNE.

Ordered logit analysis[3] was used to test whether some pressure sources systematically affect the proactiveness of the environmental management strategy. The dependent variable is the type of environmental management strategy implemented by the firm, ranked from 1 to 4 in increasing order of proactiveness. The model was estimated first for all observations pooled together, and next for the subsidiaries of foreign MNEs and for Belgian firms separately.

4.5 RESULTS

Table 4.2 summarizes the importance of each individual source of pressure for all observations together and for foreign MNEs and Belgian firms separately. In addition, Table 4.2 also includes the correlation coefficients between each pair of explanatory variables.

The greatest individual source of pressure cited by all firms appears to be domestic national and subnational regulatory pressure, irrespective of their status as Belgian firm or subsidiary of a foreign MNE. This is in accordance with hypothesis 1. It is interesting to observe that subsidiaries of foreign MNEs perceive pressures from host country environmental regulations to be much stronger than the pressures resulting from regulations prevailing in their home country, thus suggesting that hypothesis 2 should be rejected. In addition, Table 4.2 indicates that many firms, and in particular subsidiaries of foreign MNEs, believe there are economic opportunities associated with the implementation of a specific environmental strategy, suggesting the relevance of hypothesis 4. Finally, internal and external stakeholder pressures appear to exert some influence on corporate environmental strategies as well. Stakeholder pressures are perceived more strongly by subsidiaries of foreign MNEs. This result is consistent with the results shown in Table 4.1, which described the higher proactiveness of MNE environmental strategies (compare hypothesis 5).

The correlation coefficients show that some sources of individual stakeholder pressure, in particular the pressure exerted by consumers, suppliers and rivals, are strongly correlated with each other, suggesting that specific environmental strategies may be developed in response to simultaneous pressures exerted by various external stakeholders. This is a first indication that hypothesis 6 may be valid. Econometric theory argues that the presence of multicollinearity will increase the standard errors of the parameter estimates, thereby reducing their level of significance in subsequent econometric analysis. Multicollinearity may also cause coefficients to have an unexpected sign or to be sensitive to small changes in the data (Greene, 1993). Given that the significance of the individual coefficients of stakeholder pressures may be low, likelihood ratio[4] tests will be employed to test for joint significance.

A more rigorous test of the hypotheses formulated earlier is obtained by using regression analysis techniques. The parameter estimates and respective t-values of the ordered logit models are presented in column 1 for all observations, in column 2 for subsidiaries of foreign MNEs only and in column 3 for Belgian firms only. A separate analysis for foreign MNEs and Belgian firms is relevant as a benchmark for comparison and in order to explicitly test hypothesis 3.

One interesting finding is that national and sub-national regulatory pressures do not appear to be a significant factor in explaining why some firms implement more proactive environmental strategies than others in the entire sample (hypothesis 1 rejected), even though national regulatory pressures were rated high by all participants. This suggests that national regulations do not induce firms to become leaders in the development of products and processes with a low environmental impact. However, another interesting finding which is in contradiction with the results for the entire sample, is that regulatory pressures do stimulate Belgian firms to switch from reactive to more proactive environmental management. This result implies that Belgian national and sub-national environmental regulations have a stronger impact on the environmental practices of local firms than on subsidiaries of foreign MNEs (hypothesis 3 accepted). Remember though, that the typical domestic firm is a follower in the field of environmental management and that the choice of environmental strategy is often between merely reacting to environmental legislation and systematically reducing pollution at the source (Table 4.1).

The results also confirm that the impact of home country regulations as a pressure source for subsidiaries of foreign MNEs is very limited (hypothesis 2 rejected). This finding implies that MNEs do not design environmental strategies in their foreign affiliates based on their home country environmental regulations. The Porter and Van der Linde (1995) perspective, which argues that stringent environmental regulation at home can offer home producers a competitive edge as first-movers in international markets is therefore not supported by the facts.

Table 4.2 Summary statistics and correlation coefficients for key sources of environmental pressure on foreign and local firms in Belgium

	Mean: all firms	Mean: MNEs	Mean: local firms	1	2	3	4	5	6	7
1 Economic opportunities	3.867 (0.884)	4.083 (0.815)	3.700 (0.904)	1.00						
2 Employees	2.311 (1.033)	2.639 (1.073)	2.055 (0.927)	0.17	1.00					
3 Shareholders	2.576 (1.256)	2.895 (1.138)	2.327 (1.293)	0.15	0.41	1.00				
4 Customers	2.520 (1.259)	2.663 (1.298)	2.409 (1.221)	0.31	0.34	0.34	1.00			
5 Suppliers	1.755 (0.895)	1.802 (0.918)	1.718 (0.879)	0.17	0.36	0.40	0.55	1.00		
6 Rivals	2.015 (1.074)	2.151 (1.133)	1.909 (1.019)	0.22	0.40	0.34	0.50	0.48	1.00	
7 National and sub-national regulations	3.888 (0.895)	3.895 (0.882)	2.882 (1.001)	-0.04	0.20	0.06	-0.04	0.06	0.13	1.00
8 Home country regulations*		2.723 (1.464)								
9 Good relationships with host countries*		3.174 (1.285)								

Notes: Standard deviations between brackets.

• data available for subsidiaries of foreign MNEs only

Table 4.3   *Determinants of proactive environmental management: ordered logit estimations*

	Complete sample		Subsidiaries of foreign MNEs		Belgian firms	
	Coeff	t	Coeff	t	Coeff	t
Region	1.1611	-2.585***	-1.4607	-2.324**	-1.8131	-2.255**
Foreign MNE	0.7316	1.910*				
National and sub-national Belgian regulations	0.2104	1.148	-0.1762	-0.559	0.5258	2.046**
Home country regulations			0.0118	0.061		
Economic opportunities	0.6963	3.411***	1.2301	2.977***	0.7641	2.762***
Good relationships with host countries			0.9498	3.591***		
Stakeholder pressure						
Employees	-0.0458	-0.245	-0.0966	-0.333	-0.2594	-0.893
Shareholders	0.5383	3.367***	0.7479	2.405**	0.5104	2.394**
Customers	0.0408	0.237	-0.4783	-1.482	0.2029	0.864
Suppliers	-0.0043	-0.019	-0.3210	-0.760	0.3144	0.962
Rivals	0.2166	1.164	0.6847	2.077**	0.0117	0.044
Sectors						
Textile	0.9910	1.790*	3.455	2.481**	0.8739	1.299
Other light industry	-0.7877	-1.493	0.3473	0.341	-1.1432	-1.692*
Manufacturing	0.9731	1.663*	2.0459	3.391**	-0.0816	-0.095
Minerals and metals	1.2803	2.148**	2.0459	2.307**	1.2477	1.371
Chemicals	1.0773	1.827*	0.8982	1.154	1.9966	1.478
Other sectors[1]	-0.2443	-0.359			-0.1131	-0.152
Number of observations	196		86		110	
Chi2	71.81		47.51		38.13	
Likelihood ratio for all stakeholders	18.22***		11.80**		11.50**	
Likelihood ratio for external stakeholders	2.10		5.82		2.72	

Notes:

*   coefficient significant at 10% level.
**   coefficient significant at 5% level.
*** coefficient significant at 1% level.
[1] There were no observations for subsidiaries of foreign MNEs in this category.

Table 4.4 Environmental strategies implemented and stakeholder pressures perceived by MNEs: division according to location of subsidiary

	All MNEs	Wallonia	Flanders
Environmental strategies			
Fraction implementing reactive environmental strategy	10.5	10.0	11.0
Fraction implementing pollution prevention at the source	63.0	64.5	62.0
Fraction implementing green product differentiation	15.0	22.5	11.0
Fraction implementing sustainable development strategies	11.5	3.0	16.0
Stakeholder pressures			
Employees	2.639	2.871	2.509
Shareholders	2.895	3.452	2.582
Customers	2.663	3.258	2.327
Suppliers	1.802	2.258	1.545
Rivals	2.151	2.387	2.018
National and sub-national regulations	3.895	4.065	3.800
Home country regulations	2.723	3.097	2.513
Perceived economic opportunities	3.867	4.355	3.927
Good relationships with local community	3.174	3.484	3.000

Hypothesis 4 is confirmed for the entire sample as well as for the two sub-samples, that is the subsidiaries of foreign MNEs and the Belgian firms. The results show that proactive environmental management is stimulated by perceived opportunities to achieve improvements in environmental and industrial performance simultaneously. In addition, the results for the entire sample also suggest that shareholder pressures contribute positively and significantly towards strong proactive environmental management, but that other individual stakeholder pressures exert less influence. This may be due to the presence of multicollinearity between these explanatory variables, as mentioned earlier. In fact, the imputed likelihood ratio test statistic for the joint significance of internal and external stakeholder pressures indicates that their joint impact on environmental management practices is positive and important (hypothesis 5). However, the likelihood ratio, computed to test for the joint significance of external stakeholder pressures only, suggests that external stakeholder pressures are jointly insignificant, leading to the rejection of hypothesis 6. The joint impact of external stakeholder pressures appears to be somewhat stronger for subsidiaries of foreign MNEs though the likelihood ratio falls short of being significant, even at the 10 percent level of significance. The most striking result in the analysis for subsidiaries of foreign MNEs and this is in sharp contrast with the findings for the entire sample and for the domestic firms, is that proactive environmental management is responsive to rivalry pressures. This suggests that the forces of global, rather than local, competition induce MNEs to adopt more proactive environmental strategies in a small open economy. This interpretation warrants some caution though: contrary to the expectations the coefficients of customers and suppliers have a negative sign. This may simply be a consequence of multicollinearity, as mentioned earlier.

Finally, when concentrating on subsidiaries of foreign MNEs only, it can be observed that the MNE's valuation of good relationships with the local community has a very strong influence on the choice of an environmental management strategy (hypothesis 7 accepted).

A last striking observation is that the coefficient of the dummy for region is negative and significant for the entire sample as well as for both sub-samples. Considering the sub-sample of subsidiaries of foreign MNEs, Table 4.4 indicates that the subsidiaries located in Flanders implement environmental strategies that are slightly more proactive than those of the subsidiaries located in Wallonia. However, regulatory pressures as well as other stakeholder pressures are perceived more strongly by the subsidiaries located in Wallonia (see also Table 4.4).

4.6 CONCLUSIONS

This chapter identified the key determinants of proactive environmental management in a small open economy. These determinants include regulatory pressures, the pursuit of economic opportunities (that is the simultaneous pursuit of environmental and industrial performance), the valuation of good relationships with local communities in host countries and internal and external stakeholder pressures. The chapter focussed on the environmental strategies of MNEs in small open economies because of their strong involvement in highly polluting activities and their key role in the dissemination of new technologies and managerial practices across borders. One interesting finding is that the environmental practices of foreign MNEs appear to be superior to those of domestic firms in host countries, at least in the case of Belgium.

It appears that regulatory pressures exerted by the government of a small open economy have more impact on the strategic decisions of domestic companies than on the decisions of subsidiaries of foreign MNEs. Indeed, the research provides evidence that high perceived regulatory pressures induce domestic firms to adopt more proactive environmental management strategies. However, this conclusion does not extend to the case of subsidiaries of foreign MNEs. Therefore, this hypothesis could not be accepted in general. The hypothesis, which stated that subsidiaries of foreign MNEs implement environmental strategies in host countries based on regulations prevailing in their home country is also rejected, as environmental management strategies of MNE subsidiaries do not appear responsive to environmental pressures in the MNE's home country.

The perception that proactive environmental management leads to economic benefits (reputation effects, access to new markets, efficiency gains) was shown to contribute positively towards the greening of corporate strategies.

As regards the hypothesis that internal and external stakeholder pressures constitute a moderately important element affecting the choice of a specific environmental management strategy, the strongest pressure comes from shareholders, for whom poor environmental performance implies increased investment risks. Moreover, it also appears that rivalry pressures may push MNEs towards the implementation of more proactive environmental management strategies in their affiliates. In addition, the chapter's findings suggest that stakeholder pressures do not operate in isolation from each other: it is their joint effect that may raise a company's awareness of environmental issues, and motivates them to develop green FSAs. However, the joint impact of external stakeholder pressures does not appear to be as significant. Finally, the hypothesis is confirmed that the valuation of good relationships with host country actors stimulates subsidiaries of foreign MNEs to adopt stringent environmental standards worldwide was confirmed.

In sum, shareholder pressures and perceived economic opportunities are the key determinants of a proactive environmental strategy. In addition, Belgian firms respond to national and sub-national regulatory pressures when choosing between a reactive and a proactive environmental management strategy. However, government environmental regulations have less influence on the choice of an environmental strategy in the case of an MNE. This conclusion holds for both regulatory pressures prevailing in home and host countries. The chapter's findings suggest no role for strategic policy making, whereby stringent environmental regulations would lead to first mover advantages internationally, and strengthen the competitiveness of specific domestic industries (compare Nehrt, 1996). Moreover, these results also show that the impact of national regulations, whether from home or host countries, on the behavior of MNEs is rather limited.

NOTES

1. It is difficult to compare in practice the stringency of environmental regulations between countries because different countries may use different instruments to address specific pollution problems (Nehrt, 1998).

2. In each of the three cases, domestic (Belgian) and international pressure sources appeared to be closely correlated, with international pressure sources more important for MNEs.
3. Ordered logit analysis is an estimation method designed to account for the following properties of the dependent variable: (1) the dependent variable takes discrete values only, (2) the ordering is important and (3) the ordering is only a ranking. The dependent variable, EMSTYPE, has exactly these properties.
4. The likelihood ratio test is based on the change in value of the likelihood function, resulting from the introduction of a number of restrictions. In symbols: LR = chi2(J) = $-2(LnL_0 - LnL_1)$, with LnL_0 the value of the likelihood function at unconstrained parameter estimates, and LnL_1 the value of the likelihood function at restricted estimates. LR follows a Chi2 distribution with J degrees of freedom, where J corresponds to the number of parameter restrictions.

REFERENCES

Arora, S. and T.N. Cason (1996), 'Why do firms volunteer to exceed environmental regulations? Understanding participation in EPA's 33/50 Program', *Land Economics*, **72** (4), 413-32.

Barney, J. (1991), 'Firm, resources and sustained competitive advantage', *Journal of Management*, **17** (1), 99-120.

Beck, U. (1992) 'From industrial society to risk society', *Theory, Culture and Society*, **9**, 97-123.

Berry, M.A. and D.A. Rondinelli (1998), 'Proactive corporate environmental management: a new industrial revolution', *Academy of Management Executive*, **12** (2), 38-50.

Dunning, J.H. (1958), *American Investment in British Manufacturing Industry*, London: Allen & Unwin.

Dunning, J.H. (1992), 'The global economy, domestic governance strategies and transnational corporations: interactions and policy implications', *Transnational Corporations*, **1** (3), 7-46.

Florida, R. (1996) 'Lean and Green: The move to environmentally conscious manufacturing', *California Management Review*, **39** (1), 80-99.

Freeman, R. (1984), *Stakeholder Management: a Strategic Approach*, Boston: Pitman/Ballinger.

Garrod, B. (1997), 'Business Strategies, Globalization and Environment', in OECD, *Globalization and Environment*, Paris: OECD.

Gladwin, T. (1993), 'The Meaning of Greening: A Plea for Organizational Theory', in Fischer, K. and J. Schot (eds), *Environmental Strategy for Industries: International Perspectives on Research Needs and Policy Implications*, Washington, DC: Island Press.

Grant, R.M. (1991), 'The resource-based theory of competitive advantage: implications for strategy formulation', *California Management Review*, **33** (3), 114-35.

Greene, W.H. (1993), *Econometric Analysis*, Englewood Cliffs, NJ: Prentice Hall.

Hart, S.L. (1995), 'A natural-resource-based view of the firm', *Academy of Management Review*, **20** (4), 986-1001.

Henriques, I. and P. Sadorsky (1996), 'The determinants of an environmentally responsive firm: an empirical approach', *Journal of Environmental Economics and Management*, **30**, 381-95.

Hunt, C.B. and E.R. Auster (1990), 'Proactive environmental management: avoiding the toxic trap', *Sloan Management Review*, Winter 1990, 7-18.

Judge, W.Q. and T.J. Douglas (1998), 'Performance implications of incorporating environmental issues into the strategic planning process: an empirical assessment', *Journal of Management Studies*, **35** (2), 241-62.

Levy, D.L. (1995), 'The environmental practices and performance of transnational companies', *Transnational Corporations*, **4** (1), 44-67.

McGee, J. (1998), 'Commentary on corporate strategies and environmental regulation: an organizing framework', *Strategic Management Journal*, **19** (4), 377-87.

Nehrt, C. (1996), 'Timing and intensity effects of environmental investments', *Strategic Management Journal*, **17** (7), 535-47.

Nehrt, C. (1998), 'Maintainability of first mover advantages when environmental regulation differs between countries', *Academy of Management Review*, **23** (1), 77-97.

OECD (1989), *Economic Instruments for Environmental Protection*, Paris: OECD.

OECD (1993), *Taxation and the Environment*, Paris: OECD

Peteraf, M. (1993), 'The cornerstones of competitive advantage: a resource based view', *Strategic Management Journal*, **14**, 179-91.

Porter, M.E. (1990), *The Competitive Advantage of Nations*, New York: Free Press.

Porter, M.E. and C. Van der Linde (1995), 'Toward a new conception of the environment-competitiveness relationship', *Journal of Economic Perspectives*, **9** (4), 97-118.

Prahalad, C.K. and G. Hamel (1990), 'The core competence of the corporation', *Harvard Business Review*, March-April, 75-84.

Prahalad, C.K. and G. Hamel (1994), *Competing for the Future*, Boston: Harvard Business School.

Rondinelli, D. and G. Vastag (1996), 'International environmental standards and corporate policies: an integrative framework', *California Management Review*, **39** (1), 106-22.

Rugman, A. (1995), 'Environmental regulations and international competitiveness. Strategies for Canada's forest products industry', *The International Executive*, **37** (5), 97-118.

Rugman, A. and A. Verbeke (1998a), 'Corporate strategies and environmental regulation: an organizing framework', *Strategic Management Journal*, **19** (4), 363-75.

Rugman A. and A. Verbeke (1998b), 'Multinationals and public policy', *Journal of International Business Studies*, **29** (1), 115-36.

Rugman A. and A. Verbeke (1998c), 'Corporate strategy and international environmental policy', *Journal of International Business Studies*, **29** (4), 819-33.

Russo, M.V. and P.A. Fouts (1997), 'A resource based perspective on corporate environmental performance and profitability', *Academy of Management Journal*, **40** (3), 534-59.

Shrivastava, P. (1995), 'Ecocentric management for a risk society', *Academy of Management Review*, **20**, 118-37.

Steadman, M.E., T.W. Zimmerer and R.F. Green (1995), 'Pressures from stakeholders hit Japanese companies', *Long Range Planning*, **28** (6), 29-37.

United Nations (1993), *Environmental Management in Transnational Corporations: Report on the Benchmark Corporate Environmental Survey*, New York: United Nations.

Vernon, R. (1966), 'International investment and international trade in the product cycle', *Quarterly Journal of Economics*, **80**, 109-207.

Wernerfelt, B. (1984), 'A resource-based view of the firm', *Strategic Management Journal*, **5**, 171-80.

5. Globalization as a Threat and an Opportunity in a Small Open Economy. Why are Some Firms in Belgium more Protectionist than Others?

Ilse Scheerlinck, Luc Hens and Rosette S'Jegers

5.1 INTRODUCTION

Since the early 1990s firms operating in Belgium have been confronted with new regulatory and institutional arrangements concerning international trade. First, the EU Single European Act and the Maastricht Treaty have further transferred power from EU Member States to the European Union. Second, the General Agreement on Tariffs and Trade (GATT) was extended towards 'new issues' that go beyond trade in goods, such as rules on trade in services (included in the General Agreement on Trade in Services - GATS) and trade-related aspects of intellectual property rights (TRIPs, included in the TRIPs Agreement). These changes have deeply affected firms' operations, and consequently firms have good reasons for leaving their mark upon the further course of policy making. Professional organizations (industry lobbies) continuously articulate their views to policy makers in order to influence the policy outcome, and lobbying is anything but a declining sector. This fact does not necessarily conflict with John Dunning's observation in this volume's first chapter that governments have become less 'interventionist' (for example as providers of subsidies or defenders of special interests), but are becoming more important as providers of infrastructure. As Dunning indicates, infrastructure can be seen in a broad sense, including institutions to guarantee a level playing field and to enhance (international) competition. The shift in public policy preoccupations illustrates the greater coincidence of interests between governments and the private sector. At the same time of course, firms still (and maybe even more than before) try to capture rents generated by protection. In any case, the interactions between firms and governments are crucial to understand how trade policy is made. The first step is to investigate which factors shape firms' views on trade liberalization and harmonization of the conditions of competition. This is the subject of the present chapter.

In a number of empirical papers, we examined how firms operating in Belgium perceive policy options in the areas of trade liberalization and harmonization (Scheerlinck 1998; Scheerlinck, Hens and S'Jegers 1996a, 1996b, 1998; André, Hens and Scheerlinck 1997). More specifically, the following issues were addressed:

1. How do firms in Belgium behave politically towards new trade policy issues?
2. Do firm-specific characteristics have an influence on these firms' behavior?
3. Are there substantial differences between industries with respect to the influence of these firm-specific characteristics?

Observations of the firms' positions on trade policy were gathered from representative industry surveys. The total sample consisted of more than 700 returned questionnaires. CEOs had to express whether they were strongly opposed, opposed, in favor, or strongly in favor of a number of specific policy options related to each industry (such as the Single License principle for banks operating in the EU, or the gradual reduction of tariffs on textiles and clothing). Similar questions were asked about GATT principles such as reciprocity and non-discrimination. Since the emphasis was on new policy issues, we focused on industries that have recently faced important changes in market regulations: the textile and clothing industries (generally considered as a declining industry), banking and road haulage (two very different service industries), and the pharmaceutical industry (for which trade-related aspects of intellectual property rights are particularly important).

Economic theory (in particular the political economy of trade policy and the managerial approach to political behavior) suggests that a firm's positions are shaped by its self-interest. We tested whether characteristics of the firm (such as diversification of activities, the perceived threat of competition, the firm's nationality of ownership and potential pressure by employees who are afraid to lose their jobs) explained the observed variation in the responses. Readers interested in detailed discussions of the results by industry (including which proxies are used for the firms' characteristics, the numerical results of the econometric estimation exercises and alternative estimation techniques) are referred to the papers mentioned above. In this chapter, we compare the outcomes across the selected industries (textile and clothing, banking, road haulage and the pharmaceutical industry) and investigate their relation to the (apparent) paradoxes outlined by John Dunning in his contribution to this volume. The results illustrate several of the points made by Dunning; they also appear to contradict some.

5.2 A MANAGERIAL APPROACH TO THE POLITICAL ECONOMY OF TRADE POLICY

Our approach is at the crossroads of the political economy of trade policy and the managerial approach to political behavior. Political economy - firmly rooted in public choice theory - explains trade policies and trade regimes as the results of industries pursuing their self-interest. The firms are seen as maximizers of profits (or of a broader measure of stakeholders' welfare) and costs to influence the outcome of public policy (such as contributions to the industry lobby organization, or donations to a friendly politician's election fund) are included in the firms' costs. An industry's policy demand or policy outcome are thus related to structural characteristics of the industry, that is, the determinants of its competitiveness and costs. Hillman (1989), Lanjouw and Wielinga (1994), and Rodrik (1995) survey the theory; empirical work includes Pugel and Walter (1985) for the US and Tharakan (1984, 1991) for Belgium and the EU. Typically, the *industry* serves as unit of analysis and consequently the political economy approach provides little insight into motives driving the individual *firm*. Managerial views on political behavior (pioneered by Rugman and Verbeke, 1990a, 1990b, 1992, and Boddewyn and Brewer, 1994) fill this gap by focusing on the individual firm rather than the industry. The managerial approach attributes a firm's political behavior to strategic decisions and individual characteristics, but does not explicitly consider the structure of the industry in which the firm operates. We integrate the two theoretical perspectives by analyzing political behavior of individual firms in various Belgian industries. This integration is particularly relevant when studying trade interests in a Member State of the EU. The firm-level perspective is interesting because firms may disagree on policy making; the industry-level perspective because (national) industry professional organizations play a major role in serving their members' European interests (see the papers collected in Mazey and Richardson, 1993). The influence of firm-specific characteristics may also differ according to the industry in which the firm operates.

Following the above analysis, our hypotheses are:

1. Belgian businesses are increasingly confronted with supranational, long-run policy issues of liberalization and harmonization.

2.   Self-interest guides the individual firm when it expresses its preferences on new long-run (trade) policy issues applying to its industry.
3.   These policy preferences are shaped by firm-specific characteristics: the perceived international competition, strategic characteristics and structural characteristics.
4.   The impact of these firm-specific characteristics on policy preferences may differ according to the industry in which the firm operates.

5.3   RESULTS BY INDUSTRY

5.3.1   Firms within the Same Industry often Disagree

The political economy approach typically assumes that firms within the same industry take a (more or less) unanimous stance on trade policy and other (de)regulatory issues in their industry. The managerial approach to political behavior assumes that (trade) policy preferences are not homogeneous within an industry, but differ considerably across firms. Firms within an industry may differ substantially and have a wide range of political interests, and therefore may have an incentive to lobby individually. The results of our empirical research indeed suggest that firms within an industry disagree significantly. Consequently, political economy models based on a sectoral approach may miss much of the story.

Textile and clothing industries
The following types of issues were presented to the textile and clothing firms:

1.   EU Common Commercial Policy;
2.   EU internal free trade;
3.   GATT principles of non-discrimination and reciprocity;
4.   GATT tariff costs; and
5.   issues on the openness of the EU towards trade originating from low-wage countries, more specifically the reduction of restrictions on imports and the phasing out of the Multi-Fibre Arrangement.

A majority of Belgian textile and clothing firms favors the EU Common Commercial Policy and internal free trade. Nevertheless, they support exceptions to the EU Common Commercial Policy and the tariff cuts enforced by GATT. They also support restrictions on imports from low-wage countries. But there is an important degree of dissent among firms, in particular on the GATT reciprocity principle, the GATT import tariff reductions, the issue of market access for non-EU firms and the phasing-out period of the Multi-Fibre Arrangement.

Road haulage

In the road haulage industry the following types of issues were considered:

1. EU harmonization of road haulage and the European tax on heavy weight transport ('Eurovignette');
2. liberalization of road haulage within the EU;
3. liberalization of road haulage between the EU and third countries (and low-wage countries in particular);
4. market access for firms originating from other EU countries and third countries;
5. liberalization of EU road cabotage and free access for firms doing cabotage;
6. GATS liberalization of trade in (transport) services.

A majority of road hauliers operating in Belgium favors liberalization and harmonization when framed in general terms. A majority opposes the more specific issues, such as access to the Belgian or European markets by foreign competitors. Particularly striking is the strong opposition against the Eurovignette. There is an important degree of dissension among road hauliers, in particular on a possible liberalization between EU and third countries, on access for Belgian hauliers to foreign countries, on the GATT most-favored-nation clause and on worldwide liberalization of road haulage.

Banking

The following policy issues were presented to the banks:

1. the single-license principle and the home-country-control principle included in the EU Second Banking Directive;
2. the minimum capital requirements on the risk-asset ratio and on off-balance-sheet operations;
3. the law incorporating the Second EU Banking Directive into Belgian law;
4. GATS liberalization of trade in (financial) services.

Belgian credit institutions generally favor liberalization and deregulation. But they also favor exceptions, in particular to the implementation of the second EU banking directive into Belgian law and the capital standards on off-balance-sheet activities. An important degree of dissension is observed with respect to the issues on the GATS.

Pharmaceutical industry

The issues on intellectual property rights that were presented to the pharmaceutical firms relate to:

1. the TRIPs chapter included in the GATT;
2. the European Supplementary Protection Certificate;
3. the enforcement of intellectual property rights, included in the GATT.

There is overwhelming support for the general regulations on patent protection: the TRIPs Agreement, the Supplementary Protection Certificate and the enforcement of intellectual property rights. For these issues, the responses range from 'in favor' to 'strongly in favor'. A similar support is found for the World Trade Organization (WTO) sanctioning countries whose national laws are not up to TRIPs standards. Conflicts become more apparent when the firms express their opinions on more specific aspects regarding protection and enforcement of intellectual property rights.

5.3.2 Firms' Policy Preferences are Shaped by Self-interest

The fact that some (and often quite a few) firms oppose protection suggests that protection does not benefit all firms in the industry. We assume that firms take policy positions on the basis of rational behavior: they favor the trade policy that involves the lowest costs or highest benefits for the further course of their operations. This implies that the observed variation in support for protection can be explained by observable differences between firms, differences in their strategic and structural characteristics as well as in the international competition they perceive. These characteristics explain firms' positions on deregulation and trade liberalization. However, the influence of some characteristics may differ according to the industry in which the firm operates. So let us now turn to the next question: who is afraid of international trade liberalization and who is not?

Textile and clothing industries

We expect that textile and clothing firms that experience international competition are more opposed to trade liberalization. In particular, competition from non-EU countries turns out to influence a firm's policy stance (Table 5.1). Non-EU firms, originating from developing countries and Central and Eastern Europe, are Belgian textile and clothing firms' main competitors. Exports from these countries to Belgium are based on relatively abundant low-skilled labor. As for competition from other EU countries, Belgian textile and clothing firms have for many years been expressing their dissatisfaction over excessive labor costs in Belgium relative to the EU trading partners. However, EU competition does not appear to influence Belgian textile or clothing firms' policy stance (except for the issue on EU internal free trade).

Highly diversified textile and clothing firms are expected to favor trade liberalization more than weakly diversified firms. The argument is that textile and clothing firms can spread the risk of losing market share because of tariff reduction by producing a broader range of product type. This relationship is confirmed by the empirical results and goes somewhat against the perceived trend that firms increasingly focus on their 'core business', as suggested by Dunning in this book's first chapter.

A textile and clothing firm's international orientation (through foreign establishments and export orientation) contributes to its favorable stance towards liberalization. Cross-border transactions are important to firms in a small open economy like Belgium. To introduce trade restrictions might unchain retaliatory actions and impede international operations.

As far as a firm's nationality is concerned, it was expected that foreign-owned textile and clothing firms (established in Belgium) would have similar trade interests and would be somewhat more free-trade minded. This expectation is based on the argument that foreign textile and clothing firms are independent entities being highly embedded in the Belgian market and thus behave like domestic firms. However, the results point out that foreign textile and clothing firms are more protectionist than Belgian firms. Apparently, considerations of quota and tariff hopping and protection against local competitors play a role here.

A protectionist stance is also taken by firms that employ many workers. This supports the hypothesis that CEOs of firms that are labor-intensive undergo more protectionist pressure since their workers stand in direct conflict with lower-wage countries where relatively abundant labor is employed.

Road haulage industry

Competition from other EU countries (rather than from non-EU countries) influences road hauliers' policy preferences (Table 5.2): the playing field in road haulage is still the European Union, although the role of non-EU (mainly Central-European) hauliers is growing. Stronger diversification (by offering transport-related services such as assembly, inventory control, storage, or packaging) leads hauliers to favor more liberalization. Diversified hauliers do not put all their eggs in one basket in order to spread their risks more widely.

*Table 5.1   Policy preferences and characteristics of textile and clothing
              firms*

Firm's characteristics	Preferences towards liberalization and harmonization	
	(Strongly) opposed	(Strongly) in favor
Strong non-EU competition	x	
Highly diversified		x
International orientation		x
Highly export-oriented		x
Foreign owned	x	
Many laborers	x	

Internationally-oriented hauliers also take a more liberal stance.
Liberalization may foster direct investment in other countries and enhance
co-operation and alliances with foreign hauliers. Foreign hauliers established
in Belgium are more in favor of liberalization than Belgian hauliers, possibly
because foreign hauliers operate more internationally than Belgian firms by
way of cabotage operations carried out across the EU.

Two opposite arguments have been put forth with respect to the influence
of labor size. One argument is that local drivers may be more threatened by
foreign and often cheaper truckers when transport is liberalized. In that case,
a company having many drivers is inclined to oppose liberalization. Another
argument is that hauliers' high dependence makes them more vulnerable to
retaliation, invoked by foreign governments as a response to protection. As
these retaliatory actions may hit the firm and its drivers directly, road
hauliers having many drivers may be more inclined to favor liberalization.
The results in this study support the second argument: hauliers having many
drivers are more in favor of liberalization (particularly with regard to market
access).

*Table 5.2   Policy preferences and characteristics of road haulage firms in
              Belgium*

Firm's characteristics	Preferences towards liberalization and harmonization	
	(Strongly) opposed	(Strongly) in favor
Strong EU competition	x	
Highly diversified		X
International orientation		X
Foreign alliances		X
Foreign owned		X
Many laborers (drivers)		X

Banking

As expected, banks facing fierce international competition oppose liberalization of banking services (Table 5.3). The empirical results also indicate that diversified banks and banks having establishments abroad favor liberalization. Banks with establishments in foreign countries have a particular interest in simpler procedures to establish operations in other EU Member States (as provided by the Second EU Banking Directive). The results also show that foreign-owned banks are more in favor of liberalization than Belgian banks. This result is in line with the theoretical argument that foreign banks - often small branches - form an integral and legal part of a global trading network of the parent company and thus think globally. Unexpectedly, banks employing many people favor (rather than oppose) liberalization. One interpretation may be that highly skilled employees, who are well-represented in the banking industry, are more free-trade minded and suffer less from low-cost import competition.

Table 5.3 Policy preferences and characteristics of banks in Belgium

	Preferences towards liberalization and harmonization	
Firm's characteristics	(Strongly) opposed	(Strongly) in favor
Strong foreign competition	x	
Highly diversified		X
International orientation		X
Foreign owned		X
Foreign branches		X
Many employees		X

Table 5.4   Policy preferences and characteristics of pharmaceutical firms in Belgium

	Preferences towards liberalization and harmonization	
Firm's characteristics	(Strongly) opposed	(Strongly) in favor
Medium-sized		x
Highly diversified		x
Brand name products	x	x
R&D activities	x	x
Foreign owned		x

Pharmaceutical industry

Because harmonization facilitates their cross-border operations, foreign pharmaceutical firms established in Belgium favor protection of intellectual property rights more than Belgian companies (Table 5.4). Diversified firms welcome patent protection: firms operating in several market segments often have a higher propensity to engage into research.

A pharmaceutical firm's policy stance is also influenced by characteristics that have their origin in the theory of patent protection: firm size, the importance of brand name products and R&D intensity. The relationship between firm size and policy stance is non-linear: medium-sized firms favor patent protection more than smaller and larger firms. However, the influence of brand-name production and R&D operations is ambiguous. While both factors were expected to be positively related to a pharmaceutical firm's stance on harmonization of intellectual property rights, for some issues the opposite result was found. However, when a separate Belgian and foreign subsample is considered, the results are more in line with the theoretical argument.

5.4 THE INDUSTRIES COMPARED

5.4.1 Strategic Choices versus Structural Characteristics

In all industries, firm-specific characteristics that relate to strategies of internationalization (export orientation, foreign establishments, foreign alliances) and of diversification are major determinants of a firm's policy.

However, the influence of other – non-strategic – characteristics differs across industries (Table 5.5). These factors are largely outside the direct control of firms or characterize the type of industry in which the firm operates. Depending on the industry, a firm's source of international competition originates mainly from the EU or from outside the EU. Employment size and nationality of ownership have different influences depending on the industry. A firm's nationality has an influence on more issues in some industries than in others, and the sign of the coefficient may differ.

Table 5.5 Firm-specific characteristics and industry specificity

	Influence is similar in all industries	Influence differs across industries
Strategic characteristics (international Orientation, diversification)	X	
International competition (EU, non-EU)		x
Structural characteristics (nationality, employment, size, R&D)		x

The origin of international competition depends on the type of product (whether it can be produced in lower-wage countries or not) and on whether the firm operates in a service or a manufacturing industry. In a service industry such as the Belgian road haulage industry the playing field is essentially the EU, which explains the importance of EU competition, rather than non-EU competition, in shaping a road haulier's policy preferences. In the Belgian textile and clothing industry, on the other hand, the playing field extends well beyond the EU. The industry competes against products which are imported from lower-wage countries. This explains the influence of non-EU competition, rather than EU competition, on a firm's policy preferences.

The direct competition experienced from labor employed in low-wage countries may also explain why textile and clothing firms employing many laborers oppose trade liberalization. The opposite result is found in the road haulage industry: road hauliers employing many drivers are in favor of market access issues. The mobile character of road haulage operations and the fear of retaliation (increasing with the number of drivers) may be an explanation, though future research should be further scrutinized. In banking, large size in terms of employment favors liberalization, as bank employees are less threatened by cheap labor.

Foreign firms established in Belgium are supportive of free trade in more concentrated industries and industries where many foreign subsidiaries are active (banking and pharmaceutical industry). Foreign subsidiaries, at least in small open economies like Belgium, highly depend on their parent company – for example the Japanese banking 'succursales' and the pharmaceutical subsidiaries of foreign multinationals – and thus have a strong interest in liberalization. In the textile and clothing industry, foreign firms are strongly embedded in the Belgian market and act more like domestic firms: for some policy issues, they even tend to be more opposed to liberalization than Belgian firms. In the road haulage industry, foreign firms favor liberal market access.

In sum, while the influence of *strategic* firm-specific characteristics on policy preferences is similar in all industries, the influence of international competition and structural characteristics (employment, nationality) differs according to the industry in which the firm operates. Factors such as the industry structure, the boundaries of the playing field (EU or beyond EU), the type of product or activity (can it be produced in low-wage countries?) and the type of industry (service or manufacturing) all matter.

While the political economy of trade policy considers industry structure as an important determinant of the supply of protection (the policy outcome), our research shows that industry structure also explains the demand side (or policy preferences), and that both firm specificity and industry specificity shape policy preferences.

5.4.2 Trade Liberalization versus Level Playing Field Issues

An interesting distinction is the one between issues of trade liberalization (removal of trade barriers, market access) and issues that aim at attaining a level playing field (Table 5.6). Firms' preferences on most trade liberalization issues are influenced by all characteristics: international competition, diversification, international strategies, nationality of ownership (particularly in the banking industry) and employment size. On the other hand, preferences on level playing field issues are merely influenced by international competition, foreign establishments, and (in the textile and clothing industry and the banking industry) nationality.

Table 5.6 Trade liberalization and level playing field issues

Types of issues:	(+): firm favors liberalization/deregulation
	(-): firm opposes liberalization/deregulation
Trade liberalization: • removal of tariffs and non-tariff barriers • market access • trade originating from third countries (for example, lower-wage countries)	• firms having subsidiaries abroad (+) • firms having foreign alliances (+) • export-dependent firms (+) • diversified firms (+) • firms facing fierce international competition (-) • firms that employ many workers (+ for road haulage, - for textile and clothing) • foreign owned firms (+)
Level playing-field: • EU internal free trade of goods (textile and clothing) • harmonization and Eurovignette (road haulage) • capital requirement (banking)	• firms facing fierce international competition (-) • firms having foreign establishments (+) • foreign firms (+ for banks, - for textile and clothing)

5.4.3 The Industries: Contrasts and Similarities

How do industries differ with regard to the determination of policy preferences? Textile and clothing and road haulage firms face fierce import competition. High short-term labor adjustment costs force the CEOs to be more protectionist. These mostly weak knowledge- and information-based industries represent the import-competing sectors in the specific factors model. Banking and the pharmaceutical industry, on the other hand, are highly knowledge- and information-based industries. They largely base their operations on telematics or innovative activities as reflected by, among other things, their high degree of multinational integration. These internationally oriented industries behave more like the export-oriented industry in the specific factors model and thus have a stronger interest in liberalization and harmonization than have import-competing industries.

Foreign-owned establishments in the host country behave differently in manufacturing than in services. In manufacturing, establishments of multinationals may be protectionist when they expand internationally to jump tariffs or quotas, or to deter local competitors. Particularly subsidiaries, which serve the local market and do not depend much on foreign operations may be protectionist oriented. On the other hand, in service industries such as banking and road haulage, even the smallest affiliates or 'succursales' have an interest in liberalization. Two explanations stand out. First, foreign subsidiaries often use the host market as a platform that permits the seeking of new international linkages (for example, cabotage operations for road hauliers). Second, many clients of service companies are themselves highly internationally oriented (for example, the multinational clients of branches of Japanese banks).

5.5 POLICY IMPLICATIONS

5.5.1 Lobbying

European umbrella lobbying groups often represent cross-sectoral interests. Given that even within an industry of a single country there may be quite some disagreement, national industry interest groups are likely to remain important in serving their members trade interests. Interest groups from the 'core countries' (and from Belgium in particular) have the additional advantage of being simultaneously close to the European institutions and to their constituencies, lowering the transaction cost of establishing and maintaining trust based relationships. For the same reason, countries from the periphery are at a disadvantage. Countries from the periphery (at least those from the South) also tend to have a different industrial structure, that is, more sunset industries and less R&D-intensive sectors and may therefore have other policy preferences.

5.5.2 Public Policy Making

Two points can be made with regard to public policy making. First, policy makers and businesses have far less discretion to be protectionist than they used to, thanks to mechanisms built into the GATT agreement. For example, the reciprocity principle encourages exporting firms to support liberalization. Second, public policies fostering internationalization of business may contribute to a virtuous circle of trade liberalization. The empirical evidence presented in Sections 5.2 and 5.4 suggests that firms with stronger cross-border alliances are more supportive of free trade. This provides a dynamic argument against policies to promote 'national champions' or to 'anchor' firms domestically (on top of the usual static argument that such interventionist policies usually fail to correct a well-identified market failure). The recent rise of cross-border mergers (for example, in banking, the automobile industry and in telecommunications) indicates that even if some governments would want to, they can do little to prevent this type of globalization. As Dunning argues in this volume, the role of public policy is shifting towards creating a framework that allows the indigenous created assets to be upgraded (human capital, infrastructure).

5.5.3   Future Trade Negotiations

The results of our study have two implications for future trade talks. First, the relevance of firm- and industry-specificity in shaping business' policy preferences suggests that industry-specific and thus issue-specific trade negotiations remain important, besides general across-the-board negotiations. Second, some of the characteristics of the firms (the right-hand-side variables in the equations explaining the firms' preferences) may themselves be influenced by the firms' preferences. For instance, a firm that favors trade liberalization may choose to increase its international collaborative agreements, which in turn - as argued above - can foster trade liberalization. This positive-feedback scenario bodes well for the long-term future of the WTO trade talks and suggests that in a globalizing economy firms are more likely to support the government to take the road towards trade liberalization, even if that road may occasionally be bumpy.

REFERENCES

André, Ph., L. Hens and I. Scheerlinck (1997), 'Determinants of Pharmaceutical Firms' Positions on Trade-Related Aspects of Intellectual Property Rights', in Khosrow Fatemi (ed.), *International Business in the New Millennium*, vol. 2, Laredo, Texas: A&M International University, pp. 573-86.
Boddewyn, J.J. and T.L. Brewer (1994), 'International-business political behavior: new theoretical directions', *Academy of Management Review*, 19, 119-43.
Hillman, A.L. (1989), *The Political Economy of Protection*, Chur: Harwood.
Lanjouw, G.J. and M.M. Wielinga (1994), 'De politieke economie van protectie en anti-protectie', *Maandschrift Economie*, 58, 1193-228.
Mazey, S. and J. Richardson (eds) (1993), *Lobbying in the European Community*, New York: Oxford University Press.
Pugel, T. and I. Walter (1985), 'US corporate interests and the political economy of trade policy', *Review of Economics and Statistics*, 67, 465-73.
Rodrik, D. (1995), 'Political Economy of Trade Policy', in G. Grossman and K. Rogoff (eds), *Handbook of International Economics*, vol. III, Amsterdam: North-Holland/Elsevier.

Rugman, A. and A. Verbeke (1990a), *Global Corporate Strategy and Trade Policy*, London: Routledge.

Rugman, A. and A. Verbeke (1990b), 'American trade policy and corporate strategy', *World Competition*, **13**, 79-90.

Rugman A. and A. Verbeke (1992), 'Multinational Enterprise and National Economic Policy', in P.J. Buckley and M. Casson (eds), *Multinational Enterprises in the World Economy: Essays in Honor of John Dunning*, Aldershot: Edward Elgar.

Scheerlinck, I. (1998), 'Who's afraid of international trade liberalization and deregulation? An analysis of Belgian businesses' policy preferences', unpublished ph.D. dissertation, Vrije Universiteit Brussel, Brussels.

Scheerlinck, I., L. Hens and R. S'Jegers (1996a), 'Who's afraid of international deregulations? Belgian credit institutions policy preferences', *Applied Financial Economics*, **6**, 319-25.

Scheerlinck, I., L. Hens and R. S'Jegers (1996b), 'Free trade or protection? Belgian textile and clothing firms trade policy preferences', *Weltwirtschaftliches Archiv*, **132**, 723-39.

Scheerlinck, I., L. Hens and R. S'Jegers (1998), 'On the road to transport liberalization? Belgian road hauliers policy preferences', *Journal of Transport Economics and Policy*, **32** (3), 365-76.

Tharakan, P.K.M. (1984), 'Political economy of protection: an analysis of the Belgian Case', *Cahiers Economiques de Bruxelles*, **101**, 3-39.

Tharakan, P.K.M. (1991), 'The Political Economy of anti-dumping undertakings in the European communities', *European Economic Review*, **35**, 1341-59.

PART III

The Role of Inter-firm Linkages

6. Competitive and Comparative Advantages: The Performance of Belgium in a Global Context

Leo Sleuwaegen and Reinhilde Veugelers

6.1 GLOBALIZATION

There can be no doubt that the structure and performance of the Belgian economy has been strongly affected by the globalization of economic activities, characterized by some important new features (see Dunning, 1993). As also discussed by Dunning's in this book (Chapter 2), the most important distinctive features of the recent globalization process could be characterized as follows:

- The most valuable resources in the globalization of activities stem from newly created assets (new technologies, marketing and organizational innovations) rather than natural assets (land, unskilled labor, and so on).
- These resources are intangible and firm-specific, meaning that they are proprietary rights of commercial enterprises. These resources can be deployed in foreign locations insofar that national and international law systems enable and protect the execution of these rights. Hence, the importance of new international institutions, including the World Trade Organization (WTO).
- Global firms are increasingly spreading their activities not only to serve foreign markets or benefit from cheaper factor costs in other countries, but to create or acquire new assets through, for example, undertaking decentralized Research and Development activities.
- Mergers and acquisitions have been playing a prominent role in Foreign Direct Investment (FDI) in the Triad region over the past ten years.
- The motives why and modes by which firms globalize have become more diverse than ever before, with a strong growth in cross-border networking of firms through strategic alliances, international subcontracting and other cooperative agreements.
- National and sub-national governments have become active partners in the globalization process. Through growing regional and world

integration, trade and macro-policies have become increasingly harmonized, which has led national governments to put more emphasis on microeconomic policies and compete amongst each other in providing firms with the right techno-economic infrastructure to make them more competitive on a global scale.

The new distinctive features of the ongoing globalization process necessitate a reconsideration of the competitive position of Belgium along the dimensions outlined above. A traditional analysis of comparative advantages of Belgium based on the relative availability of classical factor endowments, such as capital and labor, would not only obscure many interesting factors but also neglect the role of intangible assets as well as institutional or organizational factors which are increasingly shaping the competitive advantages of firms and countries in the new global context. Section 6.2 of the chapter proposes a conceptual analytical scheme which relates the competitive position of a country to location bound advantages and specific advantages possessed by firms in the country. Using revealed measures of comparative advantages and firm-specific advantages, Section 6.3 examines the competitive position of Belgian manufacturing industries for the year 1990. Section 6.4 of the chapter examines industries sensitive to the European Single Market following their relative competitive positions and the types of mergers and acquisitions that occurred thereafter. The role of strategic alliances is discussed in section 6.5 of the chapter. Section 6.6 concludes and offers some new perspectives for further research.

6.2 LOCATION-BOUND ADVANTAGES AND COMPETITIVE ADVANTAGES OF FIRMS

The importance of firm-specific competitive advantages for trade performance has only recently gained attention in the economics literature. Recent developments in trade theory are now increasingly incorporating the logic of the international business paradigms in explaining firm-specific advantages in general equilibrium models, endogenizing the emergence and location of multinational firms. The results from these models are not equivocal, but are very sensitive to the nature and relative importance of transaction costs (Ethier, 1997). From an international business perspective, the combination of locational and firm-specific advantages has been used to explain the type of trade and integration of firms across national markets (Kogut, 1985). The transferability of firm-specific advantages and their development within transnational networks has been studied by Rugman and Verbeke (1995) and has led to criticize the Porter framework explaining competitive advantages of countries which focused too exclusively on the home basis of firms to develop competitive advantages. Dunning (1993) and Kogut and Kulatilaka (1994) add to the firm-specific advantages, systemic advantages from developing a global network by multinational firms.

Consequently, studying the structure and competitive performance of a country, one should at least distinguish between location bound advantages and firm-specific competitive advantages. The first group of advantages refers to general factor or market conditions available to all firms locating in a particular country or region while the second group of advantages refers to proprietary intangible or tangible assets. The firm-specific assets can be profitably deployed in one or more countries depending on the transferability and adaptability to local conditions. Sometimes these firm-specific advantages follow from information and knowledge sharing within a particular group structure, as for instance in the Japanese keiretsu (Belderbos and Sleuwaegen, 1996) or are systemic to the global network in which the MNE operates (economies of scale and scope and flexibility of shifting production from one country to another) (Kogut, 1994).

6.3 REVEALED MEASURES OF COMPARATIVE ADVANTAGES AND FIRM-SPECIFIC ADVANTAGES

Revealed comparative advantage measures used at the sectoral level incorporate both type of advantages. Disentangling firm-specific advantages from location-bound advantages is not an easy task. In one of the few studies dealing with the subject, Kamal Abd-el Rahman (1991) finds important trade and productivity differences across firms in industries characterized by comparative disadvantages, suggesting the importance of firm-specific advantages in these industries. The measure of comparative advantage we propose to use hereafter is the traditional Balassa-index:

$RCA_i = X_i/M_i / X/M$, that is ratio of exports to imports of industry i relative to total exports to imports ratio.

The RCA measure combines location bound and firm-specific advantages. Confronting this RCA measure with a specific measure for the firm-specific type of advantage only, will help to trace the origin of any comparative advantage position. Transferable firm-specific advantages are revealed by the relative importance of MNEs in the industry. This concerns incoming as well as outgoing investments. While the relative importance of multinational firms from local origin signals the strength of these transferable advantages possessed by firms based in the country, the presence of subsidiaries of multinationals based in other countries signals the competitive disadvantage of local firms. In order to assess the relative superiority of Belgian-based firms, a measure of firm-specific advantage is constructed similar to the revealed comparative advantage trade measure:

$RFSAi$ = BMNEi/FMNEi/BMNE/FMNE, that is ratio of sales by Belgian multinationals to sales by foreign based multinationals in industry i relative to total sales by Belgian multinationals to sales by foreign multinationals in Belgium.

Figure 6.1 Competitive position of Belgian industries

	RFSA ≤1	RFSA >1
RCA >1	**Quadrant 1** Basic chemicals Pharmaceuticals Other chemicals Tobacco Machinery for iron & steel Choc. & Confec. Beer Plastics *32.8% of total production*	**Quadrant 3** Iron & steel Steel cold-forging Metal structures Carpets Wooden furniture *17.3% of total production*
RCA ≤1	**Quadrant 2** Non-ferrous metals Basic industrial chemicals Other machinery Telecom Cars Dairy Paper & pulp Animal foods Clothing *42.9% of total production*	**Quadrant 4** Tools & cans Foundries Metal treatment Machine tools Computers Fruit & vegetables Printing & publishing *7.1% of total production*

Following the logic of the scheme developed in the previous paragraph, it is interesting to analyze the features of the industries in which Belgium shows a high RCA and RFSA. The analysis is done for the year 1990. Figure 6.1 combines the RCA and RFSA measures and displays the most important industries belonging to the different quadrants (for a full list of industries, see Appendix). To further clarify the classification, Figure 6.2 shows the average values per quadrant for trade and investment patterns underlying the RCA and RFSA characterization.

Figure 6.2 Trade and investment indicators in the Belgian industry

	RFSA <1	RFSA >1
RCA >1	**Quadrant 1** *RCA=1.40*	**Quadrant 3** *RCA=1.19*
Xi/Si / X/S	0.86	1.11
Mi/Si / M/S	0.72 *RFSA=0.17*	0.55 *RFSA=10.5*
BMNE*i*/*i* / BMNE/*S*	0.18	4.51
FMNE*i*/*Si* / FMNE/*S*	1.05	0.43
RCA <1	**Quadrant 2** *RCA=0.68*	**Quadrant 4** *RCA=0.71*
Xi/Si / X/S	1.06	1.04
Mi/Si / M/S	1.21 *RFSA=0.074*	1.32 *RFSA=2.8*
BMNEi/Si / BMNE/S	0.093	1.73
FMNEi/Si / FMNE/S	1.256	0.61

Notes:
If RCA >1, this implies $Xi/X > Mi/M$ or relative to Sales, S, $Xi/Si / X/S > Mi/Si / M/S$. The average export-intensity X/S=74.3%, while the average import-intensity M/(S+M)=40.9%.
If RFSA >1, this implies BMNE*i*/BMNE > FMNE*i*/FMNE or relative to Sales, S, BMNE*i*/Si / BMNE/*S* > FMNE*i*/Si / FMNE/*S*. The average Belgian MNE sales intensity, BMNE/S is 5.9%, while average foreign MNE sales intensity, FMNE/S=58%.

The industries belonging to quadrant 1 exhibit a strong revealed comparative advantage, with RCA>1, and relatively weak firm-specific advantages of Belgian firms, since no revealed ownership advantages can be detected (RFSA<1). The presence of foreign-based multinationals is very important for those industries. Foreign presence in these industries is even higher than the Belgian average of 58 percent. In addition, using the information that the presence of Belgian MNEs is minimal, location-bound advantages seem to be more important to explain the positive trade performance. These location-bound advantages are attracting foreign-based multinationals. The comparative advantage position with RCA>1 is built mainly through a low import penetration, while export activities are important, be it less than the high Belgian average. Important examples are the major part of the chemical sector, including the pharmaceutical industry. Also several food and drink industries are found here, including the Belgian chocolate and beer industry. In total, about one third of Belgian manufacturing production belongs to this quadrant.

Industries in quadrant 2 show no strong comparative advantage, and Belgian firms possess, relative to their foreign counterparts, less transferable firm-specific advantages, leading to almost absent Belgian MNEs in this quadrant. Foreign penetration through FDI is, however, very predominant, with the highest foreign penetration share. Despite above average export performance, the negative RCA is explained by the even more pervasive import penetration. Here one can find important industries like telecom and car manufacturing. About 43 percent of all Belgian manufacturing production is located in quadrant 2.

The best performing industries are in quadrant 3 where trade performance is strong. Export performance is even higher than the Belgian average while import penetration is limited. This trade pattern goes hand in hand with Belgian firms having developed strong, transferable firm-specific advantages. The percentage of sales accounted for by Belgian multinational firms is the highest in these industries, with more than a quarter of total Belgian production accounted for by these firms in these industries. At the same time, foreign multinational penetration is far below average. Parts of the steel industry, as well as furniture and carpets, are located in the quadrant, representing 17 percent of Belgian manufacturing.

Industries in quadrant 4 fail to display a positive trade balance, where despite high export intensity an even more pervasive import penetration applies. This negative trade performance prevails despite relatively strong firm-specific advantages possessed by Belgian firms. Belgian multinational firms account for 10 percent percent of all sales, while foreign penetration is about 35 percent below the Belgian average, explaining the positive RFSA. Industries like computers and machine tools are located here. This quadrant represents only 7 percent of Belgian industry sales.

Some basic structural characteristics of the various industries following the quadrants to which they belong in Figure 6.1 are represented in Table 6.1. Several interesting observations emerge from this table and can be summarized as in Figure 6.3.

Figure 6.3 Characteristics of Belgian industries per quadrant

	RFSA <1	RFSA >1
RCA >1	**Quadrant 1**	**Quadrant 3**
	High transport costs	*Large scale*
	High public procurement	*High concentration*
	Advertising intensive	
	Low concentration	
RCA <1	**Quadrant 2**	**Quadrant 4**
	Large scale	*No public procurement*
	High tech	*High concentration*
	Advertising intensive	*High transport costs*

Table 6.1 Industry characteristics of Belgian firms according to different quadrants

	Scale	Non-tariff barriers	Transport Costs	Public procurement & regulation	High-tech	Advertising	Concentration
All industries	22.4%	23.6%	30.7%	24.4%	26.0%	29.3%	13.5%
Quadrant 1 RCA>1;RFSA<1	8.4%	23.9%	42.5%	30.2%	29.9%	37.1%	4.9%
Quadrant 2 RCA<1;RFSA<1	29.9%	10.5%	23.8%	27.1%	36.1%	38.0%	7.2%
Quadrant 3 RCA>1;RFSA>1	39.3%	2.7%	20.6%	14.7%	0.0%	0.0%	31.6%
Quadrant 4 RCA<1;RFSA>1	0.0%	4.4%	41.6%	4.4%	10.5%	12.1%	47.8%

Notes:
Scale = % of industry sales realized in scale-intensive sectors (scale-intensive sectors are defined as those where the minimal efficient scale is larger than 500 employees).
Non-tariff barriers = % of industry sales realized in industries with high non-tariff barriers.
Transport costs = % of industry sales realized in high transport cost sectors (defined as sectors where the total transport costs relative to sales is above average).
Public procurement and regulation = % of industry sales realized in sectors with important public procurement and regulation.
High-tech = % of industry sales realized in high-tech sectors.
Advertising = % of industry sales realized in advertising intensive sectors.
Concentration = % of sales in sectors with an above average concentration.

Source: All of the industry characteristics were obtained from Davies and Lyons (1996) and were measured at the EC level.

First, the industries classified in quadrant 3 are those industries characterized by large scale and high concentration. Differentiation through R&D and advertising is limited. Second, contrary to quadrant 3, the industries classified in quadrant 1 are characterized by low scale and low concentration. At the same time, these industries are advertising intensive and have relatively high transportation costs, while public procurement and regulation is pervasive. This finding suggests that these industries are likely to be fragmented and is thus consistent with the relatively strong presence of foreign multinational firms. Third, the industries classified in quadrant 2 are in between of these two cases. The industry characteristics observed in this quadrant are large-scale and high-tech industries with relatively high advertising expenditures. These industries may be thus identified with markets which are differentiated, explaining the strong presence of foreign multinational firms as well as import flows.

The Belgian firms in the industries in quadrants 1 and 2 both face disadvantages, but the sources of competitive advantage of their base industries appear to be different. This may further imply that the motivation of foreign multinational firms, strongly present in both quadrants, to enter these industries are probably different. In quadrant 1 the low important penetration observed in Table 6.1 can be explained by the high transport costs and other non-tariff barriers, especially public procurement and regulation, which warrants local presence through FDI or alliances. In industries located in quadrant 2, the importance of intangible assets explains the pervasiveness of multinational firms. Finally, the industries in quadrant 4 are characterized by a lack of public procurement but especially high concentration.

6.4 RESTRUCTURING FOR THE EUROPEAN SINGLE MARKET

Changes in the relative competitive position of industries are the result of both changes in the location-bound advantages and firm-specific advantages. Changes over time in comparative location advantages stem from the accumulation or creation of factors of production, including the broader techno-economic infrastructure of the country. Firm-specific advantage can be acquired or accessed through licensing agreements or absorbing know-how spillovers, by attracting specialized employees or through acquiring or allying with firms in other countries. Belgian firms may also transfer these advantages to foreign firms through merger and acquisition (M&A) or strategic alliances with other firms.

Changes in the environment, such as the formation of a single market, may trigger a strategic restructuring of operations, as firms widen their home base from the national arena to the European wide arena and try to strengthen firm-specific advantages or to exploit systemic network advantages on a European scale.

Using the matrix figure combining the location-bound advantages with firm-specific advantages as a framework to interpret strategic restructuring through different modes of M&A, we expect Belgian firms in quadrant 3 to use their competitive advantage to acquire foreign firms, rather than to be taken over by foreigners. Firms belonging to the industries of quadrant 4 where domestic firms have strong transferable competitive advantages but no location advantages can either decide to take over foreign firms in countries characterized by better location conditions or sell their assets to foreign based companies.

We expect acquisitions of Belgian firms by foreign firms to be the dominant mode of restructuring in quadrant 1 where, on average, Belgian firms are at a disadvantage *vis-à-vis* foreign competitors with respect to firm-specific competitive advantages. Industries showing no revealed comparative advantage, nor firm-specific advantages of Belgian firms in quadrant 2 seem to have no other option than to rationalize operations. We expect mergers and acquisitions especially to serve that purpose, preferably domestic M&A.

Our expectations are largely supported by the findings about M&A which occurred during the period 1986-1992. Table 6.2 classifies industries following their RCA and RFSA measures in 1985 and, for each quadrant, the distribution of M&A following three distinct types of M&A: Domestic M&A, Cross-border M&A of foreign firms by Belgian firms, and acquisitions of Belgian firms by foreign firms. The dominant mode of restructuring can now be identified for each quadrant. Cross-border mergers and acquisitions of foreign firms occurred most frequently in quadrant 3 where Belgian firms show important transferable firm-specific advantages. In quadrant 1 where, on average, Belgian firms were at a competitive disadvantage, relatively more firms were taken over by foreigners. Among the different possible modes of restructuring, domestic mergers and acquisitions occurred most frequently in quadrant 2, be it that international M&A are also important. The predominance of national M&A in quadrant 4 is somewhat at variance with our conjecture, since these sectors are typically characterized by locational disadvantages. Maybe Belgian firms try to access other locations by using other internationalization modes besides M&A, such as alliances.

The table concerns only the 40 manufacturing industries that are considered to be very sensitive to the market integration program as defined by Buigues, Ilzkovitz and Lebrun (1990) and relate to a total of 90 mergers and acquisitions recorded from the financial press over the period 1986-1992.

Table 6.2 Distribution of domestic and cross-border M&As by type of industry in Belgium

	% Domestic mergers and acquisitions	% Cross-border M&A of foreign firms by Belgian firms	% Acquisitions of Belgian firms by foreign firms
All industries	41	25	34
Quadrant 1 Industries with RCA>1;RFSA<1	34	20	46
Quadrant 2 Industries with RCA<1;RFSA<1	36	30	34
Quadrant 3 Industries with RCA>1;RFSA>1	20	60	20
Quadrant 4 Industries with RCA<1;RFSA>1	67	14	19

6.5 STRATEGIC ALLIANCES AND TRANSNATIONAL NETWORKS

As emphasized in Dunning's chapter in this volume, in the age of 'alliance capitalism', firms are increasingly engaged in alliances, national or cross-border (Hagendoorn and Schakenraad, 1991; Contractor and Lorange, 1988; Porter and Fuller, 1986; Harrigan, 1985). The advantages of alliances are compelling. Alliances are an expedient way to crack new markets, gain skills and technologies, realize economies through reorganization and exploitation of complementarities, share fixed costs and resources, as well as the ability to monitor and control competitive forces. Despite these apparent benefits of cooperation, scattered evidence suggests that alliances carry a disturbingly high risk of trouble or failure, see for example Kogut (1988). Partners may fail to jointly manage the dynamics of the alliance, implementing readjustments. In addition, firms expose and develop valuable know-how through the alliance. Such information flows, when uncontrolled, can undermine the firm's long-term position in the face of opportunistic partners (Baumol, 1991; Hamel, Doz and Prahalad, 1989). Hence the importance for firms to manage, in Dunning's terminology, the yin of competition with the yang of cooperation in such alliances.

Although this networking phenomenon is not new, the recent upsurge carries new features, with more different types of firms involved and a wider diversity of intense forms of cooperation. With an increased range of sectors involved and far more international collaboration, partners tend to be more asymmetric (Harrigan, 1988). Indeed this refers to one of the paradoxes raised by Dunning, namely the renaissance or opportunities for small firms in regional networking activities with large, global firms.

Within internalization strategies, alliances are an interesting option to manage the paradox of globalization and localization. As compared to the alternative internationalization modes, sharing ownership allows firms to spread geographically at a much faster and flexible rate, as compared to full ownership investments. Besides mere access to specific local assets, as M&A equally provide, alliances also allow for joint exploitation of complementary assets, capitalizing on synergy effects. At the same time, the typical quid-pro-quo arrangements in alliances, allow better monitoring of opportunism as compared to other contracting modes such as licensing. Of course external governmental pressure exists in many countries for ownership sharing with local stakeholders.

Given these typical motives and problems of alliances, it is clear that the phenomenon of alliances, as a growing mode of internationalization, is intrinsically related to the pattern of competitive advantages. Or as Dunning puts it: 'when, with whom and how to cooperate is determined by firm, industry and country specific characteristics'. Companies actively use ventures to defend, create or rebuild their own competitive advantage. Given that alliances provide the possibility for exploiting synergies out of partner complementarities and/or that they allow access to partner's know-how, firms can indeed improve or create new competitive advantages through alliances.

Not only will the costs and benefits of alliances affect the relative advantages of partners and nations. These relative advantages which partners and nations hold are likely to shape the motives for engaging in alliances in the first place. Strong relative advantages are often necessary to be able to enter into alliances, to serve as a quid-pro-quo, or to be able to generate interesting complementarities. It furthermore strengthens the bargaining position of the company in alliance agreements, allowing for more stable and beneficial relationships. At the same time, however, the uncontrolled know-how flows among partners within the alliance and beyond the alliance may endanger any initially built up advantages, at least when partners are opportunistic. Firms may hence avoid alliances to protect strong positions.

Do comparative host country advantages and firm-specific competitive advantages determine the choice and motives of alliances as alternative internationalization modes? To answer this question, alliances in which Belgian firms are engaged, national and international, were distributed across the different quadrants of Figure 6.1, characterizing the different types of advantages in the Belgian matrix. This classification of alliances was then used to search for differences in alliance characteristics to determine the influence of the nature of relative advantages on the motives and problems of alliances. The focus on Belgium, a small, open economy, allows us to explore the issue raised by Dunning in Chapter 2 of this volume, namely whether alliances offer some extra benefits or costs to firms in closely knit smaller economies.

Alliances, as they appeared in the financial press between 1986 and 1992 have been collected and coded along structural characteristics. This procedure, common in most other alliance databases, such as MERIT, INSEAD and Harvard, may cause some misrepresentation, given that the more visible and high impact alliances have a larger probability of being announced in the press (see also Vonortas, 1998). About 670 alliances have thus been collected, involving all activities (R&D as well as non-R&D), all sectors (industry and services) and all nationalities, be it that European firms are overrepresented due to the reliance on the European financial press. For an overview of the characteristics of this dataset, see Veugelers (1993). The analysis reported here was performed on the subset of alliances involving at least one Belgian partner, leaving 194 alliances.

Comparing alliances involving at least one Belgian partner with the non-Belgian alliances in the total sample reveals some interesting differences, as Table 6.3 demonstrates (see Veugelers, 1993). Belgian alliances are significantly less of the joint venture type. Belgian companies significantly choose more simple, less involved forms of coordination, engaging more in R&D alliances (significant at p=0.011). Typically, less production activities are organized in alliances as compared to other nations. Also the technological link between the partners is different for Belgian companies, who tend to be more horizontally and less vertically related. It is important to note that especially large international Belgian companies can be found to engage in alliance activities: 34 percent of all Belgian companies in the sample belong to the top ten largest companies in Belgium. This skewed size distribution is also present in the non-Belgian alliances. Half of the Belgian companies only show up once in the database, while 65 percent of the non-Belgian partners show up more than once. Hence within the database, there is clearly less alliance experience within Belgian partners.

It is important to note that significantly more Belgian alliances are found in the service sector, typically company services and banking, while less

Belgian alliances can be found in the typical alliance-intensive industrial sectors, such as chemicals, electronics and car manufacturing. Since the comparative and firm-specific advantage measure used in this study are only constructed for industrial sectors, we have to restrict the Belgian alliances to industrial sectors only. The restricted number of alliances thus remaining (80 in total) prohibits any generalization of the results, which therefore should only be considered as an illustration and stimulus for further more elaborate analysis.

Table 6.3 Belgian versus non-Belgian alliances

	Belgian alliances	Non-Belgian alliances
Organizational structure of the alliance		
% alliances in joint venture form	48%	68%
Functional activities organized within the alliance		
% alliances including R&D activities	25%	21%
Asymmetric partner characteristics		
% alliances with vertical partners	26.5%	31.5%
Alliance experience		
% alliances in which partners are engaged only once	49%	34%

Figure 6.4 shows the distribution of Belgian alliances in manufacturing across the different quadrants. For every quadrant, the sector with the highest number of alliances is reported. Also included per quadrant (between brackets) is a measure of alliance intensity, namely the number of alliances per billion BEF sales.

Figure 6.4 Distribution of Belgian alliances in manufacturing

	RFSA <1	RFSA >1
RCA >1	**Quadrant 1** 39.4% incl. pharmaceuticals (1.25)	**Quadrant 3** 12.7% incl. cement (0.76)
RCA <1	**Quadrant 2** 35.2% incl. telecom (0.85)	**Quadrant 4** 12.7% incl. computers (1.87)

Few Belgian alliances are found in sectors where Belgium holds a comparative ownership advantage, RFSA >1. This is of course partly due to the restricted set of industries. But when relating the number of alliances to the size of industries, the lowest alliance intensity is displayed in quadrant 3 where an ownership advantage (RFSA>1) goes along with a comparative advantage (RCA>1). A similar exercise for European companies left two thirds of all European alliances in this quadrant 3. The apparent paradox of why Belgian firms who hold strong relative positions are reluctant to engage in alliances can be related to a defensive policy. Fearing opportunism of their partners, firms avoid alliances to protect their strong position. Such a defensive stance can be rationalized for Belgian firms, when they lack expertise and power in alliance management. This defensive stance can furthermore be related to the characteristics of these types of industries, which are highly concentrated and growth constrained.

When Belgian firms hold no comparative advantage despite a relative firm-specific advantage, see quadrant 4, alliance activities are also restricted with only one eighth of all alliances located here. Nevertheless, we do find a high alliance intensity here, mainly due to the computer industry, which in Belgium represents no real production activities. If these alliances are international, they may serve as an alternative to foreign acquisition which we expected but failed to observe in this quadrant.

Most of the Belgian alliances can be found in sectors where Belgium holds no relative ownership advantage, namely quadrants 1 and 2. These include important core sectors like chemicals, notably pharmaceuticals, electric manufacturing and the beverages industry. All of these industries are noted for their global alliance activities. In most cases, Belgium holds a comparative advantage; see quadrant 1. Despite the absence of firm-specific advantages, comparative locational advantages seem to be present. Whether the alliances that are found in this quadrant 1 will help to build up firm-specific advantages for Belgian companies or only serve to provide access to other companies in order to benefit from locational advantages, requires a more in-depth analysis of the types of alliances in these quadrants. Table 6.4 details the alliance characteristics for each of the sub-segments.

The limited number of alliances in quadrant 3 already suggested a defensive stance taken by Belgian companies. The alliances that do come out here are furthermore significantly more restricted to national partners, again reflecting a defensive attitude to protect firm advantages from internationally spilling over. For foreign firms, getting access to these Belgian firm-specific advantages through alliances is not obvious. But also the other internationalization modes, imports and FDI are less prevalent (see Figure 6.2), suggesting that Belgian firms actively try to protect their interests. These alliances are less R&D and distribution oriented, suggesting that alliances are mostly used for production motives in these scale-intensive industries. This also explains the larger share of horizontal alliances with symmetric partners.

Table 6.4 Characteristics of Belgian alliances by industry type

	% National	% Intra-EC	% R&D	% Distribution
All industries	25	56	29.5	52
Quadrant 1 Industries with RCA>1;RFSA<1	14	43	32	50
Quadrant 2 Industries with RCA<1;RFSA<1	28	68	40	68
Quadrant 3 Industries with RCA>1;RFSA>1	44	55	11	22
Quadrant 4 Industries with RCA<1;RFSA>1	33	67	11	44

Table 6.4 Characteristics of Belgian alliances by industry type (continued)

	% Horizontal	% Vertical	% Equal size	% Equal experience
All industries	51	35	77.5	52
Quadrant 1 Industries with RCA>1;RFSA<1	46	39	68	36
Quadrant 2 Industries with RCA<1;RFSA<1	44	48	80	48
Quadr*ant 3* Industries with RCA>1;RFSA>1	78	11	100	78
Quadrant 4 Industries with RCA<1;RFSA>1	55.5	11	78	89

Most of the Belgian alliances can be found in quadrant 1, where Belgian firms hold no comparative ownership advantage. Almost all of these alliances are international, a majority of them even beyond EC borders. For these industries, like beverages and chocolate, characterized by a revealed comparative advantage, getting access to the location-bound advantages in Belgium is possible through FDI if transaction costs are present. But alliances allow for a faster access to these advantages. For the Belgian partners, such alliances provide access to the firm-specific advantages of the foreign partner. The high share of R&D alliances and the prevalence of vertical partners indeed suggests an intensive search for the active exploitation of partners' advantages. The fact that Belgian firms are typically in an asymmetric position here is reflected in the low number of experienced partners, see Table 6.5.

If no relative ownership advantage, nor a revealed comparative advantage, can be found in the industries of quadrant 2, the motives for firms to engage in alliances are not straightforward. Domestic alliances could be used to restructure, but since most of these alliances are international, one could wonder what the foreign firms are searching for in these alliances. Table 6.5 reveals that there is a large number of vertical alliances, which suggests the development of global supply chains. The large frequency of R&D alliances is not surprising given the high-tech type of industries involved (see Figure 6.3). However, the question arises whether the relatively disadvantaged Belgian firms are able to absorb this superior external technological know-how from their partners in these alliances to improve their position. Also interesting to note is the high frequency of distribution alliances in quadrant 2. This may suggest that foreign firms may use alliances with weak Belgian partners to exercise control on the market and competition, to induce rationalization in industries like car components and machinery. Getting access to local markets which is typically faster through alliances than through FDI, may be an important drive for foreign partners. This is also suggested by the important international activities through other modes like FDI and imports. Despite the small size of the market, Belgium is an open and highly developed economy with a high GDP per capita, which leaves an interesting market for these industries characterized by product differentiation (see Table 6.3). The combination of R&D and distribution activities organized within these alliances further suggests a prevalence of technology-for-market swaps. Domestic firms trade access to their home market for the technological know-how of the foreign firm. Finally, since these sectors are also characterized by strong FDI, foreign firms might be interested in alliances with local partners as a fast entry mode, within follow-the-leader types of strategies, aimed to obtain access to markets in which competitors are already present through FDI.

In quadrant 4 where Belgian multinationals are pervasively present, alliances are less frequent. In line with the results for the sectors in quadrant 3 where the RFSA>1, this might again reflect a more defensive stance on the part of the Belgian companies to protect their ownership advantages. This defensive stance is also reflected in the lower frequency of R&D alliances, as well as truly global alliances.

6.6 CONCLUSIONS

This chapter has proposed a new research design to analyze patterns of international competition. The major finding that emerged from this chapter is that the confluence of country-specific and firm-specific advantages determines the competitive performance of industries and helps to explain industrial restructuring through mergers and strategic alliances.

The 'if and why' of mergers and alliances for local as well as foreign partners are shown to depend on the size and scope of relative comparative and competitive advantages. The analysis revealed that when Belgian firms hold strong firm-specific, but typically footloose, advantages, they take a very defensive attitude towards alliances but prefer to acquire foreign firms. This attitude may be driven by a desire to protect these advantages which may be difficult to keep proprietary within inter-firm arrangements, especially since Belgian multinationals are normally smaller in international scope and less experienced in international alliances than a typical foreign-based multinational. If they do choose to be engaged in especially international alliances, with large, more experienced players, these typically do not involve R&D, hence minimizing the flow of core know-how within these alliances. In industries where a foreign presence was strong, suggesting that Belgian firms did not possess firm-specific advantages, we find a relatively strong occurrence of acquisitions by foreign firms in the period prior to 1992.

APPENDIX I

Quadrant 1

		RCA	MTA
247	glass	2.27154	0.12410
253	other basic industrial chemicals	1.07600	0.00000
255	paint & ink	1.28657	0.26497
256	industrial & agricultural chemicals	1.07529	0.40290
257	pharmaceuticals	1.21378	0.00000
258	soap & detergents	1.05381	0.00000
259	dom. & off. chemicals	2.73915	0.00000
315	boilers & containers	1.39094	0.39216
321	tractor & agricultural machines	1.82590	0.00000
323	textile machines	1.17794	0.00000
325	mining & construction machines	1.39875	0.00000
341	insulation wires & cables	1.13945	0.00000
343	electrical equipment	1.02388	0.53720
347	electric lamps	1.07613	0.00000

412	meat products	1.84614	0.00000
420	sugar	1.80220	0.00000
421	chocolate & sugar confectionery	1.31730	0.00000
423	other foods	1.20656	0.98039
427	beer	4.21821	0.57670
428	soft drinks	1.04596	0.00000
429	tobacco	1.78839	0.00000
462	wood boards	1.64910	0.00000
464	wooden containers	1.08451	0.00000
481	rubber	1.25318	0.11671
483	plastics	1.38145	0.49020

Quadrant 2

		RCA	MTA
224	non-ferrous metals	0.74520	0.00000
231	extraction building materials	0.88296	0.00000
239	extraction other minerals	0.68174	0.00000
248	ceramics	0.49853	0.00000
252	chemicals from petroleum & coal	0.74388	0.00000
260	man-made fibres	0.32751	0.00000
312	forging	0.59357	0.00000
326	transmission equipment	0.61678	0.10430
328	other machines	0.67279	0.00000
342	electrical machines	0.80731	0.13808
344	telecom & measure equipment	0.68011	0.34602
345	radio & tv	0.97060	0.10542
346	domestic electrical appliances	0.26782	0.00000
351	motor vehicles	0.99231	0.00000
353	motor vehicle parts	0.57216	0.00000
362	rail stock	0.84683	0.00000
363	cycles & motorcycles	0.57161	0.00000
364	aerospace	0.97302	0.45600
371	measuring instruments	0.51387	0.00000
372	medical instruments	0.79085	0.00000
373	optical instruments	0.38543	0.00000
413	dairy products	0.93076	0.00000
416	grain milling	0.88344	0.00000
417	pasta	0.66016	0.00000
418	starch	0.33357	0.52709
422	animal foods	0.80988	0.00000
424	distilling products	0.06278	0.00000
425	wine & cider	0.13194	0.00000
436	knitting	0.40921	0.00000
442	leather products	0.40551	0.00000
453	clothing	0.62965	0.17825
461	wood sawing	0.22348	0.46685
463	wooden structures	0.94159	0.00000
466	cork & brushes	0.57592	0.00000

471	paper & pulp	0.33608	0.67150
472	processed paper	0.95151	0.36311
482	retreading rubber tyres	0.85117	0.00000
493	photo labs	0.78634	0.00000

Quadrant 3

			RCA		MTA
			RCA		**MTA**
221	iron & steel		3.28204		11.2457
222	steel tubes		1.43876		4.9020
223	steel cold-forging	2.19728		17.5794	
241	clay products		1.24256		4.9020
242	cement		4.28357		5.6282
243	concrete		2.50635		5.8824
314	metal structures		1.59342		1.6340
352	bodies motor vehicles		1.93667		20.1525
361	ship building		1.78433		68.6275
419	bread & biscuit		1.59529		1.1250
438	carpets		6.99065		65.3595
439	miscellaneous textiles		2.05388		1.1765
455	household textiles		1.32215		2.1008
467	wooden furniture		1.71587		49.0196

Quadrant 4

		RCA	**MTA**
245	stone products	0.87051	1.153
311	foundries	0.64636	5.767
313	metal treatment	0.42563	1.089
316	tools & cans	0.78211	1.110
322	machine tools	0.76697	5.279
324	food & chem. mach.	0.87801	1.140
327	pap. & wood etc. mach.	0.44135	176.471
330	computer & off. mach.	0.45976	1.279
414	fruit & veg. products	0.85074	2.401
415	fish products	0.30155	1.730
451	footwear	0.13564	1.225
473	print & publishing	0.79925	8.824
494	toys & sports	0.48684	3.676

REFERENCES

Abd-el Rahman, K. (1991), 'Firms' Competitive and national comparative advantages as joint determinants of trade composition', *Weltwirtschaftliches Archiv*, **127**, 83-97.

Baumol, W. (1991), *Technology Cartels, Speed of Technology Transmission and the Market Mechanism*, Working Paper, Princeton University.

Belderbos, R. and L. Sleuwaegen (1996), 'Japanese firms and the decision to invest abroad: business groups and regional core networks', *The Review of Economics and Statistics*, **78**, 214-20.

Buigues, P., F. Ilzkovitz and J.F. Lebrun (1990), 'The impact of the internal market by industrial sector: the challenge for the member states', *European Economy*, Office for Official Publications, Luxembourg.

Caves, R.E. (1996), *Multinational Enterprise and Economic Analysis*, Cambridge: Cambridge University Press.

Contractor, F. and P. Lorange (eds) (1988), *Cooperative Strategies in International Business*, Lexington: D.C. Heath.

Davies, S. and B. Lyons (1996), *Industrial Organization in the European Union*, Oxford: Clarendon Press.

Dunning, J.H. (1993), *Multinational Enterprises and the Global Economy*, Wokingham, UK: Addison-Wesley.

Ethier, W. (1997), *Firmes Multinationales, Comportements Strategiques et Localisation*, Working Paper, Université de Paris I Panthéon-Sorbonne.

Hagedoorn, J. and J. Schakenraad (1991), 'The role of interfirm cooperation agreements in the globalization of economy and technology', *Prospective Dossier*, 2, 8, Maastricht: MERIT.

Hamel, G., Y. Doz and C. Prahalad (1989), 'Collaborate with your competitor and win', *Harvard Business Review*, 133-9.

Harrigan, K. (1985), *Strategies for Joint Ventures*, Lexington: Lexington Books.

Kogut, B. (1985), 'Designing global strategies: comparative and competitive value-added chains', *Sloan Management Review*, Summer, 15-27.

Kogut, B. (1988), 'A Study of the Life Cycle of Joint Ventures', in F. Contractor and P. Lorange (eds), *Cooperative Strategies in International Business,* Lexington: D.C. Heath.

Kogut, B. and N. Kulatilaka (1994), 'Operating flexibility, global manufacturing, and the option value of a multinational network', *Management Science*, **40**, 123-39.

Markusen, J. (1995), 'The Boundaries of multinational enterprises and the theory of international trade', *Journal of Economic Perspectives*, **9**, 169-89.

Porter, M. and M. Fuller, (1986), 'Coalitions and Global Strategy', in M. Porter (ed.), *Competition in Global Industries*, Boston: Harvard Business School Press.

Rugman, A. and A. Verbeke (1995), 'Transnational Networks and Global Competition', in A. Rugman, J. van den Broeck and A. Verbeke (eds), *Research in Global Strategic Management, Beyond the Diamond*, Greenwich, CT: JAI Press Inc.

Veugelers, R. (1993), *Global Cooperation: A Profile of Companies in Alliances*, Onderzoeksrapport 9325, Leuven: KULeuven.

Vonortos, N. (1998), 'Research joint ventures in the US', *Research Policy*, **26**, 577-98.

7. Internationalization through Strategic Technology Partnering: The Role of Multinationals in the Netherlands

Geert Duysters and John Hagedoorn

7.1 INTRODUCTION

The globalization of the world economy has received widespread interest from scholars in business as well as in economics (see for example Vernon, 1966; Hirschey and Caves, 1981; Pearce, 1989: Bartlett, Doz and Hedlund, 1990: Dunning, 1988 and in this volume). Globalization is often described as a process that will eventually lead to a single global world market in which companies have become 'footloose' with no particular commitment to any specific country. In such a global market, large companies would have a global presence in virtually all countries (Reich, 1991).[1] The globalization tendencies which are widely portrayed and heralded in the literature have, however, been questioned by others (see for example Porter, 1986, 1990; Patel and Pavitt, 1991; Hu, 1992).

In the present contribution we place our research in the context of the discussion above. We will first try to identify some major trends in the internationalization of corporate technological activity as found in the output of research and development. In addition, we will also pay attention to international strategic technology partnering that plays an important role in the international strategies of major companies. For both topics, the internationalization of research and development and strategic technology partnering, specific attention will be paid to the role played by multinational companies in one small open economy, that is the Netherlands.

7.1.1 The Internationalization of Research and Development

As John Dunning has explained in several publications (see for example Dunning, 1988, 1993, and in this volume) companies are increasingly engaged in foreign production activities. Subsequent research has established that the internationalization of R&D follows the establishment of production

113

activities with a certain time lag (Pearce, 1989; Cantwell, 1991). In the literature on multinational enterprises, several advantages of an international dispersed network of R&D facilities have been reported (Granstrand, Hakanson and Sjolander, 1992; Miller, 1994; Pearce and Singh, 1992). The traditional rationale for the creation of foreign R&D facilities was to adapt products to the local market or to satisfy host country government regulations. By creating local R&D facilities firms can be in close contact with their customers and major local suppliers. This enables them to respond quickly to differences in demand among the various countries and allows them to interact with their major local suppliers. Sometimes local R&D is a necessity to gain government contracts, for example; in telecommunications and military equipment or to facilitate local clinical testing, for instance, in pharmaceuticals (Granstrand, Hakanson and Sjolander, 1992). However, there are also a number of factors that favor the geographical centralization of R&D facilities in the home country. The main reason to centralize R&D within the home country is the existence of economies of scale and scope in R&D. If economies of scale and scope exist, then one large R&D facility is often more efficient than several smaller facilities. The establishment of centralized R&D facilities near the major production centers can also be used to improve the interaction between the production, marketing and R&D departments. It has also been noted that centralization of R&D aids the protection of firm-specific technologies (Rugman, 1981). In the case of centralized R&D there seems to be less danger of knowledge 'leaking' to competitors (Granstrand, Hakanson and Sjolander, 1992).

A number of recent studies suggest that multinational companies have gradually increased their foreign R&D activities. An increase of overseas R&D has been reported by, among others, Lee and Reid (1991), Reich (1991), Graves (1991) and Miller (1994). These studies suggest that foreign R&D has grown more rapidly than domestic R&D expenditures. Others have reported a strong increase in the number of overseas R&D facilities of major multinational companies (Peters, 1992; Pearce and Singh, 1992). In addition to innovation input statistics, measures of innovation output have also been subject to a number of studies (Cantwell and Hodson, 1991; Patel and Pavitt, 1991). Patel and Pavitt (1991) made use of US patent statistics to analyze international patenting activities of large multinational corporations. In their study they distinguished between patents obtained in the US by 'national' companies in each country and patents obtained by foreign subsidiaries of those same companies. Their study confirmed that although foreign subsidiaries of multinational companies do indeed contribute significantly to world innovative activities, this contribution was less than 10 percent of world patenting during the first half of the 1980s.[2] Other authors (Cantwell and Hodson, 1991) found somewhat higher shares of international patenting.

They estimate the share of US patents attributable to research in foreign locations for the world's largest firms during the first half of the 1980s at about 10 percent. These differences are partly due to the fact that whereas Patel and Pavitt include small and medium-sized companies, universities and government laboratories, Cantwell and Hodson include only the largest companies. However, the latter research indicates also 'that the world's largest firms witnessed a mild trend towards the internationalization of technological activity over the 1969-1986 period' (Cantwell and Hodson, 1991, p. 137).

In the next section we will try to assess the importance of foreign R&D for a small open economy such as the Netherlands. In that context we will look in particular at patents as a measure of R&D output.

7.1.2 The Role of Foreign R&D for Companies in a Small Open Economy

The European Patent Office statistics show that about 35 percent of all the patent applications by Dutch firms are a result of research outside the Netherlands (see Table 7.1).

Table 7.1 Patent application from research outside the home country as a percentage of total patent applications, 1991

Country	Percentage	Country	Percentage
The Netherlands	35	Greece	6
United Kingdom	15	Spain	5
Belgium	12	Germany	5
Sweden	12	Switzerland	4
Austria	9	Finland	4
Norway	8	Italy	2
Denmark	6	Ireland	1
France	6	Japan	1
USA	6	Portugal	0

Source: MERIT, based on EPO data.

In terms of patents obtained outside the home country, the Netherlands appear to lead the internationalization process of R&D. There are two major factors that account for this high percentage of foreign R&D in the Netherlands (Duysters and Verspagen, 1994):

- The Dutch economy is dominated by a relatively small group of large multinational corporations. The five leading multinational firms in the Netherlands account for more than half of all the corporate R&D expenses.
- The Netherlands is a relatively small country. In such a small country it is impossible to find all the necessary technological and other resources that are necessary to compete in today's global marketplace (see also Dunning in this volume).

Further analysis shows that a considerable part of foreign research of Dutch companies takes place in Germany and the United Kingdom and to a somewhat lesser extent in the US and France (see Table 7.2). These countries are also the major trading partners of the Netherlands.

Table 7.2   Patent applications of Dutch companies, ranked according to country of innovation, 1979-1993

Country	Percentage
The Netherlands	67.0
Germany	10.6
United Kingdom	10.4
USA	6.2
France	5.3
Switzerland	1.2
Japan	0.5

Source: MERIT, based on EPO data.

7.2 INTERNATIONALIZATION THROUGH STRATEGIC TECHNOLOGY PARTNERING

In the literature on internationalization it is sometimes suggested that strategic alliances are essential to international corporate strategies (Ohmae, 1990; de Woot, 1990: OECD, 1992a). Before the 1980s, co-operative agreements (usually joint ventures) were typically undertaken between somewhat smaller companies. During the 1980s large multinational Enterprises (MNEs) came to play a role in the establishment of strategic alliances (Hladik, 1988). Traditionally most of these alliances were undertaken in order to gain access to foreign markets or to bypass government regulations (Contractor and Lorange, 1988; Hamel, Doz and

Prahalad, 1986; Haklisch, 1989; Porter and Fuller, 1986). Today we observe an increasing number of multinational corporations, more or less comparable in size, that link up with each other. The scope of these alliances is usually global and the modes of co-operation can take numerous forms: for example consortia, cross-licensing agreements, joint ventures, research partnerships, franchising and so on. Whereas co-operative agreements used to be undertaken on the basis of short-term objectives, today firms are increasingly recognizing the strategic importance of these agreements (Harrigan, 1985b; Porter and Fuller, 1986; Contractor and Lorange, 1988). In today's global markets, where technological progress is extremely rapid, boundary-spanning strategic technology alliances have become an important factor for the overall competitive position of a company. Before the mid-1970s there appeared to be an inverse relationship between R&D intensity and co-operative alliances (Stopford and Wells, 1972; Friedman, Berg and Duncan, 1979; Haklisch, 1989). Today, high-technology sectors account for the majority of all newly established alliances (Fusfeld and Haklisch, 1985; Osborn and Baughn, 1990; Mytelka, 1991; Hagedoorn 1993). Changes in the relative importance of strategic technology alliances for high technology sectors are above all due to fundamental shifts in the structure of the global environment and in the process of technological change (Haklisch 1989). Fierce competition, the homogenization of markets and ongoing Globalization tendencies account for most of the structural changes, whereas rapid growing capital and R&D costs, the ever increasing complexity of products and a significant increase in the speed of technological developments are important drivers from a technological point of view (Haklisch, 1989). The rapidly changing technological and competitive settings induced firms to search for new ways to increase their flexibility. In the late 1970s and early 1980s a number of companies started to trade their traditional practices like mergers and foreign direct investments for various types of technology sharing agreements. These new forms of agreements gave firms a previously unknown degree of flexibility in terms of the acquisition of technology and foreign market entry. (Vonortas, 1989).

The data presented in this chapter are based on the MERIT-CATI database (see also Appendix 1). The concept 'inter-firm co-operation' is used to refer to those co-operative agreements between partners that are not coordinated through (majority) ownership. Although co-operative agreements can take numerous forms such as marketing, production and research agreements we will limit our analysis to technology driven agreements. Before 1975, this type of agreement was virtually unknown (Hladik, 1985). In the 1980s however, several authors started to report a strong and steady increase in the number of strategic technology alliances (Hagedoorn and Schakenraad, 1990; Hergert and Morris, 1988). In order to safeguard the strategic element in our sample, we will study only those alliances that are assumed to affect the long-term product market positioning of at least one partner. Because alliances between public agencies or academic institutions and private companies are often undertaken for different reasons than the alliances between two or more private companies (see for example Haklisch, 1989), we will restrict our attention to those alliances that are established between private companies. For the same reason, we do not pay attention to government initiated or EU-wide R&D cost-sharing programs such as ESPRIT, EUREKA or JESSI.

In order to assess the importance and magnitude of (international) strategic alliance activity we calculated the number of newly established strategic technology alliances as they appear in our CATI database. Figure 7.1 shows that the number of newly established (international) strategic technology alliances increased rapidly during the 1980s.

Figure 7.1 New strategic technology alliances (1980-1994)

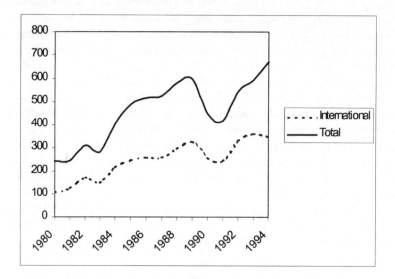

Previous work has shown that during the early 1970s co-operative activity remained at a rather modest level in the information technology industry. During the second half of the 1970s, as companies were slowly becoming more aware of the advantages associated with the use of strategic alliances, the number of newly established alliances started to increase gradually.[3] It was not, however, until the late 1970s that the number of alliances really took off. Apart from a short period of stabilization in the mid-1980s growth persisted until the end of the decade. The overall increase in alliance activity during the 1980s coincides with a period of worldwide structural and technological turbulence in many key industry sectors. During this period both production and R&D costs have been rising rapidly whereas ongoing internationalization tendencies have increased the 'global' character of the industry.

All these factors seem to have increased the need to establish strategic alliances. At the end of the decade, the growth rate in the number of newly established alliances seemed to level off. An explanation for this slower growth rate can be found in difficulties associated with the management and control of strategic alliances. As companies become more aware of the risks and dangers of co-operation, they tend to become more careful in closing strategic alliances as their most preferred contractual form (Hagedoorn, 1993). In the early 1990s, we again find a growth in the number of newly established alliances. Companies started to use newly developed management techniques that allowed them to cope with the difficulties associated with strategic partnering, whereas increased competitive pressures and ever rising R&D costs in combination with shrinking life cycles increased the need for technology/cost sharing even more.

An indicator of the possible internationalization of strategic technology partnering is found in a relative internationalization index, which we calculated by taking the percentage of international alliances as a percentage of all newly established alliances (see Figure 7.2).

Figure 7.2 Relative share of international technology alliances in newly established alliances (1980-1994)

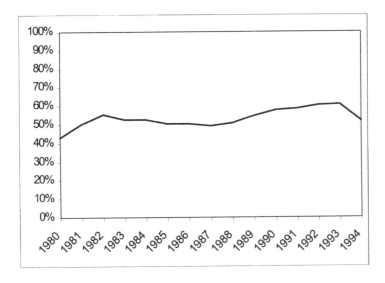

International strategic technology alliances have always accounted for a relatively high percentage of all strategic technology alliances. In the eighties, they represented about 50 percent of all strategic technology alliances. In the early 1990s, their number increased to about 60 percent. In 1994, however, the percentage decreased again to slightly more than 50 percent.

Table 7.3   Distribution of strategic technology alliances according to home country of partner(s), 1980-1994

MNE	Total	Netherlands	USA	Japan	Germany	France	UK	Switzerland
Shell	104	16	25	4	6	2	9	2
		15.4%	24%	3.8%	5.8%	1.9%	8.7%	1.9%
Philips	260	19	59	30	31	24	11	4
		7.3%	22.7%	11.5%	11.9%	9.2%	4.2%	1.5%
Unilever	23	4	5	2	0	0	6	1
		17.4%	21.7%	8.7%	0%	0%	26.1%	4.3%
DSM	43	5	4	7	1	2	2	1
		11.6%	9.3%	16.3%	2.3%	4.7%	4.7%	2.3%
AKZO	47	5	14	6	3	3	1	0
		10.6%	29.8%	12.8%	6.4%	6.4%	2.1%	0%
Total	477	49	107	49	41	31	29	8
		10.3%	22.4%	10.3%	8.6%	6.5%	6.1%	1.7%

Source: MERIT-CATI database.

Table 7.3 illustrates the distribution of strategic technology partnerships of the five leading Dutch multinationals (Shell, Philips, Unilever, DSM and AKZO) in the period 1980-1994. Only 10.3 percent of all alliances were undertaken with a domestic (Dutch) partner. This confirms the assumption that strategic alliances are a very important part of the internationalization strategy of Dutch multinationals. Philips stands out as the most outward-oriented organization in terms of its strategic technology alliances. If we compare Table 7.3 with the findings in Table 7.2 we find large similarities in terms of the countries in which Dutch firms try to find the required technological knowledge. However, Japanese firms seem to play a more important role in international strategic technology alliances with Dutch multinationals than as a home base for foreign laboratories. This illustrates the position of Japan as a knowledge-intensive, but difficult to penetrate, market (at least without a Japanese partner). US firms also seem to play a more important role in the strategic alliances of Dutch multinationals. In other words, proximity seems to play a more important role in the establishment of foreign laboratories than in the case of strategic technology alliances.

7.3 CONCLUSIONS

In this chapter we analyzed patterns of internationalization of corporate technological activity. The empirical analysis shows that only a relatively small degree of corporate technological activity takes place abroad. A noticeable exception is the position of companies from the Netherlands. The Netherlands seem to have, by far, the highest amount of international R&D, measured in terms of the percentage of patents that result from foreign R&D. This leading position in the internationalization process of R&D is due to two major factors: (1) the dominance of a relatively small group of large multinational corporations and (2) the size of the Dutch economy.

Whereas foreign R&D facilities play a relatively minor role in the R&D strategies of international firms (with the exception of the Netherlands), strategic alliances seem to play a much more important role in the internationalization strategies of companies worldwide. During the 1980s and early 1990s we find that between 50 and 60 percent of all strategic alliances were undertaken by partners from different home countries. The increase in the absolute number of international strategic technology alliances, however, does not indicate an increasing trend towards internationalization. The growth in the number of international strategic technology alliances was met by similar growth in the number of newly established domestic strategic technology alliances. Strategic technology partnering has therefore not necessarily become more internationalized, in contrast to the case of foreign R&D by Dutch multinationals which seem to be very internationally oriented in terms of their strategic technology partnerships. Only about 10 percent of all the alliances of Dutch multinationals are undertaken with a domestic partner.

These findings indicate that firms in the Netherlands are particularly outward-oriented. A certain degree of internationalization of R&D can be useful for an open economy such as the Netherlands and the fact that this occurs is certainly not surprising given the small scale of the Dutch economy. However, such a strong outward orientation might lead to a situation whereby domestic companies cannot benefit from the spillover effects of the R&D activities of large multinationals that undertake a disproportionate share of their R&D in other countries. The Dutch government could try to encourage more domestic R&D by actively creating a strong technological infrastructure, for example by government stimulation of R&D and by providing high quality education to engineering students. This would not only invite Dutch multinational companies to keep some of their R&D facilities in a well-developed technological infrastructure, it would also invite other companies to set up additional R&D activities in the Netherlands.

APPENDIX 1: THE CO-OPERATIVE AGREEMENTS AND TECHNOLOGY INDICATORS (CATI) INFORMATION SYSTEM

The CATI data bank is a relational database that contains separate data files that can be linked to each other and provides (dis)aggregated and combined information from several files. The CATI database contains three major entities. The first entity includes information on over 14,000 co-operative agreements involving some 6500 different parent companies. The data bank contains information on each agreement and some information on companies participating in these agreements. We define co-operative agreements as common interests between independent (industrial) partners which are not connected through (majority) ownership. In the CATI database only those inter-firm agreements are being collected, that contain some arrangements for transferring technology or joint research. Joint research pacts, second-sourcing and licensing agreements are clear-cut examples. We also collect information on joint ventures in which new technology is received from at least one of the partners, or joint ventures having some R&D program. Mere production or marketing joint ventures are excluded. In other words, our analysis is primarily related to technology co-operation. We are discussing those forms of co-operation and agreements for which a combined innovative activity or an exchange of technology is at least part of the agreement. Consequently, partnerships are omitted that regulate no more than the sharing of production facilities, the setting of standards, collusive behavior in price-setting and raising entry barriers - although all of these may be side effects of inter-firm co-operation as we define it.

We regard as a relevant input of information for each alliance the number of companies involved; names of companies (or important subsidiaries); year of establishment, time-horizon, duration and year of dissolution; capital investment and involvement of banks and research institutes or universities; field(s) of technology;[4] modes of co-operation;[5] and some comment or available information about progress. Depending on the very form of co-operation we collect information on the operational context; the name of the agreement or project; equity sharing; the direction of capital or technology flows; the degree of participation in case of minority holdings; some information about motives underlying the alliance; the character of co-operation, such as basic research, applied research, or product development possibly associated with production and/or marketing arrangements. In some cases we also indicate who has benefited most.

The second major entity is the individual subsidiary or parent company involved in one (registered) alliance at least. In the first place we assess the company's co-operative strategy by adding its alliances and computing its network centrality. Second, we ascertain its nationality, its possible (majority) owner in case this is an industrial firm. Changes in (majority) ownership in the 1980s were also registered. Next, we determine the main branch in which it is operating and classify its number of employees. In addition, for three separate subsets of firms time-series for employment, turnover, net income, R&D expenditures and numbers of assigned US patents have been stored. The first subset is based on the *Business Week* R&D scoreboard, the second on Fortune's International 500 and the third group was retrieved from the US Department of Commerce's patent tapes. From the *Business Week* R&D Scoreboard we took R&D expenditure, net income, sales and number of employees in 1980. Some 750 companies were filed; during the next years this number gradually increased to 900 companies in 1988, which were spread among 40 industry groups. The *Fortune International 500* of the largest corporations outside the US provides amongst others information about sales (upon which the rankings are based), net income and number of employees.

A third entity was recently added in order to perform more in-depth research in the information technology field. For this purpose, detailed information on leading companies in the three major segments of the information technology industry was included in the database. These major segments comprise the data processing, telecommunication and microelectronics industry. For all these industries, information on the direction of technology flows and on technology to market ratios of major players in these industries were processed from the CATI alliance database and stored in a separate entity. Information on technology flows is used to measure the degree to which the strategic partnerships of companies diffuse technology to their partners or absorb technology from them. Technology-to-market ratios are created in order to measure whether a company's alliances are primarily focused on research or used for market-entry purposes. This information was subsequently complemented by information technology diversification patterns of the same firms which we were able to obtain from Elsevier's *World Electronics Company File*. In order to measure the research activities of these firms, detailed patenting behavior information was processed from the US Department of Commerce patent tapes. In addition we included complementary data from various sources. The Gartner Group provided us with a comprehensive data set which comprised information on corporate sales, data processing sales, R&D expenditures and operating income of the 100 largest worldwide data processing companies. Data on the telecommunications industry was gathered from various sources. Publications of telecommunications sales of major telecommunications firms were found in specialized journals and newspapers, books and annual reports. Sources include DATA, DATAQUEST and BIPE. R&D

expenditures were already available from the CATI database, or taken from annual reports or Elsevier's *World Electronics Company File.* Microelectronics sales data were also obtained from various specialized journals and from newspapers. All journals and newspapers we used for our sample made use of Dataquest data. Once again R&D expenditure data as well as total sales data were obtained from the CATI database as well as from annual reports and Elsevier's *World Electronics Company File.*

NOTES

1. The foreign subsidiaries of these multinational enterprises (MNEs) would then be linked through major information networks that enable the corporate headquarters to communicate with their subsidiaries and to maintain control at relatively low cost.
2. Only in the case of Dutch and Swiss companies does the number of patents from subsidiaries rise to a very high proportion. This is mainly due to the existence of a few very large Dutch and Swiss companies that have strong manufacturing and R&D asets outside their small domestic base.
3. This so-called 'initiation effect' is dealt with more extensively in Hagedoorn (1993).
4. The most important fields in terms of frequency are information technology (computers, industrial automation, telecommunication, software, microelectronics), biotechnology (with fields such as pharmaceuticals and agro-biotechnology), new materials technology, chemicals, automotive, defense, consumer electronics, heavy electrical equipment, food and beverages, and so on. All fields have important subfields.
5. As principal modes of co-operation we regard equity joint ventures, joint R&D projects, technology exchange agreements, minority and cross-holdings, particular customer-supplier relations, one-directional technology flows. Each mode of co-operation has a number of particular categories.

REFERENCES

Bartlett, C.A., Y. Doz and G. Hedlund (1990), *Managing the Global Firm*, London: Routledge.
Cantwell, J. (1991), 'The International Agglomeration of R&D', in M. Casson (ed.), *Global Research Strategy and International Competitiveness*, Oxford: Blackwell.
Cantwell, J. and C. Hodson (1991), 'Global R&D and UK Competitiveness', in M. Casson (ed.), *Global Strategy and International Competitiveness*, Oxford: Blackwell.
Contractor, F.J. and P. Lorange (1988), *Cooperative Strategies in International Business*, Lexington, MA: D.C. Heath and Company.
Dunning, J.H. (1988), *Multinationals, Technology and Competitiveness*, London: Unwin Hyman.
Dunning, J.H. (1993), *Multinational Enterprises and the Global Economy*, Workingham: Addison-Wesley Publishing Company.
Duysters, G. and B. Verspagen (1994), 'Internationalisering van technologische activiteiten', *Economische Statistische Berichten*, **79**, 853-60.
Friedman, P., S.V. Berg and J. Duncan (1979), 'External vs. internal knowledge acquisition: joint venture activity and R&D intensity', *Journal of Economics and Business*, **32**, 103-10.

Fusfezld, H.I. and C.S. Haklisch (1985), 'Cooperative R&D for competitors', *Harvard Business Review*, **85**, 60-76.

Granstrand, O., L. Hakanson and S. Sjolander (1992), *Technology Management and International Business: Internationalization of R&D and Technology*, Chichester: John Wiley & Sons.

Graves, A. (1991), *International Competitiveness and Technological Development in the World Automobile Industry*, D.Phil Thesis, Brighton: University of Sussex.

Hagedoorn, J. (1993), 'Understanding the rationale of strategic technology partnering interorganizational modes of co-operation and sectoral differences', *Strategic Management Journal*, **14**, 371-85.

Hagedoorn, J. and J. Schakenraad (1990), 'Inter-firm Partnerships and Cooperative Strategies in Core Technologies', in C. Freeman and L. Soete (eds), *New Explorations in the Economics of Technological Change*, London: Pinter Publishers.

Hamel, G., Y. Doz and C.K. Prahalad (1986), *Strategic Partnership: Success or Surrender?*, Colloquium on cooperative strategies in international business, New Brunswick, N.J.: Rutgers/Wharton.

Haklisch, C.S. (1989), 'Technical Alliances in the Semiconductor Industry: Effects on Corporate Strategy and R&D', in Background Papers for conference on Changing Global Patterns of Industrial Research and Development, Stockholm, June 20-22.

Harrigan, K.R. (1985b), *Strategies for Joint Ventures*, Lexington, MA: Lexington Books.

Hergert, M. and D. Morris (1988), 'Trends in International Collaborative Agreements', in F.J. Contractor and P. Lorange (eds), *Cooperative Strategies in International Business*, Lexington: D.C. Heath and Company.

Hirschey, R.C. and R.E. Caves (1981), 'Internationalization of research and transfer of technology by multinational enterprises', *Oxford Bulletin of Economics and Statistics*, **42**, 115-30.

Hladik, K.J. (1988), 'R&D and International Joint Ventures', in F.J. Contractor and P. Lorange (eds), *Cooperative Strategies in International Business*, Lexington: D.C. Heath and Company.

Hu, Y.S. (1992), 'Global or transnational corporations and national firms with international operations', *California Management Review*, **34**, 107-27.

Lee, T. and P. Reid (1991), *National Interests in an Age of Global Technology*, Washington: NAP.

Miller, R. (1994), 'Global R&D networks and large-scale innovations: the case of the automobile industry', *Research Policy*, **23**, 27-46.

Mytelka, L. (1991), *Strategic Partnerships and the World Economy*, London: Pinter Publishers.

Organisation for Economic Co-operation and Development (1992a), *Technology and the Economy: The Key Relationships*, Paris: OECD.

Organisation for Economic Co-operation and Development (1992b), *Telecommunications and Broadcasting: Convergence or Collison?*, Paris: OECD.

Ohmae, K. (1990), *The Borderless World*, New York: Harper.

Osborn, R.N. and C.C. Baughn (1990), 'Forms of interorganizational governance for multinational alliances', *Academy of Management Journal*, **33**, 503-19.

Patel, P. and K. Pavitt (1991), 'Large firms in the production of the world technology: an important case of non-globalization', *Journal of International Business Studies*, **22** (1), 1-22.

Pearce, R.D. (1989), *The Internationalization of Research and Development by Multinational Enterprises*, London: Macmillan.

Pearce, R.D. and S. Singh (1992), *Internationalization of R&D among the World's Leading Enterprises*, London: Macmillan.

Peters, L.S. (1992), *Technology Management and the R&D Activities of Multinational Enterprises*, CSTP-RPI paper.

Porter, M.E. (1986), *Competition in Global Industries*, Boston: Harvard Business School Press.

Porter, M.E. (1990), *The Competitive Advantage of Nations*, New York: The Free Press.

Porter, M.E. and M.B. Fuller (1986), 'Coalitions and Global Strategies', in M.E. Porter (ed.), *Competition in Global Industries*, Boston: Harvard Business School Press.

Reich, R.B. (1991), *The Work of Nations*, New York: Vintage Books.

Rugman, A.M. (1981), *Inside the Multinationals*, New York: Columbia University Press.

Stopford, J.J. and L.T. Wells (1972), *Managing the Multinational Enterprise: Organization of the Firm and Overlap of Subsidiaries*, New York: Basic Books.

Vernon, R. (1966), 'International investment and international trade in the product cycle', *Quarterly Journal of Economics*, **88**, 190-207.

Vonortas, N.S. (1989), *The Changing Economic Context: Strategic Alliances among Multinationals*, Mimeo, New York: Center for Science and Technology Policy.

Woot de, P. (1990), *High Technology Europe: Strategic Issues for Global Competitiveness*, Oxford: Blackwell.

PART IV

The Role of Inward and Outward FDI: The Case of Belgium

8. The Ownership Structure of Belgian Companies: Evidence about a Small Open Economy in the Globalization Process

Haiyan Zhang and Daniel Van Den Bulcke

8.1 INTRODUCTION

Given its relatively small economic size (that is only 2.9 percent of EU GDP in 1998), Belgium has established a very strong foreign direct investment (FDI) position in the EU. The Belgian inward FDI stock, which reached US$164 billion by the end of 1998, accounted for 11 percent of the total EU inward FDI stock (UN/UNCTAD, 1999). Belgium is among the leading host economies in the world as it ranks second in terms of inward FDI per capita (after Singapore) and sixth in terms of absolute value. Belgium is also highly ranked as a home country of FDI. Its cumulative outward FDI (including Luxembourg) reached US$129 billion at the end of 1998, and accounted for about 6.6 percent of the total EU outward FDI stock. The ratio of the inward and outward FDI stock to Belgium's GDP increased respectively from 5.9 and 4.9 percent in 1980 to 55.1 and 40.7 percent in 1997, while the comparable ratio for all EU countries only went up from 5.5 and 6.2 percent to 15.2 and 20 percent during the same period.

This high level of 'globalization' of the Belgian economy has several specific characteristics as compared to other European Union (EU) small open economies (SOEs) with regard to both the inward and outward FDI operations. First, the patterns of Belgian inward and outward FDI flows show a strong regional concentration along the lines of geographical proximity and historical ties (Bernard, Van Sebroeck et al., 1998). The high geographical concentration of Belgian inward and outward FDI can partially be explained by the strong intra-firm and inter-firm linkages that are the results of its hosting of and/or the participation in cross-border industrial clusters. The existence of a highly developed transport and communication network in the region has also been found to act as a significant factor to attract FDI (Bartik, 1985; Hill and Munday, 1992).

Secondly, Belgium may be considered as a 'host' rather than a 'home' country because of its relatively lower level of outward FDI as compared to its inward investment. This makes Belgium quite distinct from other European SOEs that are often more active in investing abroad. The weakness of Belgian firms in outward FDI expansion has been often attributed to the limited size of its largest firms as compared to the 'big companies' in other small countries, as is the case in the Netherlands and Sweden (Van Den Bulcke and De Lombaerde, 1992). Belgium has 14 companies in the list of the largest 500 European enterprises in 1998, while the Netherlands and Sweden accounted for respectively 29 and 27. The average size of these largest Belgian companies was also smaller: they employed on average 17,997 persons as compared to 37,400 and 23,902 for the above-mentioned two countries. While Belgium counts only one firm among the 100 largest multinational enterprises (MNEs) in the world, the Netherlands and Sweden list respectively five and three (UN/UNCTAD, 1999).

Thirdly, the foreign investment pattern of Belgian companies has been affected by the increasing presence of foreign enterprises in Belgium itself, especially as a result of takeover operations. Belgium was ranked eighth among the global buyers and ninth among global sellers in the world's mergers and acquisition (M&As) in 1999 (KPMG, 2000). Although it is difficult to estimate the number of Belgian MNEs which are actually themselvesforeign-owned 'subsidiaries', the presence of such highly internationalized foreign MNEs in the Belgian economy has somehow extended the global strategic options of the Belgian companies not only by improving their competitiveness, but also by allowing them to continue and even extend their outward investment operations. The experience of these foreign-owned companies in operating as relatively autonomous firms on the one hand, and as subsidiaries within the global networks of MNEs on the other hand, may even result in a management system that is more flexible and more local-oriented (Daems and Van De Weyer, 1993).

Fourthly, in reviewing the spatial configuration of Belgian inward and outward FDI, it has to be noted that the dynamic linkages between inward and outward FDI operations - that is the crucial position of Belgium as a 'platform'[1] for many EU and non-EU MNEs in their cross-border value-added activities - constitutes a major feature of the Belgian globalizing economy. According to the database 'Who Owns Whom' (Dun & Bradstreet, 1998), 17 percent of Belgian overseas subsidiaries were established by foreign-owned subsidiaries operating in Belgium in 1997, while this relative proportion was only 4 percent for Sweden, 7 percent for Ireland, 8 percent for Denmark and 11 percent for Austria. The high participation of foreign firms in outward FDI activities was also observed in the case of the Netherlands (27 percent) and Luxembourg (14 percent). The central geographical location of these SOEs and the fact that they are surrounded by relatively large markets in the neighboring countries are probably the most significant factor to explain the 'platform' position and role of the Benelux countries (Beije and Nuys, 1995).

Given the specific features of the Belgian economy as compared to other European SOEs and based on recent theoretical insights on globalization (Dunning, 1997), this chapter attempts to make an extensive statistical analysis of the ownership structure of the Belgian economy in general and to provide an aggregate analysis of Belgian inward, outward and platform FDI in particular. The second section provides an analytical framework and summarizes the major characteristics of the database that are used in this study. The third section gives an overview of specific features of Belgian-based enterprises according to their ownership structure and FDI operations. In the fourth section, the Belgian-based firms' inward, outward and platform FDI operations are analyzed. Also the ownership advantages of Belgian-owned MNEs are compared to those of foreign subsidiaries established in Belgium. The concluding part attempts to summarize the main findings of this study and to shed more light on the specific characteristics of Belgium's globalization as an SOE.

8.2 DATA SOURCES AND ANALYTICAL FRAMEWORK

8.2.1 Data Sources

The data used in this study are collected and compiled from Bel-First (Bureau Van Dijk, 1999), a corporate database of Belgian- and Luxembourg-based companies. On the basis of data included in the National Bank of Belgium's (NBB) Central Balance,[2] Bel-First provides information on the direct and indirect participations of Belgian-based companies in the equity capital of other domestic and foreign companies on the one hand and the domestic and foreign shareholders of Belgian-based companies on the other hand. This data set consequently allows analyzing the ownership pattern of Belgian-based companies.[3]

The Bel-First database as compiled in April, 1999 counts a total of 272,803 Belgian-based companies, of which 37,572 were removed from the current study because they terminated their activities before this date for reasons such as bankruptcy (14,619 firms), liquidation (15,787) and other motives. The number of companies with consolidated accounts was 349. These firms are excluded from the analysis with regard to employment, sales and financial indicators in order to avoid double counting with the companies that are taken up separately. This database can be considered to some extent as an aggregate picture of the Belgian economy, because it accounts for about 40 percent of all firms included in Belgium's value added tax (VAT) statistics in 1996 in terms of number of companies,[4] 50 percent in terms of the number of employees and 82 percent in terms of turnover.

8.2.2 Analytical Framework

The Belgian-based companies included in the database can be divided into three groups according to their ownership structure and nationality. The first category of firms includes Belgian-owned companies that are neither subsidiaries nor shareholders in other firms. These firms are defined as 'Belgian (domestic) independent (single) firms'. The second category consists of 'Belgian (domestic) enterprise groups' that have either equity participations in or are themselves controlled by other domestic firms.[5] Since shareholders of these companies as well as their subsidiaries are domestic firms, they might be called uninational firms. By contrast, the companies that are included in the third category are firms that either have subsidiaries abroad or are controlled by foreign MNEs. Therefore, they are considered as 'Belgian-based multinational firms'.

Among the 235,231 Belgian-based enterprises that are included in the Bel-First database, 192,923 are independent firms, 30,385 are parent or subsidiary firms belonging to 15,990 domestic/uninational groups and 11,923 are parent or subsidiary firms of 4,968 Belgian-owned and 922 foreign multinational groups. This study focuses on the last group of enterprises, that is the 11,932 companies of Belgian-based multinationals. The major objective is therefore to emphasize the extent and patterns of Belgian inward, outward and platform FDI operations. On the basis of the conceptual model (Figure 8.1), the companies included in the third group - that is the Belgian-based multinationals - are further divided into four categories. The first category, Category A, consists of 5,950 companies that are part of Belgian-owned MNEs and are not directly involved in FDI operations themselves. In other words, although these companies are subsidiaries of multinational groups and are in some cases involved as local partners of foreign inward investors in Belgium, they have no equity participation abroad. The 4,133 companies included in Category B are Belgian-owned companies that directly participate in the equity capital of companies located abroad, that is they are parent companies and control wholly-owned affiliates or joint ventures abroad. The 1,401 companies in Category C are Belgian-based subsidiaries of foreign-owned MNEs. When these latter companies themselves have equity participation in firms located outside of Belgium, they are classified in Category D and are called platform investors. There are 439 foreign-owned subsidiaries established in Belgium that are involved in this particular form of FDI. The first and third categories in this typology consist of inward FDI operations, while the second and fourth group of enterprises are outward investors that are either operating from their Belgian home basis or as a platform in Belgium on behalf of their foreign parent companies. Of course, enterprises included in Category D have also to be considered as inward investors as they are foreign subsidiaries established in Belgium.

Figure 8.1   Typology of Belgian-based firms involved in foreign direct investment

Direction of FDI

		Inward FDI	Outward FDI
		Category A Belgian companies involved in international joint ventures as local partners (n=5,950)	**Category B** Belgian companies involved in outward FDI operations (n=4,133)
Nationality of Shareholders (parent companies)	Belgian		
	Foreign	**Category C** Foreign subsidiaries based in Belgium (n=1,401)	**Category D** Foreign subsidiaries located in Belgium and involved in platform FDI (n=439)

8.3 OWNERSHIP CHARACTERISTICS OF BELGIAN COMPANIES

8.3.1 Overview

Belgian independent (single) firms accounted for 82 percent of all companies included in the Bel-First database. They play a substantial role in the Belgian economy, especially with regard to employment. These companies controlled BEF5,659 billion of assets (27 percent of all Belgian-based companies in the database), employed 508 thousand people (37 percent), realized BEF3,287 billion of turnover (25 percent) and generated BEF1,118 billion of net added value (31 percent) in 1997 (Table 8.1). However, single firms represent a very small proportion in the manufacturing sector as compared to their position in the total economy, especially in terms of assets and sales. They accounted for less than 15 percent of the total assets of Belgian manufacturing, 17 percent of net added value, 14 percent of sales and 23 percent of employment.

As compared to single firms, domestic groups created intra-firm linkages through equity participation in other local companies and benefit from economies of scale and scope at the national level. Although these companies accounted for less than 13 percent of all Belgian-based firms, they play a relatively important role in the Belgian economy. The 30,385 enterprises of domestic groups employed 299 thousand people and generated sales of BEF2,340 billion in 1997, accounting respectively for 21 percent of Belgian employment and 18 percent of the sales of all companies in Belgium included in the database. Their net added value and total assets amounted respectively to BEF692 and BEF3,316 billion in 1997, representing 19 and 16 percent of the database. These Belgian domestic enterprise groups take up a similar position in the Belgian manufacturing sector, as they accounted for 16 percent of the total number of manufacturing enterprises, 14 percent of the total assets, 17 percent of the sales, 17 percent of the net added value and employment in 1997.

As far as Belgian-based multinational companies are concerned - although they represent only a small proportion (about 5 percent) in terms of the number of firms - they accounted for 57 percent of total turnover and 42 percent of the employment of all firms included in the database. Contrary to the independent single enterprises and domestic groups, these companies are highly involved in inward, outward and platform FDI operations. The inter- and intra-firm linkages of these multinational groups provide in fact the dynamic substance of the globalizing Belgian economy in terms of FDI, as they have established international joint ventures and concluded alliances in both domestic and foreign markets (see further). The Belgian-based multinational companies occupy an even more important position in the Belgian manufacturing industry, as they control more than 70 percent of assets, create 59 percent of employment, realize 70 percent of sales and generate 66 percent of net added value in 1997. These indicators show that the internationalization process is much more advanced in Belgian manufacturing than in agriculture and services.

Table 8.1 *Main indicators of Belgian companies by ownership structure, 1997*

	Domestic single firms	%	Domestic groups	%	Multinational groups	%	Total
All industries							
Number of companies	192,923	82.01	30,385	12.92	11,923	5.07	235,231
Total assets (BEF billion)	5,659	26.95	3,316	15.79	12,023	57.26	20,999
Net added value (BEF billion)	1,118	31.26	692	19.35	1,767	49.39	3,578
Sales (BEF billion)	3,287	25.09	2,340	17.87	7,472	57.04	13,098
Number of employees ('000)	508	36.78	299	21.64	575	41.58	1,382
Manufacturing							
Number of companies	15,771	72.80	3,545	16.36	2,347	10.83	21,663
Total assets (BEF billion)	506	14.57	498	14.35	2,470	71.08	3,475
Net added value (BEF billion)	209	17.44	201	16.75	788	65.81	1,197
Sales (BEF billion)	517	13.53	655	17.12	2,653	69.35	3,825
Number of employees ('000)	106	23.33	81	17.79	268	58.88	454

8.3.2 Industrial Concentration

The industrial concentration/specialization of each group of companies is measured by the ratio of its share in net added value of one particular industry to that of all industries, that is the industrial concentration ratio (ICR). When the ICR of a group of companies is higher than 1 in an industry, it means that these companies are more frequently present in this particular industry as compared to their overall position in all industries. When the ICR is below 1, the presence of a group of companies in a particular industry is considered to be weaker as compared to its overall position in all industries together.

The companies that are included in the database as single firms are highly concentrated in agriculture, accounting for 68 percent of net added value in this sector. They also have a strong presence in non-classified manufacturing, construction, business and consumer services, commerce, financial, insurance and real estate services and fabricated metals (Table 8.2). Because these companies have neither domestic nor overseas subsidiaries, the sectors in which they have a strong presence are evidently characterized by low intra-firm integration in terms of ownership control and weak internationalization in terms of direct investment.

The sectors in which domestic/uninational groups have a high ICR are construction, transportation and communication services, textiles and apparel, wood and paper products and finance, insurance and real estate. As a result, these sectors are typically characterized by the presence of intra-firm linkages, although these relationships are limited to the domestic firms.

Most of the Belgian manufacturing industries, especially electronic and electric equipment, mining, chemicals, basic metals, machinery, instruments and transport, are in fact highly involved into inward and outward FDI operations. A large proportion of these industrial sectors are controlled by Belgian-based multinational enterprises. For instance, 77 percent of the net added value of the chemical industry can be attributed to companies that are part of Belgian and foreign MNE groups. In the mining sector, these multinational firms realized together 80 percent of net added value. The transport and communication services as well as the distribution of gas and electricity in Belgium are also becoming more involved into the internationalization process in terms of FDI as a result of the market liberalization of service sectors in the EU. The differences among groups of enterprises with regard to their ICR can be explained not only by the characteristics of the industries and firms, but also by the national and supranational sectoral policy that has significantly affected corporate restructuring and market openness and liberalization (European Commission, 1998).

Table 8.2 Industrial distribution and index of specialization of Belgian-based companies by categories, 1997

Sectors	% of net added value			ICR (in terms of net added value)		
	Independent firms	Domestic groups	Multinational groups	Independent firms	Domestic groups	Multinational groups
Agriculture, forestry and fishing	67.84	19.13	13.03	2.17	0.99	0.26
Mining	15.77	4.07	80.16	0.50	0.21	1.62
Construction	53.13	23.86	23.00	1.70	1.23	0.47
Food and kindred products	18.29	17.08	64.63	0.59	0.88	1.31
Textiles and apparel	24.54	22.82	52.64	0.79	1.18	1.07
Wood and paper products	30.00	22.78	47.22	0.96	1.18	0.96
Chemical and allied products	5.69	17.64	76.68	0.18	0.91	1.55
Rubber and plastics	17.30	13.17	69.52	0.55	0.68	1.41
Non-metal minerals	15.30	17.41	67.29	0.49	0.90	1.36
Primary metal products	10.19	14.05	75.75	0.33	0.73	1.53
Fabricated metal products	33.58	19.41	47.01	1.07	1.00	0.95
Machinery and equipment	13.91	10.62	75.47	0.45	0.55	1.53
Electrical and electronic equipment	7.38	6.82	85.81	0.24	0.35	1.74
Transportation equipment	17.96	14.03	68.01	0.57	0.72	1.38
Instruments and related equipment	19.79	6.87	73.34	0.63	0.36	1.48
Other manufacturing industries	54.12	13.12	32.77	1.73	0.68	0.66
Transport and communication	23.70	23.30	53.00	0.76	1.20	1.07
Electricity, gas and sanitary services	11.86	15.32	72.82	0.38	0.79	1.47
Wholesale and retail	41.86	19.77	38.37	1.34	1.02	0.78
Finance, insurance and real estate	37.00	22.43	40.58	1.18	1.16	0.82
Other services	49.62	18.90	31.49	1.59	0.98	0.64
All industry	31.25	19.36	49.39	1.00	1.00	1.00

Source: Bel-First (1999).

8.3.3 Operational Aspects

The comparative analysis of several operational aspects of Belgian-based companies shows a number of differences (Table 8.3). The multinational enterprises are relatively large as they employed on average 81 persons per company in Belgium in 1997 as compared to 20 persons for the domestic groups and 7 for the single firms. The average turnover of this former group of companies amounted to BEF1,017 million as compared to BEF 185 million for domestic groups and BEF40 million for independent firms. The size difference between these three groups of companies is also apparent from the intra-industrial comparison. The multinational groups are much larger as compared to domestic groups and independent firms in all industries in terms of employment as well as sales, assets and net added value. Only in mining/energy and public utility sectors are the average employment and net added value of Belgian single firms higher than for the average of the domestic groups.

The productivity measures that are used here are gross added value, operating revenue and profits per employee. They provide an indication of the productivity of each employee in the value creating activities. The calculations show that labor productivity in independent firms and domestic groups is substantially lower than for the average of multinational groups. Each person employed by independent firms created on average BEF2.25 million of gross value added in 1997, while the mean for domestic and multinational groups was respectively BEF2.91 and BEF4.61 million. Yet, labor costs, that is wages and salaries including social security contributions, were also much higher in domestic and multinational groups and offset, to some extent, the higher productivity of these enterprises.

The combination of labor costs per employee and productivity, that is value added per employee (labor costs/value added per employee) provides a so-called 'unit labor cost' index that illustrates the absolute costs of labor inputs (CEFIC, 1995). This index shows no significant difference between independent firms and domestic groups in the level of absolute labor costs, but multinational groups have a higher index, meaning that - in absolute terms - they spend more on their personnel.

The variation in labor productivity among firms may reflect differences in the use of other inputs, such as capital, technology and intermediate goods. The high labor productivity of multinational groups can to some extent be explained by their concentration in capital-intensive and high-tech industries - such as chemicals, transport equipment and primary metals - that rely relatively more on automated processing technology. However, apart from this cross-industry difference, labor productivity is also largely influenced by other firm-specific factors, such as plant size (in terms of sales) and the skill levels of employees. The intra-industry comparison shows that the productivity of multinational groups was higher in 17 out of 22 industries as compared to domestic groups and independent firms in terms of gross added value per employee. The larger size of multinational enterprises, as compared to other firms, undoubtedly contributes to their higher productivity.

In addition to size and productivity, profitability offers another interesting approach to measure the performance and competitiveness of companies. Profitability can be approximated by using the gross and net operating revenue expressed as a percentage of total turnover, that is the gross and net profit margin. Belgian-based multinational groups tend to be less profitable than other companies located in Belgium, especially as compared to domestic groups. The gross profit margin of multinational groups (subsidiaries and parent companies) reached on average 7.85 percent (median value) in 1997, while the relative ratio was 9.86 percent for independent firms and 10.23 percent for domestic groups. Yet, the differences in the net profit margins were not substantial, as they reached 3.37 percent for multinational groups as compared to 3.71 percent for domestic groups and 3.29 percent for independent firms. The intra-industrial comparison shows that the net profit margin of Belgian-based multinational groups was lower than the average of the database in 11 of 22 industries. However, it has to be noted that the presence of multinational groups in most of these industries is not important (Table 8.2).

8.4 CHARACTERISTICS OF BELGIAN-BASED MULTINATIONAL COMPANIES

This section focuses on two comparative analyses. The first comparison deals with Belgian-owned multinational companies (Categories A and B in Figure 8.1) and foreign subsidiaries established in Belgium (Categories C and D), while the second one studies differences between firms involved into inward FDI activities (Categories A and C) and those with outward FDI operations (Categories B and D). The purpose of these comparisons is to emphasize some major characteristics of different types of Belgian-based multinational companies with regard to their industrial specialization, operational size, productivity, profitability and labor costs. These analyses also provide additional information on the ownership-specific advantages of MNEs and location-specific advantages of the Belgian economy from a double perspective. First, the comparison between Belgian-owned multinational groups and foreign-owned subsidiaries operating in Belgium allows us to emphasize the ownership-specific advantages of Belgian-based companies in relation to their country of origin. Secondly, the distinction between firms

Table 8.3 Some characteristics of Belgian companies according to ownership, 1997

	Independent single firms			Domestic groups		
	Mean	N	Std. Deviation	Mean	N	Std. Deviation
Size						
Sales (million BEF)	40.25	81,648	309.16	184.99	12,650	1,051.18
No. of employees	6.55	77,584	50.46	19.75	15,140	108.49
Total assets (million BEF)	29.39	192,532	999.26	109.36	30,324	1,456.78
Net added value (million BEF)	5.85	191,164	59.41	22.99	30,124	245.36
Profitability						
Gross profit margin before tax (%)*	9.86	79,954	25.25	10.23	12,435	28.94
Net profit margin before tax (%)*	3.29	79,258	21.19	3.91	12,357	25.42
Productivity						
Gross added value per employee (million BEF)	2.25	76,153	3.49	2.91	14,820	7.36
Operating revenue per employee (million BEF)	13.69	34,993	41.78	17.09	7,769	42.49
Profit per employee (million BEF)	0.60	50,099	1.74	1.01	10,342	3.33
Labor costs						
Average cost of employee/year (million BEF)	1.17	77,480	6.29	1.35	15,125	0.60
Costs of employees/operating revenues (%)*	14.63	48,780	23.83	16.95	8,788	30.27
Index of unit labor cost	0.79	76,071	4.17	0.79	14,807	3.28

Table 8.3 (continued)

	Multinational groups			Total		
	Mean	N	Std. Deviation	Mean	N	Std. Deviation
Size						
Sales (million BEF)	1,016.70	7,349	5,538.78	128.86	101,647	1,579.77
No. of employees	81.09	7,087	593.34	13.85	99,811	170.66
Total assets (million BEF)	1,036.83	11,596	5,540.24	89.57	234,452	1,630.91
Net added value (million BEF)	153.36	11,522	983.99	15.37	232,810	244.19
Profitability						
Gross profit margin before tax (%)*	7.85	7,377	26.97	9.73	99,766	25.92
Net profit margin before tax (%)*	3.37	7,339	23.82	3.37	98,954	22.04
Productivity						
Gross added value per employee (million BEF)	4.61	6,820	19.89	2.52	97,793	6.76
Operating revenue per employee (million BEF)	24.18	5,816	65.91	15.49	48,578	45.59
Profit per employee (million BEF)	2.27	5,032	7.33	0.79	65,473	2.90
Labor costs						
Average cost of employee/year (million BEF)	1.79	7,067	0.91	1.24	99,672	0.67
Costs of employees/operating revenues (%)*	18.58	6,087	43.01	15.28	63,655	27.28
Index of unit labor cost	0.84	6,810	2.42	0.79	97,688	3.95

Note: * Median.

with domestic and inward FDI operations on the one hand, and those with outward FDI operations on the other hand, may shed some light on the comparative and competitive advantages of Belgian industrial sectors. The industries with strong inward FDI are those where Belgium has some comparative locational advantages, while sectors where outward FDI dominate might have high competitive advantages.

8.4.1 Belgian-Owned versus Foreign-Owned Multinational Enterprises

There are 10,083 Belgian-owned multinational firms (Categories A and B) and 1,840 foreign-owned subsidiaries (Categories C and D) in the Bel-First database. Belgian-owned MNEs control BEF6,694 billion of assets, accounting for 32 percent of that of all Belgian-based companies in 1997 (Table 8.4). These enterprises generate 28 percent of net added value of all Belgian companies, realized 31 percent of sales and 26 percent of employment. Although the number of foreign subsidiaries that were established in Belgium (Categories C and D) accounted only for about 0.8 percent of all Belgian-based firms, their importance in the Belgian economy is quite significant: they controlled one quarter of total assets, created about one fifth of net added value (21 percent) and realized more than one quarter of the sales (26 percent) of all Belgian-based companies in 1997. Yet, their employment contribution was markedly lower and reached only 15 percent.

In the manufacturing sector, Belgian-owned multinational enterprises have either a higher or at least a similar position as compared to their overall position in all industries. While these firms accounted for 0.79 percent of all Belgian manufacturing enterprises, they realized about one third of sales (34.5 percent), controlled 34 percent of assets, generated 30 percent of net added value and created 32 percent of employment in 1997. Yet, it is interesting to notice that although foreign-owned subsidiaries accounted only for about one fourth of Belgian-owned multinational companies in the manufacturing sector, they took up twice as large a proportion in Belgian manufacturing in terms of assets (52.5 percent), net added value (54 percent), with the exception of employment where it was only slightly lower (45.3 percent). The importance of foreign-owned subsidiaries in the Belgian economy, especially in manufacturing sectors, has significantly increased during the last two decades. In 1968, foreign-owned subsidiaries in the Belgian industry realized one fourth of production, 30 percent of total sales and provided jobs for one fifth of all industrial employees (Van Den Bulcke, 1971). In 1990, a survey of the 3,515 largest Belgian manufacturing and service companies showed that 30 percent of these enterprises were foreign-owned and generated 43.8 percent of added value (Daems and Van De Weyer, 1993).

Table 8.4 Significance of domestic and foreign-owned multinational companies in the Belgian economy, 1997

	Belgian-owned MNEs (Categories A and B)			Foreign subsidiaries (Categories C and D)		
		% of all MNE groups	% of all Belgian-based companies		% of all MNE groups	% of all Belgian-based companies
All industries						
Number of companies	10,083	84.57	4.29	1,840	15.43	0.78
Total assets (BEF billion)	6,694	55.68	31.88	5,329	44.32	25.38
Net added value (BEF billion)	1,001	56.65	27.98	766	43.35	21.40
Sales (BEF billion)	4,076	54.55	31.12	3,396	45.45	25.92
No. of employees ('000)	366	63.65	26.48	209	36.35	15.11
Manufacturing						
Number of companies	1,847	78.70	0.79	500	21.30	0.21
Total assets (BEF billion)	1,174	47.54	33.79	1,296	52.46	37.29
Net added value (BEF billion)	363	46.04	30.30	425	53.96	35.51
Sales (BEF billion)	1,320	49.75	34.50	1,333	50.25	34.85
No. of employees ('000)	146	54.71	32.24	121	45.29	26.69

Source: Bel-First (1999).

Table 8.5 Characteristics of Belgian-based multinational companies according to ownership, 1997

	Belgian MNEs (Categories A and B)			Foreign MNEs (Categories C and D)		
	Mean	N	Std. Deviation	Mean	N	Std. Deviation
Size						
Sales (million BEF)	688.99	5,916	3,328.40	2,369.60	1,433	10,458.62
No. of employees	64.29	5,692	616.65	149.68	1,395	480.94
Total assets (million BEF)	678.35	9,868	3,698.76	3,083.99	1,728	11,090.02
Net added value (million BEF)	102.13	9,803	793.91	445.48	1,719	1,672.29
Profitability						
Gross profit margin before tax (%)*	8.25	5,913	27.98	6.85	1,464	22.06
Net profit margin before tax (%)*	3.39	5,875	24.73	3.28	1,464	19.63
Productivity						
Gross added value per employee (million BEF)	4.51	5,469	20.35	5.01	1,351	17.93
Operating revenue per employee (million BEF)	23.15	4,476	66.82	27.63	1,340	62.66
Profit per employee (million BEF)	1.95	3,997	6.19	3.50	1,035	10.53
Labor costs						
Average cost of employee/year (million BEF)	1.69	5,681	0.83	2.19	1,386	1.09
Costs of employees/operating revenues (%)*	18.50	4,722	41.70	18.77	1,365	47.29
Index of unit labor cost	0.84	5,464	2.60	0.81	1,346	1.49

Note: * Median.

The foreign participation in different Belgian industries is measured by the share of foreign subsidiaries in net added value of industrial sectors on the one hand, and the industrial concentration ratio (ICR) on the other hand. Industries with a high foreign participation reflect the attractiveness or comparative advantages of these industries in the Belgian economy. Foreign subsidiaries in Belgium contributed highly to the net added value in chemicals (65 percent of net added value of the sector), mining and energy (58 percent), transport equipment (49 percent), machinery (47 percent) and instruments (40 percent). The ICR in each of these sectors reached respectively 3.04, 2.72, 2.22 and 1.86. All these sectors can be considered as capital- and scale-intensive industries.

As compared to foreign subsidiaries, Belgian-owned multinational companies are highly represented in resource- and labor-intensive manufacturing and strongly regulated service sectors, such as public utilities (for example electricity, gas and sanitary services), primary metal products, electrical and electronic equipment and food and kindred products. The proportion of the net added value that these firms realized in these industries accounted respectively for 73, 56 and 48 percent.

Foreign-owned subsidiaries in Belgium have larger sized operations as compared to other local firms. On average they employed 150 persons and controlled BEF3,084 million of assets in 1997, while the comparative figures for companies of Belgian-owned multinational groups were only 64 employees and BEF678 million (Table 8.5). The intra-industry comparison shows that these differences in size are typical for most sectors. Only in primary metals, transport and communication as well as public services and public utilities were foreign subsidiaries smaller than Belgian groups.

The productivity of foreign subsidiaries in Belgium was higher than for Belgian-owned multinational enterprises in terms of gross added value, operating revenue and profits per employee. The intra-industrial comparison shows that the profitability of foreign subsidiaries was higher than Belgian-owned multinational groups in 12 out of 21 industries in terms of profits per employee, especially in financial services, chemicals, rubber and plastics, transport equipment and machinery. Industries in which foreign subsidiaries achieved a lower level of productivity than their Belgian counterparts are public utilities, mining and energy, non-metallic minerals, instrument equipments, construction, and so on.

An examination of the index of unit labor costs does not bring forward a significant difference between Belgian-owned MNEs and foreign subsidiaries at the industry level as a whole. However, the intra-industry comparison shows that foreign subsidiaries have lower unit labor costs in most of the sectors where they established a strong presence, such as chemicals (30 percent lower than for Belgian MNEs), primary metals (24 percent lower), instruments (17 percent lower) and rubber and plastics (10 percent lower). An explanation for this specific characteristic might be found in the competitive advantages of global MNEs with regard to the capital- and technology-intensive production process.

8.4.2 Inward versus Outward FDI Operations

There are 4,572 Belgian-based firms that have established subsidiaries abroad. These MNEs represent about 2 percent of all Belgian-based firms in terms of numbers, while they controlled 22 percent of total assets, generated 23 percent of net added value and created 21 percent of Belgian employment in 1997. The number of firms that are involved in inward FDI, that is foreign subsidiaries in Belgium or Belgian firms as partner companies of foreign inward investors, amount to 7,351 in 1997, accounting for about 3 percent of all Belgian-based firms (Table 8.6). This latter group of companies takes up 35 percent in terms of total assets, 26 percent of net added value, 30 percent in sales and 21 percent of employment in Belgium. The comparison between these two groups of companies confirms that the Belgian economy is more oriented towards inward than outward FDI. Even in Belgium itself the impact of inward investors is more important than those with outward investment operations. In the manufacturing sector, the proportion of firms involved in outward FDI is less large than for those with inward FDI operation in terms of number of companies. However, with regard to their position in terms of assets, net added value, sales and employment it is relatively higher

Table 8.7 compares the importance of different categories of Belgian-based enterprises according to their involvement in inward and outward FDI operations. Several conclusions can be drawn from this comparative analysis. First, Belgian public utility industries (electricity, gas and sanitary services) are strongly dominated by domestic subsidiaries of Belgian-owned MNEs (Category A), which realized 73 percent of all added value in these industries. By contrast, firms in these sectors did not carry out significant outward FDI operations. However, since these service sectors have been liberalized within the EU, the inward and outward investment have become more important as a result of cross-border M&As. The take over of Tractebel by the French group Suez Lyonnaise des Eaux is a perfect illustration of the rapid entry of foreign MNEs in the Belgian public utilities sector, while the acquisition of German THL by ABX Logistics provides an example of the outward expansion of Belgian public service sectors.

Table 8.6 Characteristics of Belgian companies with inward and outward FDI, 1997

	Belgian MNEs (Categories A and B)			Foreign MNEs (Categories C and D)		
	Mean	N	Std. Deviation	Mean	N	Std. Deviation
Size						
Sales (million BEF)	688.99	5,916	3,328.40	2,369.60	1,433	10,458.62
No. of employees	64.29	5,692	616.65	149.68	1,395	480.94
Total assets (million BEF)	678.35	9,868	3,698.76	3,083.99	1,728	11,090.02
Net added value (million BEF)	102.13	9,803	793.91	445.48	1,719	1,672.29
Profitability						
Gross profit margin before tax (%)*	8.25	5,913	27.98	6.85	1,464	22.06
Net profit margin before tax (%)*	3.39	5,875	24.73	3.28	1,464	19.63
Productivity						
Gross added value per employee (million BEF)	4.51	5,469	20.35	5.01	1,351	17.93
Operating revenue per employee (million BEF)	23.15	4,476	66.82	27.63	1,340	62.66
Profit per employee (million BEF)	1.95	3,997	6.19	3.50	1,035	10.53
Labor costs						
Average cost of employee/year (million BEF)	1.69	5,681	0.83	2.19	1,386	1.09
Costs of employees/operating revenues (%)*	18.50	4,722	41.70	18.77	1,365	47.29
Index of unit labor cost	0.84	5,464	2.60	0.81	1,346	1.49

Note: * Median.

Source: Bel-First (1999).

Table 8.7   Industrial concentration of Belgian-based multinational enterprises with inward and outward FDI, 1997

Sectors	% of net added value		ICR (in terms of net added value)	
	Inward FDI	Outward FDI	Inward FDI	Outward FDI
Agriculture, forestry and fishing	4.96	8.07	0.19	0.34
Mining	34.60	45.56	1.33	1.95
Construction	10.61	12.39	0.41	0.53
Food and kindred products	20.69	43.94	0.80	1.88
Textiles and apparel	15.92	36.73	0.61	1.57
Wood and paper products	19.92	27.30	0.77	1.17
Chemical and allied products	34.85	41.83	1.34	1.79
Rubber and plastics	26.85	42.67	1.03	1.82
Non metal minerals	23.83	43.46	0.92	1.86
Primary metal products	29.48	46.27	1.13	1.98
Fabricated metal products	17.74	29.27	0.68	1.25
Machinery and equipment	26.63	48.84	1.02	2.09
Electrical and electronic equipment	45.02	40.78	1.73	1.74
Transportation equipment	49.62	18.39	1.91	0.79
Instruments and related equipment	17.99	55.34	0.69	2.36
Other manufacturing industries	16.66	16.11	0.64	0.69
Transport and communication	24.76	28.24	0.95	1.21
Electricity, gas and sanitary services	72.82	0.00	2.80	0.00
Wholesale and retail	24.49	13.88	0.94	0.59
Finance, insurance and real estate	26.90	13.68	1.04	0.58
Other services	12.12	19.37	0.47	0.83
All industries	25.99	23.41	1.00	1.00

Source: Bel-First (1999).

Secondly, Belgian sectors with high inward FDI operations but without significant outward FDI are those dominated by foreign subsidiaries, such as transport equipment and chemicals. In these two industries, foreign subsidiaries take up respectively about 50 and 65 percent of added value. By contrast, the Belgian sectors that are characterized by a high outward internationalization but without any significant inward FDI operations are sectors with an ICR higher than one for firms with outward FDI (Categories

B and D) and lower than one for those with inward FDI operation (Categories A and C). These industries are food (1.88 of outward ICR as compared to 0.8 of inward ICR), textiles and apparel, non-metallic minerals, fabricated metal products and instruments and related equipment. The high outward multinationalization of these industries can be explained by the strong competitive advantages of companies operating in these sectors or by their massive 'delocalization' due to high production costs in Belgium. Because of low attractiveness of these industries, the presence of foreign subsidiaries in these sectors is very limited.

Thirdly, the industries that have a high ICR in both categories with inward (Categories A and C) and outward (Categories B and D) FDI operations can be considered as relatively highly globalized sectors, as they are dominated not only by firms with strong inward but also with strong outward FDI operations. The strongly globalized Belgian industries are electrical and electronic equipment, mining, primary metals, rubber and plastics and machinery and equipment. For instance, in the electrical and electronic equipment sector, firms with inward FDI operations realized 45 percent of net added value of the sector in 1997, while firms with outward FDI activities had a share of 41 percent. The relative shares in the chemical industry were respectively 35 and 42 percent.

The comparison between firms with domestic and inward FDI and those with outward FDI emphasizes the comparative and competitive advantages of Belgian firms and industries (that is through an aggregation of the firms) in terms of size, productivity, labor costs and profitability (Table 8.8). Belgian firms with domestic operations and foreign subsidiaries in Belgium are much smaller than the firms involved in outward FDI activities. The former group of companies employed on average 65 persons as compared to 108 persons in the latter group. The substantial difference between these two groups of companies is also found in sales and added value, although their size in terms of total assets is rather similar. The intra-industrial comparison shows that in most industries Belgian firms with outward FDI are large sized, especially in mining and energy, primary metals, food, non metallic minerals, machinery and instrument equipment.

8.5 BELGIAN INWARD, OUTWARD AND PLATFORM INVESTMENT

After comparing Belgian-owned multinationals with foreign subsidiaries established in Belgium on the one hand, and Belgian inward with outward investing companies on the other hand, this section provides more information about their inward, outward and platform operations.

Table 8.8 Major characteristics of Belgian-based multinational companies according to ownership control and FDI activities, 1997

	Belgian firms involved in inward FDI operations (Categories A and C)			Belgian firms with outward FDI operations (Categories B and D)		
	Mean	N	Std. Deviation	Mean	N	Std. Deviation
Size						
Sales (million BEF)	843.24	4,728	5,652.59	1,329.59	2,621	5,314.08
No. of employees	64.95	4,441	328.42	108.19	2,646	872.31
Total assets (million BEF)	1,015.39	7,276	5,974.24	1,072.93	4,320	4,720.37
Net added value (million BEF)	128.53	7,232	723.94	195.20	4,290	1,309.38
Profitability						
Gross profit margin before tax (%)*	8.11	4,795	28.26	7.54	2,582	24.34
Net profit margin before tax (%)*	3.22	4,766	24.78	3.57	2,573	21.93
Productivity						
Gross added value per employee (million BEF)	4.10	4,277	13.80	5.46	2,543	27.20
Operating revenue per employee (million BEF)	20.77	3,656	54.23	29.95	2,160	81.66
Profit per employee (million BEF)	2.25	3,087	7.39	2.31	1,945	7.22
Labor costs						
Average cost of employee/year (million BEF)	1.79	4,426	0.93	1.80	2,641	0.87
Costs of employees/operating revenues (%)*	20.13	3,834	39.78	16.25	2,253	47.92
Index of unit labor cost	0.84	4,270	2.15	0.84	2,540	2.82

Note: * Median.

Source: Bel-First (1999).

8.5.1 Inward Investment

Among the 1,840 foreign subsidiaries that are included in the Bel-First database (Categories C and D), 1,056 (57.4 percent) originated from Belgium's five neighboring countries, that is 466 from France, 206 from the Netherlands, 158 from Germany, 134 from the UK and 92 from Luxembourg (Table 8.9). Apart from these neighboring countries, other European countries have also a substantial presence in Belgium, especially Switzerland with 106 and Sweden with 30 companies. All non-neighboring European subsidiaries reached 226, accounting for 12.3 percent of all foreign subsidiaries established in Belgium. North American firms (the US and Canada) owned 440 subsidiaries, accounting for 24 percent of all firms, while the number of Japanese subsidiaries amounted to 70, representing less than 4 percent.

Table 8.9 Belgian-based foreign subsidiaries by origin, 1997

	Number of companies	%	Net added value (BEF million)	%	Number of Employees	%
Neighboring countries	1,056	57.39	366	47.25	114,007	53.33
Other European countries	226	12.28	102	13.15	20,861	9.76
North America	440	23.91	269	34.66	67,108	31.39
Japan	70	3.80	22	2.85	6,585	3.08
Others	48	2.61	16	2.08	5,226	2.44
Total	1,840	100.00	775	100.00	213,787	100.00

Source: Bel-First (1999).

The subsidiaries established by firms located in Belgium's neighboring countries generate BEF366 billion of net added value and employ 114 thousands of people, accounting respectively for 47 and 53 percent of added value and employment of all foreign subsidiaries based in Belgium. Subsidiaries from North America are also quite substantial in the Belgian economy, as they account for 35 percent of the net added value of all Belgian-based foreign subsidiaries and 31 percent in terms of employment. The Japanese subsidiaries in Belgium are relatively less important (about 3 percent in terms of number of companies, employment and added value) as compared to their European and American counterparts.

The importance of foreign subsidiaries varies substantially according to the sectors. The analysis of ICR in terms of net added value shows that foreign subsidiaries established by the neighboring countries in Belgium are more concentrated in public utilities, agriculture, construction, primary metals, fabricated metals, electrical and electronic equipment and textiles and apparel. As compared to these investors from neighboring countries, firms from other European countries, especially Switzerland and Sweden, are highly concentrated in machinery and equipment, mining and energy and non-financial services. The industrial structure of American subsidiaries is more diversified, although they have a high ICR in the instrumental equipment industry, transport equipment, rubber and plastics, mining and energy, transport and communication services, machinery and chemicals. As compared to their American counterparts, Japanese firms were highly concentrated in a very small number of industries, such as non-metallic minerals, wholesale and retail and electrical and electronic equipment.

The size of the subsidiaries that are controlled by neighboring countries is much smaller than for the foreign subsidiaries from other countries of origin in terms of sales and assets. Small and medium-sized companies from neighboring countries are of course able to participate more easily in the Belgian economy as a result of their geographic and cultural proximity. Yet, there is no significant difference between subsidiaries from different countries of origin in terms of employment size. The relatively higher labor input of firms from neighboring countries as compared to their lower level of assets (that is lower ratio of assets to number of employees) might be related to the relatively low intensity of capital investment and labor-intensive technology of the sectors in which they dominate.

The profitability of foreign subsidiaries in terms of gross profit margin and net profit margin was not significantly different among firms from different countries of origin, although the Japanese ones were less profitable than the others. The gross profit margin before tax of Japanese subsidiaries amounted to 4.4 percent in 1997 as compared to 6.8 percent for neighboring invested firms, 8 percent for other European firms and 6.5 percent for American companies. The lower profitability of Japanese subsidiaries is probably related to the low labor productivity that might be originally affected by the industries in which they are concentrated. The profit per employee in firms from neighboring countries reached BEF3.7 million in 1997, while the relative value was only BEF1.6 million for Japanese subsidiaries. The comparison of the high operating revenue with the low profits per employee showed that the operating costs of Japanese companies in Belgium were relatively higher than those of other subsidiaries. However, the absolute (measured by costs of employees/operating revenues) and unit (index of unit labor costs) of Japanese subsidiaries were lower than for other subsidiaries from other countries, meaning that the lower profitability of Japanese subsidiaries in Belgium was not due to labor costs.

8.5.2 Outward Investment

There are 4,280 Belgian-owned MNEs which control 8,683 subsidiaries abroad, while 443 foreign subsidiaries located in Belgium have equity participations in another 1,919 foreign firms (for example platform investors, see further). Consequently, these two groups of companies own together 10,602 subsidiaries abroad (Table 8.10). On average each Belgian-based multinational company established 2.2 subsidiaries abroad, while the largest one controlled 149 overseas subsidiaries. About 63 percent (2,971) of these Belgian-based multinationals have one overseas subsidiary that accounted for 28 percent of the total number of Belgian invested enterprises abroad. Almost one third (31 percent) of them (1,445) own two to five overseas subsidiaries, accounting for 37 percent of all Belgian subsidiaries abroad. Only about 2 percent of the parent companies in the database are in charge of more than 10 subsidiaries abroad and take up 22 percent of all overseas subsidiaries.

Table 8.10 Belgian overseas subsidiaries and the nationality of their parent companies

	Parent companies		Subsidiaries abroad	
	N	%	N	%
Belgian-owned	4,280	90.62	8,683	81.90
Platform investment	443	9.38	1,919	18.09
Neighboring countries	264	5.59	1,102	10.39
Other European countries	51	1.08	239	2.25
North America	95	2.01	397	3.74
Japan	20	0.42	106	1.00
Others	13	0.28	75	0.71
Total	4,723	100.00	10,602	100.00

Source: Bel-First (1999).

Among the 10,602 Belgian subsidiaries abroad, 8,783 are located in Europe (82.8 percent) (Table 8.11). The neighboring countries are the most important destination of Belgian outward FDI, as 2,588 of the Belgian overseas subsidiaries are located in France (24.4 percent), 1,858 in the Netherlands (17.5 percent), 989 in Luxembourg (9.3 percent), 723 in Germany (6.8 percent) and 527 in the UK (5 percent). These five neighboring countries host 63 percent of the Belgian subsidiaries abroad and 76 percent of all Belgian subsidiaries in Europe. North America hosts 627 Belgian subsidiaries that account for 5.9 percent of total Belgian-owned subsidiaries abroad, while the relative share of Latin America and Africa is respectively 2.2 and 3.8 percent. Asia as a whole attracted 378 Belgian subsidiaries, of which 120 are located in the Asian NIEs, 62 in Japan, 101 in ASEAN-5 and 77 in China and India. Like its inward FDI operations, Belgian outward FDI is strongly concentrated in the neighboring countries, especially in France and the Netherlands mainly because of the historical links and geographic proximity.

Table 8.11 Location of Belgian subsidiaries abroad by host region, 1997

	Belgian-owned MNEs		Platform investors		Total	
	N	%	N	%	N	%
Neighboring countries	5,679	65.40	1,006	52.42	6,685	63.05
Other European countries	1,623	18.69	475	24.75	2,098	19.79
North America	397	4.57	83	4.33	480	4.53
Other developed countries	103	1.19	44	2.29	147	1.39
Africa	292	3.36	109	5.68	401	3.78
Latin America and the Caribbean	156	1.80	72	3.75	228	2.15
Asia	272	3.13	106	5.52	378	3.57
Others	161	1.85	24	1.25	185	1.74
Total	8,683	100.00	1,919	100.00	10,602	100.00

Source: Bel-First (1999).

In the Belgian manufacturing sector, there are 971 MNEs that established 2,766 overseas subsidiaries abroad, accounting for 21 percent of the total number of all parent companies and 26 percent of all subsidiaries. Within the manufacturing sector, the firms in food, wood and paper products, textiles, fabricated metals and chemicals are more active abroad, as they accounted together for about two thirds of all manufacturing parent companies (62 percent). The firms in those sectors invested in 1,591 subsidiaries abroad that accounted for 15 percent of all Belgian overseas subsidiaries or 58 percent of the subsidiaries established by manufacturing companies.

The number of Belgian companies in the service sectors with subsidiaries abroad amounted to 3,682, accounting for more than three quarters (78 percent) of all Belgian parent companies in the database. These companies established 7,684 subsidiaries abroad, accounting for 73 percent of all Belgian overseas subsidiaries. Among the Belgian service companies, the trade and finance sectors dominate both in the number of parent companies (respectively 23 and 40 percent) and subsidiaries (20 and 40 percent).

8.5.3 Platform Investment

Almost 10 percent of Belgian parent companies that are involved in outward FDI operation are platform investors and control about 18 percent of Belgian invested companies abroad (Table 8.10). This indicates that platform investors have a higher degree of internationalization as compared to other Belgian parent companies, as they control on average more than four overseas subsidiaries, while the latter group owned only two. Among the 443 foreign subsidiaries engaged in platform investment, 60 percent originated from the neighboring countries (Table 8.10). These companies represented 5.6 percent of all outward investing companies from Belgium and established 1,102 overseas subsidiaries, accounting for more than 10 percent of all Belgian subsidiaries abroad. American subsidiaries based in Belgium were also actively involved in outward FDI operations, as they control 397 subsidiaries abroad. A smaller number of firms from other European countries and Japan also rely on Belgium for this type of investment. Yet most, but not all, of this platform investment resulted from the takeover of Belgian parent companies and their subsidiaries abroad by foreign MNEs. It is, however, difficult to estimate the proportion of such acquisitions in the total outward FDI by foreign companies from Belgium.

With regard to location, platform investors are relatively different from Belgian-owned MNEs. While Belgian-owned MNEs tend to highly concentrate their overseas subsidiaries in neighboring countries (that is about 65 percent of their subsidiaries), platform investors have a further geographical coverage. They invested more in non-neighboring countries, especially in Central and Eastern Europe, Asia and Africa (Table 8.11). This might partly be explained by Belgium's specific locational advantages for foreign investors to establish regional or international headquarters (coordination centers) for investing and managing their operations in other regions.

The comparison between Belgian-owned MNEs and foreign platform investors show that the latter groups of enterprises are more active in sectors such as chemicals, non-metal minerals, rubber and plastics and machinery, while the former group of companies are highly concentrated in industries, such as mining and energy and textile and clothing. For instance, chemical companies are responsible for 16 percent of all overseas subsidiaries established by platform investors, while this proportion for Belgian-owned enterprises is only about 2.4 percent.

8.6 CONCLUSION

This chapter has examined the ownership structure of Belgian-based companies and described their inward, outward and platform FDI operations. The statistical analysis of a large Belgian corporate database, that is Bel-First, confirmed the major findings of previous studies (see the introduction) and updated information on the patterns and extent of the globalization of Belgium as a small open economy. First, the Belgian economy is highly global both in terms of inward and outward FDI operations, although there are major differences according to the industries. In the Belgian manufacturing two thirds of the assets, sales and added value are generated by multinational firms with inward, outward and platform FDI operations, while the agricultural sector and services are still dominated by independent and domestic enterprise groups. It is clear that the sustainable value added in the Belgian economy, especially in manufacturing, is the result of not only domestically-owned but also foreign-owned firms. Firms from small countries target resources and markets not just in a domestic context, because their sustainable development requires a geographic configuration spanning many countries, whereby firm-specific and location advantages present in several nations may complement each other (Moon, Rugman and Verbeke, Chapter 3 in this volume).

Secondly, the pattern and the extent of the globalization of the Belgian manufacturing sectors are different according to their location and firm-specific advantages. In the industries with high inward but low outward investments, especially in the automobile industry, Belgium has low competitive advantages despite its long established locational advantages (for example supplying activities and skilled labor). Because of the lack of its own leading companies, the Belgian automotive industry will be seriously challenged by increasing competition from low wage countries unless its supplying industries move towards a more global oriented strategy. The international competition has also strongly affected a large number of traditional Belgian industries, such as textiles, food and metals. Outward FDI by firms from these sectors has become quite important, while the inward FDI remained rather at a low level. The low attractiveness of these industries to foreign investors combined with their low competitive advantages have obliged local firms to 'delocalize' their activities abroad. The restructuring of these industries is needed, especially for technological upgrading and product innovation. Yet, the role of foreign enterprises in these specific Belgian industries is still very limited. It has to be noted that Belgium has a number of very competitive industries - such as chemicals, mining and machinery - in which foreign companies play a substantial role through their inward and outward FDI operation. The dynamic interaction between inward and outward FDI in these better Belgian industries provides Belgium with comparative advantages to attract foreign investors and allows them to further shape clusters of manufacturing activities. It is also interesting to note that within the single market program of the EU, the Belgian public utility sectors have been targeted by inward and outward investors, although these initiatives are still very limited.

Thirdly, Belgium as small open economy has been used by many foreign MNEs as a platform for their FDI in Central and Eastern Europe, Asia and Africa. These platform investors are usually large sized and have achieved a better performance than other Belgian-based domestic and foreign enterprises. They are concentrated in sectors where Belgium has established a global competitive position, such as chemicals, machinery, instrument and mining. These companies not only play a substantial role in the Belgian economy in terms of assets, added value and sales, but they also take up a very large proportion in Belgian outward FDI.

NOTES

1. When a foreign-owned subsidiary invested abroad from its Belgian host country on behalf of its multinational group, this investment is considered as a 'platform' investment.
2. According to the Royal Decree of October 8, 1976, more than 250,000 companies in Belgium are obliged to submit their annual accounts to the Central Balance of the NBB. They are (1) all companies with limited liability; (2) all economic joint ventures and European economic joint ventures; (3) all companies with unlimited liability which are regarded as large and one or more of whose partners with unlimited liability is/are legal persons; and (4) all foreign companies which have a branch or a centre of activities in Belgium.
3. Yet, a number of limitations have to be taken into account. First, the information provided by the NBB's Central Balance is not really complete because only the large firms have to present the total version of their accounts, while the small and medium-sized ones are only asked to submit an abbreviated form. A large number of missing values in the dataset might affect statistical results, especially when a comparative analysis is carried out. Secondly, the database on corporate governance of Belgian companies is based on the ownership control (equity participation) rather than on the organizational structure and managerial influence. As a result, the non-equity linkages among firms, especially their collaborative relationships, such as sourcing, distribution, joint R&D arrangements and other types of strategic alliances, are not included. Thirdly, the reliability of the database of the NBB's Central Balance is influenced by a number of factors that are related to the annual reporting as carried out by the individual companies (Jegers and Buijink, 1987). Consequently, the results of the analysis have to be interpreted with the necessary care.
4. The remaining companies are mostly self-employed 'physical persons'.
5. The equity participation is regarded as a direct investment only if it reaches at least 10 percent of the total equity share of the company. Otherwise it is considered as portfolio or indirect investment.

REFERENCES

Bartik, T.J. (1985), 'Business location decisions in the United States: estimates of the effects of urbanization, taxes and other characteristics of states', *Journal of Business and Economic Statistics*, 14-22.

Beije, P.R. and H.O. Nuys (1995), *The Dutch Diamond? The Usefulness of Porter in Analyzing Small Countries*, Leuven: Garant.

Bernard, P., H. Van Sebroeck, et al. (1998), *Delocalisation, Mondialisation: Un rapport d'actualisation pour la Belgique*, Brussels: Bureau Fédéral du Plan.

Bureau Van Dijk (1999) *Bel-First: Financial Reports and Statistics on Belgian and Luxemburg Companies*, Brussels.

CEFIC (1995), *Annual Report*, 1995, The European Chemical Industry Council, Brussels.

Daems, H. and P. Van De Weyer (1993), *L'Economie Belge sous l'influence: Investissements Etrangers en Belgique et Conséquences sur le Pouvoir de Décision Stratégique*, Brussels: Fondation Roi Baudouin.

Dunning, J.H. (1997), *Resolving some Paradoxes of the Emerging Global Economy: Small Nations as Trailblazers*, CIMDA Discussion Paper, 33, Antwerp: University of Antwerp.

European Commission (1998), *The Single Market Review: Impact on Trade and Investment: Foreign Direct Investment*, Luxembourg: Office of Official Publications of the European Communities.

Hill, S. and M. Munday (1992), 'The UK regional distribution of foreign direct investment: analysis and determinants', *Regional Studies*, 533-44.

Jegers, M. and W. Buijink (1987), The reliability of financial accounting data bases: some Belgian evidence, *Financial Journal of Accounting*, No. 1.

KPMG (2000), *Cross-Border M&A Reaches AllTtime High*.

UNCTAD (1999), *World Investment Report: Foreign Direct Investment and the Challenge of Development*, New York and Geneva: United Nations.

Van Den Bulcke, D. (1971), Les Entreprises Etrangères dans L'Industrie Belge, Brussels: OBAP.

Van Den Bulcke, D. and P. De Lombaerde (1992), 'The Belgian Metalworking Industries and the Large European Internal Market: The Role of Multinational Investment', in J. Cantwell (ed.), *Multinational Investment in Modern Europe: Strategic Interaction in the Integrated Community*, London: Edward Elgar, pp. 107-49.

9. Industrial Clusters and Japanese Manufacturing Affiliates in the Belgian Small Open Economy

Filip De Beule and Daniel Van Den Bulcke

9.1 INTRODUCTION

In 'Location and the Multinational Enterprise: A Neglected Factor?' John Dunning (1998) asserts that a critical choice of a multi-activity firm is whether it should internalize its intermediate product markets within its home country or in foreign locations and that the outcome of this choice is primarily determined by the costs and benefits of adding value to these products in alternative locations. Primarily, because the geography of international business activity is also dependent on its entry mode and, indeed, on the competitive advantages of the investing firms. The earlier emphasis on the firm-specific determinants of international economic activity has recently been complemented by a more profound interest in the spatial aspects of Foreign Direct Investment (FDI) and how they affect both the competitive advantages of firms and their modes of entry into and expansion in foreign markets.

The liberalization of markets, more outward-looking development policies, and the current attractions of regional economic integration have all helped to push out the territorial boundaries of firms. While FDI is the main route by which this extension is being accomplished, cross-border alliances - varying from international subcontracting and 'keiretsu' type relationships, to R&D consortia among rival firms - have become more significant (Dunning, 1997).

The ease with which Multinational Enterprises (MNEs) can transfer tangible and especially intangible assets across borders is being constrained by the fact that the location of the creative activities and use of these assets is becoming increasingly influenced by the presence of immobile clusters of complementary value-added activities. Silicon Valley (Saxenian, 1990) and Hollywood (Christopherson and Storper, 1986) may be the world's best-known clusters, but examples abound in every international, national, regional, state and even metropolitan economy, especially in the more advanced nations (Porter, 1998). Thus, while globalization suggests that the location and ownership of production is becoming geographically more dispersed, other economic forces are making for a more pronounced geographical concentration of economic activity both within particular regions and countries (Dunning, 1998). The spatial widening of economic activities (that is globalization) on the one hand, and the increasing pressure on firms, nations and localities to reassert their distinctive clusters (corporate and regional integration) on the other hand constitutes the so called 'paradox of economic space'.

This 'paradoxical' evolution, that is, the growing significance of the 'externalities' in industry (cluster) sustainability - that is the ability of any given industrial sector to maintain or enhance its competitive position over longer periods of time - is particularly relevant for small open economies, such as in the case of Belgium. Belgium is among the fastest globalizing economies in Europe, especially with regard to the inward and outward FDI operations. The FDI stock to GDP ratio of Belgium increased from 5.6 percent to 27.8 percent between 1980 and 1994, while the comparable ratio for all EU countries augmented from 5.6 percent to 13.6 percent for the same period (Zhang and Van Den Bulcke, 1997).[1]

While the observation that firms tend to cluster in particular regions is hardly novel (Smith, 1776; von Thünen, 1826; Marshall, 1890), it has recently been taken up in explaining the stickiness of certain locations in an increasingly slippery world (Markusen, 1994). Theories suggest that firms may be drawn to the same locations because proximity generates positive externalities or agglomeration effects. Economists have proposed agglomeration effects in the form of both static (pecuniary) and dynamic (technological) externalities to explain industry localization (Baptista, 1998). Theoretical attempts to formalize agglomeration effects have focused on three mechanisms that would yield such positive feedback loops: inter-firm technological spillovers, specialized labor and intermediate inputs (Marshall, 1890).

The empirical literature largely conceptualizes the industrial location of firms as a process of location scanning and choice (Smith and Florida, 1994). Econometric models treat the location decisions as a form of revealed preference for: (1) the classical variables of comparative advantage, such as relative wages, market size, degree of openness, and transport costs; (2) the attributes of a given area, such as (un)employment, unionization, education, population size and density, minority concentration, transportation access, infrastructure, and tax rate variables and (3) agglomeration factors (Kravis and Lipsey, 1982; Bartik, 1985; Coughlin, Terza et al., 1991; Veugelers, 1991; Woodward, 1992; Brainard, 1993a, 1993b). Several studies have found evidence of spatial concentration, or agglomeration effects in the location of FDI (Knickerbocker, 1973; Vernon, 1974; Wheeler and Mody, 1992; Florida and Kenney, 1994; Smith and Florida, 1994; Head, Ries et al., 1995; Braunerhjelm and Svensson, 1996; Ford and Strange, 1999). Clustering is a selfreinforcing process in which initial FDI accounts for additional FDI (Arthur, 1990; Markusen, 1990; Wheeler and Mody, 1992). Chance events and government inducements can have a lasting influence on the geographical pattern of manufacturing.

Agglomeration economies may be particularly strong in the case of Japanese firms, in comparison to firms from other countries, as inter-firm linkages within Japanese business groups (keiretsu) may lead members to set up affiliates close to other members (Smith and Florida, 1994; Head, Ries et al., 1995; Ford and Strange, 1999). Further evidence of agglomeration is found in the pattern of Japanese ventures, which has been argued to strengthen the prevalent specialization of countries and regions but also to create new patterns (Micossi and Viesti, 1991; Andersson, 1993; Head, Ries et al., 1995). Japanese firms have predominantly entered into industries in which the host countries have already revealed comparative advantages. However, Japanese ventures do not simply mimic the geographical pattern of local establishments in their industry. Instead, initial investments by Japanese firms spur subsequent investors in the same industry to select the same country, region or state. This pattern supports an agglomeration theory of industry localization rather than a theory based on differences in endowments of natural resources, labor and infrastructure (Head, Ries et al., 1995).

This chapter does not add to the literature of investment location and the impact of agglomeration as such, but rather uses it as a framework to analyze the characteristics of foreign subsidiaries in different sectors, in particular Japanese manufacturing affiliates in Belgium on the basis of a Japanese subsidiary-level data set.

There are obviously different reasons why multinational firms set up affiliates abroad. Dunning (1993), drawing on Behrman's typology (Behrman, 1972), suggests four different foreign subsidiary roles:

1. market-seeking subsidiaries, locating abroad because of the importance of the foreign market for the parent company's products;
2. resource-seeking subsidiaries, locating abroad to access specialized inputs, well-trained labor, or low-cost factor inputs;
3. efficiency-seeking subsidiaries, locating abroad to achieve global economies of scale on behalf of the parent company;
4. strategic asset-seeking subsidiaries, typically acquisitions of foreign firms to leverage the MNE's competitive position or to counter its competitors.

One would expect to find the relatively high value-adding subsidiaries in industry cluster locations, because they are attractive locations for foreign-owned subsidiaries, both in terms of the opportunities for learning and knowledge transfer and in terms of the specialized inputs and labor they provide. They can be seen as 'tapping into' the sources of knowledge and ideas, and scientific and technical talent which are embedded in cutting-edge regional innovation complexes (Florida, 1995). There will obviously also be foreign subsidiaries in non-cluster locations, but they are more likely to be of the market-seeking type or resource-seeking type (cheap factors of production), rather than the higher value-adding subsidiaries in industry clusters.

The chapter is organized as follows. Section 9.2 treats the literature with regard to agglomeration economies in more detail. Section 9.3 describes the dataset of Japanese affiliates, attempt to identify industry clusters and describe indigenous and transplanted sectors in Belgium, which will serve as a framework of analysis for the said manufacturing subsidiaries. Section 9.4 subsequently analyzes the locational and organizational characteristics of Japanese manufacturing subsidiaries in different industrial sectors and the final section consists of some conclusions.

9.2 AGGLOMERATIONS OR CLUSTERS

A distinction should be made between two broad types of agglomeration economies. One type relates to general economies of regional and urban concentration that apply to all firms and industries in a particular location. Such external economies lead to the emergence of manufacturing belts or metropolitan regions (Porter and Sölvell, 1997). These urbanization economies do not consist of increased efficiency of the enterprises themselves but of reduced transport and search costs for the customers and, therefore, lead to more customers than the individual enterprise would have been able to attract (Pedersen, 1994).

A second type of agglomeration is localization economies. As advances in transportation and information obliterate distance,[2] cities and regions face a tougher time attracting and anchoring income-generating activities (Markusen, 1996). The problem is most acute in advanced capitalist countries, in particular small and open economies such as Belgium, where wage levels and standards of living are substantially higher than in low-wage, labor-abundant and increasingly technically competent countries (Howes, 1993). Production space in these small and open countries has become extremely 'slippery'. Economists, geographers and economic development planners have sought for more than a decade for alternative models of development in which activities are sustained or transformed in ways that maintain relatively high wage levels, social contributions and quality of life. They have searched for 'sticky places' in 'slippery space' (Markusen, 1996), examining the structure and operation of these geographic concentrations of interconnected companies and institutions.

One extensively researched formulation is that of the flexibly specialized industrial district. In the original formulation of the industrial district, Marshall (1890) envisioned a region where the business structure is comprised of small, locally-owned firms that make investment and production decisions locally. Scale economies are relatively minimal, forestalling the rise of large firms. Within the district, substantial trade is transacted between many small firms buying and selling from each other for eventual export from the region. What makes the industrial district so special and vibrant, in Marshall's account, is the existence of a pooled market for workers with specialized skills,[3] the provision of specialized inputs from suppliers and service providers,[4] the relatively rapid flow of business-related knowledge between firms,[5] which result in what are now called technological spillovers.

All of these factors are covered by the notion of agglomeration, which suggests that the stickiness of a place resides not in the individual locational calculus of firms or workers, but in the external economies available to each firm from its spatial conjunction with other firms and suppliers of services. In Marshall's formulation, it was not necessary that any of these actors should be consciously co-operating with each other, in order for the district to exist and operate as such. But in a more recent adaptation (Piore and Sabel, 1984), based on the phenomenon of successful expansion of mature industries in the so-called Third Italy[6] (Goodman and Bamford, 1989), and extended to other venues in Europe and the United States (Scott, 1988; Storper, 1989; Paniccia, 1998), researchers have argued that concerted efforts to co-operate among district members to improve district-wide competitiveness can increase the stickiness of the district. While agglomeration economies signal external economies passively obtained by enterprises located close to each other, collective efficiency (Schmitz, 1989; Pedersen, 1994) indicates advantages which enterprises may achieve through active collaboration. Localized information flows, technological spillovers and specialized pools of knowledge and skills will ensure the revitalization of these seedbeds of innovation in these clusters. Clusters are considered as networks of production of strongly interdependent firms, knowledge producing agents and customers, linked to each other in a value adding production chain (OECD, 1999a).

However, many of the faster-growing regions of the world turn out not to be formed by small, locally owned, vertically or horizontally specialized enterprises. There exist regions where a number of key firms or facilities act as anchors or hubs to the regional economy. These clusters are dominated by one or several large, locally headquartered firms, in one or more sectors, surrounded by smaller and less powerful suppliers. These hub-and-spoke districts thrive on market power and strategy rather than on networking (Gray, Golob et al., 1996; Markusen, 1996). Yet a third variant of rapidly growing industrial districts may be termed satellite platforms (Markusen, 1996), a congregation of branch plant facilities of externally based firms. Tenants of satellite platforms may range from routine assembly functions to relatively sophisticated research. They stand alone, detachable spatially from either up- or downstream operations within the same firm or from agglomerations of competitors and external suppliers or customers (Glasmeier, 1988).

Another way of discerning different clusters is based on the origin of the industry in a specific location: indigenous or transplanted. Some industries grew up as indigenous industries and were afterwards exposed to a globalizing economy of increasing levels of international trade and investment. In the beginning, indigenous (hub-and-spoke) clusters are characterized by tightly linked local firms and relatively small numbers of foreign-owned subsidiaries. Over time, the number of foreign subsidiaries in indigenous industries increases as a result of the globalizing economy. More specifically, successful industries attract multinationals that set up or acquire local companies to have access to the available strategic assets. Other industries originate as a direct result of the increasing levels of international trade and investment between countries and regions. These transplanted (satellite platform) industries are originally characterized by a limited number of local firms and by (relatively many) foreign branch plants that are rather weakly embedded in the local economy. Transplanted industries are likely to continue to rely on their parent company or keiretsu members back home for key supplies or core technologies for some time, and will only slowly develop strong 'local' ties, set up R&D units and grow to become clusters. Alternatively, the virtuous circle of economic development by embedding foreign plants in the local economy does not materialize and the agglomeration of firms remains a satellite district.

With regard to Japanese direct investment, this could be translated, on the one hand, to the hypothesis that Japanese investors have transplanted industries in which they possess competitive advantages, such as electronics, setting up greenfield screwdriver plants that are weakly embedded in the local economy, importing supplies either from the parent company or other affiliates, or from keiretsu network suppliers, and giving limited decision-making autonomy and value-adding activities to these assembly subsidiaries. This chapter will check whether these subsidiaries (still) fit this profile of satellite platforms or not. On the other hand, Japanese multinationals have supposedly tapped into industries in which their European counterparts possess strong competitive advantages, such as chemicals, acquiring existing companies.

9.3 THE DATASET

The research focuses on Japanese manufacturing affiliates in Belgium. Data was collected primarily through a postal questionnaire. Information was also obtained from secondary sources, such as the Annual Accounts database (NBB, 1996) and the Main Industrial Indicators database (OECD, 1999b).

The subsidiary-specific data for this study were collected on the basis of a postal survey that was forwarded to all operational Japanese manufacturing affiliates located in Belgium at the end of 1995. This list of Japanese manufacturing subsidiaries in Belgium was compiled on the basis of the annual 'Survey of European Operations of Japanese Companies in the Manufacturing Sector' published by the Japan External Trade Organization (JETRO, several years). The survey covered the period from October 1995 until January 1996 and was sent to 41 companies in which Japanese firms owned at least 10 percent of the equity capital. Only companies that were incorporated in Belgium and operational at that time were included in the survey. As three companies had not yet started production, while two others were already in liquidation and another two had been sold to a local Belgian firm, there were at that time 34 active Japanese subsidiaries in Belgium. Two of those subsidiaries were controlled by other Japanese subsidiaries that were already established in Belgium. Only one reply for both of these latter production facilities was received, however. Because another three companies refused to co-operate, 29 companies out of a total of 34 operational production facilities under Japanese ownership in Belgium participated in the survey, that is, a response rate of 85 percent. Although most of the questionnaires were fully answered, the response rate for some specific questions is sometimes lower. In terms of employment (88 percent) and turnover (90 percent) the response rates were even higher than for the number of firms, because the largest companies sent in their questionnaire. Table 9.1 indicates the number of production facilities in Belgium under Japanese ownership for the various time periods in the major manufacturing sectors.

The 34 Japanese manufacturing facilities established in Belgium employed 7,783 persons at the end of 1994,[7] which is an average of 229 employees per company. Nineteen companies counted less than 100 employees, while 14 companies employed between 100 and 1,000 people.

One company provided employment to more than 1,000 persons during 1994. However, if this largest firm is left out, the average number of employees drops to 149, which is still about five times larger than the average number of employees for all the manufacturing companies in Belgium at 32 per firm[8] in 1993. The total number of Japanese nationals employed in the affiliates in Belgium approximately numbered 150,[9] that is, almost 2 percent of total employment in the Japanese manufacturing companies in Belgium. Nineteen Japanese subsidiaries had a turnover of less than BF1 billion, while the total sales of another 14 companies were situated between BF1 billion and BF10 billion. The largest firm reached BF10 billion in turnover. In total, the Japanese manufacturing subsidiaries had a turnover of approximately BF75 billion in 1994. This represented only about 2 percent of the sales of all manufacturing firms in Belgium and about 0.5 percent of the total sales of all companies in Belgium. The sales of all US affiliates in Belgium, for instance, reached almost 13 percent of the turnover of all Belgian companies (Van Den Bulcke and Zhang, 1998). In 1995, 542 so-called US non-bank affiliates employed 108 thousand persons in Belgium, of which 65.8 thousand (62 percent) in manufacturing, 14.6 thousand (14 percent) in commercial activities and 16.4 thousand (16 percent) in services. Chemicals, the dominant industry in the manufacturing sector, employed 18,300 persons, that is, 17.3 percent of the total employment of US affiliates in Belgium. The employment by American subsidiaries in Belgium accounted for 6.2 percent of the total Belgian employment in the private sector in 1995 (BEA, several years).

Belgium was the first country in Europe in which a Japanese manufacturing company was set up, when Honda Motors decided to establish its motorcycle plant in Aalst as early as 1963. Before the first oil crisis in 1973, another five Japanese plants located in Belgium. Out of the total population of 34 subsidiaries in 1995, seven were established between 1974 and 1978. From 1979 until 1985, five companies started production under Japanese ownership, including the acquisition in 1981 of Glaverbel - the largest company in Belgium under Japanese control - by Asahi Glass. More than one third of all Japanese firms located in Belgium between 1986 and 1990, that is, the period during which the European Single Market was being formed. Although Japanese FDI in Belgium almost doubled every year until 1989, the growth rate of such investment became quite sluggish after 1990 (Mason and Encarnation, 1994; JETRO's white paper, several years). During 1991-1995 only another four Japanese manufacturing affiliates decided to locate in Belgium.

The dominant sector for Japanese manufacturing companies in Belgium in terms of the number of manufacturing affiliates is the chemical sector. This industry accounted for almost half of the number of Japanese

Table 9.1   Sectoral distribution of Japanese manufacturing plants in Belgium according to period of establishment, number of plants, sales and employment (1995)

Sector	Before 1973	1974-1978	1979-1985	1986-1990	1991-1995	Total (Units)	Plants (%)	Sales (%)	Employment (%)
Chemicals and related products	3	5	1	5	2	16	47.1	35.5	28.7
Electrical and electronic equipment	1	1	1	4	-	7	20.6	15.2	12.6
Transport equipment and components	1	-	-	1	1	3	8.8	11.8	6.3
Non-metallic mineral products	-	1	2	1	1	5	14.7	33.9	49.4
Other manufacturing	1	-	1	1	-	3	8.8	3.6	3.0
Total (Units)	6	7	5	12	4	34	34	34	34
Total (%)	17.6	20.6	14.7	35.3	11.7	100	100	100	100

production units in 1995 and represented more than a third of their turnover (Table 9.1). The non-metallic mineral affiliates also figure prominently in Belgium in terms of sales and especially employment, due to the acquisition of Glaverbel, the largest glass producer in Belgium. Subsidiaries in the non-metallic mineral sector, although not that important in terms of number of plants (only 5), carried out a third of all sales of Japanese affiliates and almost half of their total employment. Japanese companies apparently only invested in a limited number of industries in Belgium, in particular in those industries for which Belgium already had a prevalent specialization, such as the originally indigenous sectors of chemicals and non-metallic minerals (glass), and the transplanted transport equipment sector. Some new patterns were also created by the Japanese in the electronics sector, although the Dutch multinational Philips had already found it convenient to locate a large part of its production capacity in Belgium. The geographical proximity must have played an important role in that decision.

For several Japanese companies, the establishment of a production facility in Belgium represented their first plant in Europe (Van Den Bulcke and Janssen, 1988). For 15 of the Japanese companies, that is almost 60 percent, their plant in Belgium still was the only one in Europe at the time of the survey. Seven of those single European subsidiaries are in the chemical industry, as compared with four in electronics and two in transportation. Nine corporate parents controlled from two to five plants in Europe, while another four owned approximately 20 plants all over Europe. Three of the latter corporate parents were chemical manufacturers.

9.4 CLUSTER IDENTIFICATION

The identification of meaningful industry clusters is not an exact science. Besides descriptive case study material of clusters (Christopherson and Storper, 1986; Scott, 1986; Goodman and Bamford, 1989; Storper, 1989; Best, 1990; Saxenian, 1990; Scott and Paul, 1990; Saxenian, 1991, 1994; Gray, Golob et al., 1996), several measures have been used to approximate agglomeration, including employment, production and export figures (Porter, 1990; Krugman, 1991; Braunerhjelm and Svensson, 1996). In order to perform a diversified approach to determining clusters in Belgium, a quantitative and qualitative approach is followed. First, several industrial indicators - that are calculated with data from the Industry, Science and Technology chapter in the Main Industrial Indicators database (OECD, 1999b) - are used to determine industrial clusters in Belgium. This analysis is then applied to the Japanese manufacturing subsidiaries, before describing in short some salient features of the sectors, in which these firms invested.

Clusters are determined on the basis of the following selected indicators for the different manufacturing sectors in Belgium (see Table 9.2 for more information):

1. Export specialization (RCA) shows Belgium's exports for an industry as a proportion of total manufacturing exports divided by OECD exports of the same industry as a proportion of OECD total manufacturing exports. A value above 100 in a certain industry implies that, relative to the OECD average, Belgium specializes in exports in that industry. The indicator is commonly known as the revealed comparative advantage (RCA) index.
2. Export import ratios (X/I) consist of exports as a percentage of imports for each industry.
3. Production share ratios (PS) are calculated as production in each industry for Belgium as a percentage of production in that industry for the OECD area.
4. Employment concentration (EC) shows Belgium's employment for an industry as a proportion of total manufacturing employment divided by OECD employment in the same industry as a proportion of OECD total manufacturing employment. A value above 100 in a certain industry implies that, relative to the OECD average, Belgium has an employment concentration in that industry.

The RCA is used to measure the international success of the various sectors. It is complemented by the export/import ratio to discriminate against agglomerations of weakly embedded 'screwdriver plants' that import most of their inputs for assembly. The production and employment shares are added to determine concentration. These shares are determined as the ratio of production and employees in Belgium against the OECD average to control for industry size and labor intensiveness.

These four characteristics provide strong (figures in bold) or partial (figures in italic) support whether Belgian industries are clustered or not. In other words, industries with a revealed comparative advantage, an export-import ratio, production share, or employment share above the OECD or national average are earmarked as weakly (italic) or strongly (bold) clustered. As such, food, beverages and tobacco; textiles, apparel and leather; chemical products (including industrial chemicals, chemicals excluding drugs, other chemicals, drugs and medicines, petroleum refineries and products, and rubber and plastic products); non-metallic mineral products; basic metal industries (including iron and steel and non-ferrous metals), metal products, and transport equipment and motor vehicles show strong or partial signs of industry clustering in Belgium.

Although the above-mentioned Belgian industries showed clustering signs compared to other OECD countries, the RCA calculation was also applied to Belgian exports on the basis of the UN's World Trade Database (1993) in order to find corroborative evidence. The products that scored high were again found to come largely from the above-mentioned industries, confirming the cluster hypothesis. There was only the odd product category in other industries. For instance, there were two product categories in wood products and furniture (that is, improved wood and reconstituted wood; wooden packing cases, boxes, crates and drums); and one product category in paper, paper products and printing (boxes, bags and other packing containers of paper) that also form a strong indication of an industry cluster in paper and wooden containers. There were still some other product categories with a high RCA such as electric insulating equipment; batteries, accumulators and parts; boilers and radiators for central heating; and live animals, but no indication of industrial clusters was apparent.

Given that Japanese companies invested in a limited number of industries in Belgium (see Table 9.1), Table 9.3 lists only those industries relevant to this study, that is chemical products, electronics, metalworking, non-metallic mineral products and transport equipment. It indicates whether these sectors are clustered or not, and whether they are indigenous or transplanted.

For the glass sector (non-metallic mineral products), for instance, the Belgian specialization goes back to the nineteenth century, more in particular to the production of blown glass. By the 1970s the Belgian glass industry's competitive position had become seriously eroded, however. The industry went through a painful but effective restructuring process. The flagship company Glaverbel was acquired by Asahi Glass in 1981. A new production process which increased the productivity and decreased the energy consumption was adopted. The output was diversified to meet new patterns of demand arising from the increased attention by consumers to safety, insulation and decorative uses of glass.

The chemical industry is another example of an indigenous industry - for example companies such as Solvay, Union Chimique Belge (UCB), Gevaert, and so on - that has globalized over time (OECD, 1992). The locational advantages have played an important role in the chemical industry as it includes both intermediate products and finished ones and in this respect the Belgian chemical industry has a definite advantage over its main competitors in France and Germany (Tharakan, Waelbroeck et al., 1989).

Table 9.2   Cluster measures of industrial sectors in Belgium (1996)

Industry	RCA	X/I	PS[a]	EC
Food, beverages & tobacco	**132.81**	**126.17**	**248**	**130.98**
Textiles, apparel & leather	**124.60**	**119.50**	**163**	96.03
Wood products & furniture	80.32	84.64	**136**	**101.72**
Paper, paper products & printing	75.19	87.30	93	83.48
Chemical products	**147.84**	**127.12**	**169**	**126.27**
Industrial chemicals	**149.72**	**116.15**	**298**	**294.07**ᶜ
Chemicals excluding drugs	**143.85**	**123.67**	**209**	
Other chemicals	**129.90**	**144.05**	95	85.05
Drugs & medicines	**133.36**	**129.91**	**172**	
Petroleum refineries & products	**182.59**	**126.11**	*107*	98.21ᶜ
Rubber & plastic products	**107.84**	*100.68*	**159**	65.37ᶜ
Non-metallic mineral products	**141.02**	**166.42**	**136**	**136.06**
Basic metal industries	**161.19**	**158.24**	*122*	**138.39**
Iron & steel	**189.21**	**196.83**	*119*	**167.91**ᶜ
Non-ferrous metals	**119.23**	*107.96*	*129*	**104.85**ᶜ
Fabricated metal products	63.25	103.22	92	82.86
Metal products	77.56	97.29	**142**	**119.48**ᶜ
Non-electrical machinery	46.18	87.72	*111*	*57.62ᶜ*
Machinery & equipment, n.e.c.	51.09	95.26		
Office & computing machinery	34.24	68.15		
Electrical machinery	44.45	94.15	85ᵇ	69.25ᶜ
Electrical apparatus, n.e.c.	46.61	85.98		
Radio, TV & communication Equipment	42.35	*100.17*		
Transport equipment	94.93	**124.80**	71	103.36ᶜ
Shipbuilding & repairing	*5.03*	56.33		
Motor vehicles	**119.16**	**131.18**		
Aircraft	14.82	53.43		
Other transport equipment	45.28	71.77		
Professional goods	41.78	83.57	65ᵇ	32.61ᶜ
Other manufacturing, n.e.c.	**436.38**	*100.06*	78	80.32
Total Manufacturing	100.00	114.71	136	100.00

Notes:
[a] Data for 1995
[b] Data for 1994
[c] Data for 1992
n.e.c. stands for not elsewhere classified
RCAs for industries that are higher than the Belgian export specialization average are marked in bold. The export import ratio above the Belgian average (114.71) are also indicated in bold, while the ratios above 100 are put in italic. The same method is used for the production share ratios. The industries with more than the OECD average number of employees are also marked in bold.
Source: OECD (1999b).

Table 9.3   Classification of industries

Industries	Cluster/Non-cluster	Indigenous/Transplanted
Chemical products	Cluster	Indigenous
Electronics	Non-cluster	Transplanted
Metal working	Non-cluster	Indigenous
Non-metallic mineral products	Cluster	Indigenous
Transport equipment	Cluster	Transplanted

In the electronics equipment industry, one Dutch firm Philips has become the largest producer in Europe. It located a substantial part of its production capacity in nearby Belgium. The Belgian domestic sector of electronic goods is as a result largely dominated by foreign multinationals. For instance, Philips set up a battery producing joint venture, together with Matsushita, in the 1970s.

Although Belgium ranks first in the world as far as the production and assembly of cars per head is concerned, the car industry in Belgium is dominated by four foreign car manufacturers: General Motors in Antwerp, Ford near Hasselt, Volkswagen near Brussels and Volvo in Gent. The port of Antwerp is also an important attraction pole for the motor vehicle industry because it is specialized in automobile distribution, allowing for easy export.

9.5 JAPANESE MANUFACTURING SUBSIDIARIES IN BELGIUM

9.5.1 Location Motives

According to the survey, the principal motive for those Japanese investors that preferred Belgium to other countries is its central location as a supply base for their European customers. With the establishment of the Single European Market, Belgium's central location in Europe is supposed to have become an even larger locational advantage (Belgium Japan Association, 1997). Three quarters (N=21) of the Japanese companies that invested in Belgium supplied their customers all over Europe rather than limit themselves to Belgium's small local market.

However, six subsidiaries in the chemical industry mentioned specifically that they invested in Belgium to be close to their customers, while six affiliates acquired a local chemical plant. One Japanese company first took over a local producer of chemicals before setting up several other plants right next door. The same approach was followed by the Japanese company in the non-metallic mineral sector.

Figure 9.1   The importance of foreign markets for Japanese subsidiaries in Belgium (1995)

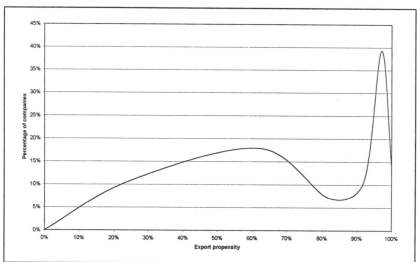

Good transport connections are also quite important, especially because three out of four affiliates export more than half of their total turnover, as the small Belgian market obviously has a too limited scope. Figure 9.1 indicates that for almost two thirds of the Japanese subsidiaries in Belgium, 90 percent or more of their total sales are directed to foreign markets. Only for one out of ten subsidiaries was the Belgian domestic market more important than exports. The smoothed line shows the increasing export propensity of Japanese subsidiaries (more companies exporting more). Instead of having a steady increase (straight line), the dip in the curve indicates skewness towards exporting nearly all (95 percent of) turnover.

The market area of Japanese subsidiaries in Belgium ranges from the countries of the European Union to a worldwide market coverage.[10] Respectively seven and eight affiliates indicated that the EU and Europe were their main export market. Thirteen companies listed Europe and certain selected other parts of the world as their market (Table 9.4). However, there was quite a change in the market area covered by these firms in 1990 and the projected markets by the year 2000. Table 9.4 illustrates the relative decline of the EU as a market for Japanese subsidiaries and the increasing attention given to the enlarged European regional market after the expected opening up of Central and Eastern Europe (CEE). The number of Japanese subsidiaries in Belgium that were concentrating on the EU market as such was due to fall from eight to two by the year 2000, because of the envisaged extension of their European or global reach. This was the case for all industries. One subsidiary in the non-metallic mineral and one in the transport industry indicated a loss in market coverage.

Table 9.4   Market area covered by Japanese manufacturing subsidiaries in Belgium (1990, 1995, 2000)

Market area (N = 29)	1990	1995	2000
European Union	8	7	2
Europe	8	8	12
Europe and selected other parts of the world	10	13	12
Worldwide with specific exclusions	-	-	2
Worldwide	3	1	1

Despite the 'European' aspirations of the Japanese investors in Belgium, the consequences of the Single European Market and the opening up of markets in other parts of Central Europe and the former Soviet Union are rather limited. The changes that occurred as a result of the fall of the Iron Curtain were deemed 'neutral' by 13 Japanese subsidiaries. Twelve Japanese subsidiaries called the effect 'positive', however. Nine firms replied that the changing situation in Central and Eastern Europe had caused an adaptation to the markets that were serviced, while for more than half of the subsidiaries the opening up of the former 'East Bloc' was of little or no consequence. If anything, subsidiaries in the more competitive clustered industries were slightly - although insignificantly - more favorable towards the fall of the iron curtain.

   More than half of the responding companies (N=16) also judged the completion of the European integration into a unified market as 'neither positive nor negative', while about one fourth of the companies (N=8) believed it to consist of an improvement. Two subsidiaries even evaluated the establishment of the Single European Market as negative, probably because they had become exposed to more intense competition. Thirteen companies replied that the European integration implied no consequences for the Belgian plant, while for nine others it resulted in adaptations of the markets that were serviced. Table 9.5 illustrates that none of these changes had a profound effect on the business activity of the Japanese manufacturing affiliates in Belgium, except for the market area that was covered. In only a few cases did Japanese subsidiaries adapt the products that were manufactured to the new situation. Changes in the investment priorities and in performance measures were rather exceptional.

Table 9.5 Perception of changes and effects of the fall of the 'Iron Curtain' and the establishment of the Single European Market for Japanese subsidiaries in Belgium (1995)

	Fall Iron Curtain		Single European Market	
Perception of changes	N = 26	%	N = 26	%
Positive	12	46	8	31
Negative	1	4	2	8
Neutral	13	50	16	61
Effects	N = 28	%	N = 28	%
None	16	57	13	46
Change in products manufactured	-	-	3	11
Change in markets serviced	9	32	9	32
Change in performance measures	1	4	2	7
Change in investment priorities	2	7	1	4

9.5.2 Different Modes of Japanese Involvement

In general, Japanese investors are assumed to prefer greenfield investments over acquisitions. Indeed, three quarters of the total number of subsidiaries in the US as well as in Europe were established through greenfield investments (Dunning, 1986, 1994; Hennart, 1993; Yamawaki, 1994). In Belgium, 17 Japanese corporations built a new plant, while 12 Belgian-owned companies and one foreign-owned firm in Belgium were acquired by Japanese investors (Table 9.6). Four of these acquisitions had already a customer relationship with the Japanese corporate parent before they were taken over, while seven of them did not entertain any prior relationship. The motive of faster market access was quoted by two thirds (8 out of 12) of the acquired local companies. The diversification strategy and the synergistic advantages were cited by respectively one and two firms.

The modes of international involvement of Japanese investment have changed, however. Acquisitions and joint ventures have become more desirable options than greenfield investments and wholly-owned subsidiaries. During the boom period of Japanese FDI in Europe from 1986 until 1990, there were relatively more acquisitions than greenfield investments. In the fiscal year 1988-1989, no less than 40 percent of the value of new Japanese investment in the EU were the result of acquisitions or mergers (Kirkland, 1990).

Table 9.6   Method of entry of Japanese investors in Belgium until 1995
according to period of establishment

Entry method	Before	1974-	1979-	1986-	1991-	Total	
(N=29)	1973	1978	1985	1990	1995	N	%
Greenfield	4	3	3	4	3	17	59
Acquisition	1	3	2	5	1	12	41

The method of entry not only changed over time, but also differs among industries. Half of the Japanese acquisitions in Belgium occurred in the chemical industry. This might to some extent be explained by the fact that the European producers in the chemical industry were considered to have more competitive advantages than their Japanese rivals (Porter, 1990). In order to improve their international competitive position within a relative short period of time, Japanese companies typically acquired local producers (Sachwald, 1994). Likewise, two out of the four investments in the sector of the non-metallic minerals were the result of takeovers. One of the acquired Belgian companies, for instance, indicated that it had provided technical assistance to the Japanese company before it was finally acquired and became part of the Japanese group. On the other hand, all the plants in the sector of electrical and electronic equipment consisted of greenfield investments.

Eighty percent of the Japanese subsidiaries in the US and Europe were majority owned, while more than half of them were wholly owned. While the average degree of ownership was quite similar for Japanese subsidiaries in the US and Europe, it was different from Asia and other regions (MITI, several years). In Belgium, the preference for complete ownership was even more pronounced, as more than two thirds of the Japanese manufacturing facilities in Belgium were wholly-owned subsidiaries as compared to only 17 percent that are majority-owned ones (Table 9.7). Four Japanese subsidiaries were equally controlled companies (50/50 percent), while one was a minority-owned Japanese plant. However, as the local partner of this minority-owned company was also majority-owned (2/3 participation) by another Japanese multinational, it has been included in the category of the majority-owned subsidiaries.

Table 9.7 shows that joint ventures have become more common since the 1980s. Again, not only has there been a change over time but also between sectors. All four of the Japanese investments in Belgium in the non-metallic mineral industry were joint ventures. In the chemical sector, three of the plants were equally-owned joint ventures, while ten took the form of wholly-owned subsidiaries. The three investments in the transport industry and five out of six investments in the electrical and electronics industry were also wholly-owned subsidiaries. Japanese investors clearly prefer complete ownership, especially when they possess strong competitive advantages.

Table 9.7   Ownership degree of Japanese manufacturing firms in Belgium according to period of establishment (1995)

Ownership (N=29)	Before 1973	1974-1978	1979-1985	1986-1990	1991-1995	Total N	%
100%	5	5	2	6	2	20	69.0
> 50%	-	1	2	1	1	5	17.2
50% / 50%	-	-	1	2	1	4	13.8
Total	5	6	5	9	4	29	100

9.5.3 Changing Organizational Strategies

The shift towards more investment in Europe, as a key strategic location for Japanese corporations, is likely to have an impact on the organization of their cross-border production operations. The organizational strategy of Japanese firms increasingly reflected the character and needs of the regional, rather than the national, market with integrated production and distribution systems (Gittelman and Dunning, 1992). A common response to the European unification was to Europeanize operations, granting more autonomy and responsibility to the European subsidiaries (JETRO, 1994). If more value-adding production activities were being located abroad, then those activities had to be supported and sustained with additional co-ordinating and control functions, including research and development, as well as establishing linkages in the local economy.

9.5.3.1 Sourcing

Japanese manufacturing firms are known to develop long-term and tight relationships with the suppliers of their components and semi-finished products (Lincoln, 1993). When a member of a Japanese keiretsu invests abroad, the suppliers to that firm benefit from an advantage when it comes to negotiating contracts for the delivery of, for example, components to the subsidiary. It is therefore not altogether surprising to find that Japanese investors choose to import semi-finished products and parts from their suppliers back home, since the suppliers in the home country will hesitate to start production abroad and will need convincing arguments and time to actually do so. The main reasons - indicated by almost all Japanese subsidiaries in Belgium - for importing at least certain parts are that local suppliers were not available or were not able to respect the production standards put forward by the group. In some cases, local suppliers were also considered to be insufficiently competitive.

However, as plants generate their own routines, they will consider alternative suppliers in the host country both in terms of equipment and consumables (Emmot, 1992). Over time, firms will be inclined to buy from local suppliers or keiretsu suppliers that have located in Belgium or Europe with the intention to Europeanize operations as quickly as possible. Japanese manufacturing subsidiaries in Belgium, for instance, seemed to rely increasingly on 'local' suppliers rather than imports from the home country. The share of outside suppliers, especially European ones, has increased for the Japanese subsidiaries in Belgium. At the risk of oversimplifying, it can be stated that Japanese companies established a plant in Belgium to supply their European customers, using suppliers in Europe (including Belgium) for their inputs. The expansion of imports from other subsidiaries of the group, especially from Asia, for example Malaysia and China, should not be overlooked either. The percentage of production directed to other plants of the multinational group has also slightly increased over the years. The relative share of imports from the corporate parent itself has declined sharply, however. These developments tend to indicate that the Japanese subsidiaries in Belgium are becoming more integrated in the group network and that the corporate parents in Japan have lost some or most of their locational advantage.

Positioning themselves on a scale between (1) 'assembly only' and (5) 'fully-fledged manufacturing', 15 or about half of the Japanese subsidiaries ranked themselves as fully-fledged manufacturers. While the number of Japanese firms that only engaged in assembly operations amounted to four in 1990, this number decreased to only two plants in 1995, and only one was expected to still retain this status by the year 2000. The so-called 'screwdriver' plants that are fully dependent upon the parent company for management decision-making and control, inputs and full product and process specifications, are apparently on their way out. This is almost entirely due to the upgrading of the factories in the Belgian electronics industry, that is an increase from an average score of 2.83 in 1990 to an average of 4.17 by the year 2000. In fact, the only assembly plant (score of 1) that would still be active in the year 2000 was a chemical plant. The three manufacturing plants in the transport sector would also remain fairly low-grade production units (score of 2), despite the increase over time by two factories from a score of 1 in 1990 to a score of 2 by 1995 or 2000. One plant even foresaw a decrease in production responsibilities by the year 2000.

9.5.3.2 Research and development

Three out of four (N=22) subsidiaries in the survey performed at least some research and development activities in Belgium, for example customer technical services, adaptation of manufacturing technology, development of new or improved products for European markets, development of new products and processes for world markets, or generation of new technology for the corporate parent. In 1990 about two out of five Japanese companies in the sample (N=10) did not engage in any R&D, while in 1995 one out of four (N=7) carried out neither fundamental nor applied R&D in Belgium. Four companies (14 percent) declared that no research activities were planned in Belgium before the year 2000 (Table 9.8).

Approximately a third of the responding companies established customer technical services and adapted their manufacturing technology to the local situation. The number of Japanese subsidiaries that engaged in research and developed new or improved products for the European markets in 1990 increased by 50 percent five years later and was expected to double in another five years. By the year 2000, more than half of the Japanese subsidiaries in Belgium were supposed to carry out research and development activities aimed at the European market. The number of companies that developed new products or production processes for the world market increased from three plants in 1990 to seven in 2000. One subsidiary even developed new technology for the corporate parent. Table 9.8 indicates that not only the number of companies that performed R&D activities increased over the years, but also that more complete R&D activities were and will be taken up in the future. Several Japanese corporations no longer restricted the high value adding activities to Japan alone. This is not only the case for the chemical and non-metallic mineral industry, but even more so for the transport and electronics/electrical equipment industry, as the latter sectors are new to this trend of increasing R&D activities.

Table 9.8   R&D activities performed by Japanese subsidiaries in Belgium (1990, 1995, 2000)

R&D activities	1990	1995	2000
None	10	7	4
Customer technical services	8	9	9
Adaptation of manufacturing technology	7	10	9
Development of new or improved products for European markets	8	12	16
Development of new products and processes for world markets	3	4	7
Generation of new technology for corporate parent	0	1	2

9.5.3.3 Decision-making authority

Over a ten-year period the decision-making authority of Japanese subsidiaries in Belgium generally increased. The decision-making index,[11] on a scale from 1 to 4, where at one extreme (1) the parent company decides everything itself and at the other (4) the subsidiary can decide autonomously, went up from 1.97 in 1990, to 2 in 1995, and to 2.07 in 2000 on the issue of R&D activities. This is partly due to the increasing number of companies that took up research and development. There appears to be a shift away from these extremes, on the one hand, from exclusive local decision-making and, on the other hand, from complete centralized corporate control, towards more shared decisions. The answers from managers of Japanese subsidiaries in Belgium indicated that the number of corporate parents that solely decided about R&D dropped from ten in 1990 to five in 2000. The number of subsidiaries that could decide about R&D issues themselves, at least after having consulted the corporate parent, increased from three to seven. However, three out of these seven subsidiaries had formerly been solely responsible for R&D.

This increasing autonomy of the Japanese subsidiaries is again mainly apparent in the transplanted industries, and even more so in the electronics sector than in the transport equipment industry. Subsidiaries in the indigenous sectors of chemicals and glass just maintained or had a slight reduction of their research and development decision-making autonomy, although it remains higher than in the other industries. Apparently, the subsidiaries that are active in the industries where Japan had distinctive competitive advantages, such as electronics and transport equipment, have gained credibility and capability within the group and are now increasingly allowed to decide themselves. Certain subsidiaries in the chemical and glass sector, in which the Japanese parent companies had less competitive advantages, on the other hand, were set up or acquired for different reasons (acquisition of strategic assets) and are now increasingly being integrated within the group. Other more basic chemical plants have gained autonomy, making the shift towards more shared decision-making even more evident.

A more outspoken shift towards a higher decision-making authority for Japanese subsidiaries, more particularly towards decisions mainly taken by the local company - after consulting with the corporate parent or regional headquarters - occurred about specific decisions, for example about the market area, the product range, the process and product technology and financial issues. This was again definitely the case for the - what might be called - Japanese sectors and less convincingly so for the Belgian sectors, although it only applied for certain decision-making areas such as product range and production technology. Figure 9.2 illustrates this movement

Figure 9.2 Decision-making autonomy index of Japanese subsidiaries in Belgium (1990, 1995, 2000)

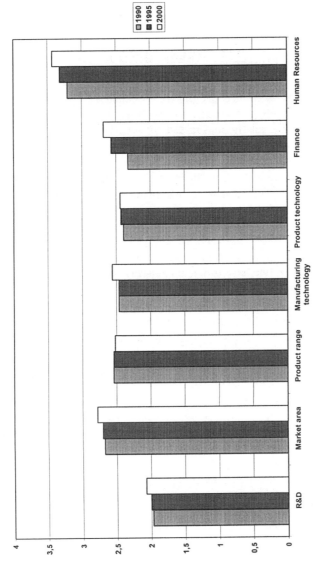

Note: Subsidiaries ranked their decision-making authority on a scale from 1 to 4, with 1 being the most centralized and 4 the most decentralized decision making structure.

towards more shared decision-making in the Japanese subsidiaries in Belgium.

The decision-making authority with regard to human resources was completely controlled by the local management in Belgium. Almost all the companies in the sample could decide about human resources either autonomously (N=12) or after having consulted with the parent company's regional headquarters (N=13). Companies in the electronics industry seem to have the highest decision-making autonomy index of all.

9.6 CONCLUSION

This chapter has examined the pattern of Japanese FDI in Europe, more particularly in the Belgian manufacturing sector. It has provided information - on the basis of a newly constructed subsidiary-level data set - about the activities of Japanese firms in Belgium. Japanese investment in Europe has a long history, especially in non-manufacturing branches such as trading, banking and insurance, dating back to the 1870s. It was not until 1963, however, that the first manufacturing plant was set up in Europe, when Honda Motor decided to establish a motorcycle plant in Belgium. The quantity and impact of Japanese investment in Europe remained quite limited until the 1970s. Back then Japanese FDI was a response to, rather than a factor determining, Japanese economic progress (Gittelman and Dunning, 1992). Rationalization and efficiency improvements of business activities mainly took place in Japan, with outward manufacturing FDI aimed towards maintaining or advancing markets for Japanese exports (in industrialized countries) and relocating uncompetitive activities (in developing - Asian - economies). The primary purpose of these investments in sectors where Japanese firms already had strong ownership advantages, such as the electrical and electronic equipment industry, was to establish operations in Europe to protect the acquired market shares via export, either in response to actual or potential trade barriers, or to counter the moves of competitors which threatened to disrupt domestic operations. In short, much of this overseas production substituted for goods previously exported from Japan, and was undertaken to secure a more permanent access to the European market (Strange, 1993).

During the 1980s Japan achieved outstanding economic successes. For years, businessmen and bureaucrats from other countries made the long pilgrimage to Japan to observe first hand the so-called economic miracle and its special management style and techniques. The explanations which have been advanced to explain this success abound and include the Confucian work ethic and the Japanese national culture, the close business-government collaboration ('Japan Incorporated'), the 'unfair' trade practices towards foreign companies, the specific management styles and techniques, the long-term orientation as far as profitability is concerned, the intercompany linkages (keiretsu), and so on.

During the second half of the 1990s Japan's future looked bleak and especially the Japanese government was condemned for its persistent failure to relaunch the economy. Even though Japan had grown into the second largest economy in the world, it was confronted with a serious and persistent structural recession after the bursting of the so-called bubble economy. Some economic pundits even raised serious doubts about the possible end of the era of Japanese dominance of global markets for manufactured goods (Van Wolferen, 1993). In contrast, others have rejected this pessimistic view and suggested that the 1990s were only a pause in the continuing growth of the Japanese economy and the start of a new stage of global expansion of Japanese firms (Lorriman and Kenjo, 1994). As a matter of fact, some of these same factors are also put forward as an explanation for the Japanese crisis of the 1990s, meaning that the Japanese system had become too complacent. While each of these factors has some validity, the rise and fall of the Japanese economy is undoubtedly a multicausal phenomenon.

These developments encouraged Japanese firms even more than before to create or acquire new competitive advantages abroad, as there was now a rapidly expiring time limit on how long firms could defend and exploit their existing strengths. The implication was that offensive FDI became a more attractive strategy than it had been in previous years. In contrast to the defensive market-seeking investments, which were based upon the exploitation of existing competitive advantages, these offensive investments were targeted at gaining access to the information and technology required to upgrade and rationalize not only their domestic operations, but also to advance their global competitive strategy. Generally the high value activities, such as design, research and development, marketing strategy, and financial control were still concentrated and retained in Japan. The new or extended role of the foreign affiliate became more and more oriented towards the continuing upgrading and rationalization of the parent company's operations by feeding it with new information about markets, products and technologies.

Japanese FDI in general has shown a remarkable strategic dexterity in response to the rapidly changing environment facing Japanese firms (Dunning, 1979, 1993). The companies moved from exporting to defensive investment strategies in order to maintain their ownership advantages in an increasingly competitive European market in the 1980s. When the existing ownership advantages of Japanese firms became increasingly threatened, Japanese firms created or acquired new ownership advantages abroad. The increased location advantages of Europe as a result of the Single Market and the EU enlargement resulted in an expansion of offensive Japanese FDI in Europe. For sectors where Japanese firms possess strong ownership advantages, such as the electronics industry, the possible threat of a 'Fortress Europe' was quite influential in the surge of Japanese direct investment. In other industries, such as chemicals, where the firm-specific advantages of the Japanese MNEs are less pronounced, the lure of a large and integrated market of the EU itself provided an important attraction for the Japanese firms. Due to the rapidly expiring time limit on how Japanese firms could defend and exploit their existing ownership advantages, they made relatively more use of takeovers than before. The well known preference of Japanese investors for greenfield investments over acquisitions consequently diminished.

However, there is a significant sectoral difference in Belgium with regard to the entry mode. Acquisitions appear a far more acceptable practice in the competitive industry clusters, such as chemicals and non-metallic minerals, than in the transplanted sectors, such as electrical and electronic equipment industry. The ownership structure is similarly skewed towards complete ownership for the more 'Japanese' sectors in comparison with the more 'Belgian' sectors.

The Japanese corporations apparently no longer concentrate their higher value adding activities, such as R&D, as strongly in Japan as before, which possibly indicates that the location advantages of Japan itself have been declining. A catching up process of some sort can be distinguished in the transplanted industries compared to the industry clusters, although it remains higher on average in the clustered industries. Also, they are granting more local decision-making authority to their subsidiaries in Belgium. The subsidiaries that are active in the industries where Japan had distinctive competitive advantages, have gained credibility within the group, leading to an increase in decision autonomy. Subsidiaries in the industries where Japan had less competitive advantages are now being integrated within the group, leading to a shift towards more shared decision-making.

Apparently, as a response to EU unification, Japanese MNEs seem to be 'Europeanizing' their operations through increasing local sourcing and granting more managerial autonomy to the subsidiary management. Japanese firms continue to upgrade their industrial infrastructure outside of Japan, while the economic conditions in Japan itself have become less advantageous.

In conclusion, there has been a radical change in the nature of the so-called 'Japanese challenge'. Through the mechanism of FDI the challenge has as a result of the increasingly global reach of Japanese MNEs, on the one hand, intensified, and, on the other, become less Japanese (Gittelman and Dunning, 1992).

NOTES

1. However, the highly open Belgian economy is characterised by its European orientation. Belgian inward FDI is strongly linked with its neighbouring countries: that is France with 25 percent, Germany with 20 percent, the Netherlands with 19 percent and the UK with 4 percent (Zhang and Van Den Bulcke, 1997). The regional concentration of inward (and outward) FDI activities of Belgium with its neighbouring countries/regions might be related to the high intra-firms and inter-firms linkages which are often the result from the hosting of and/or the participating in industrial clusters.

2. The dismissal of transport and communication costs as a factor of location is somewhat of a paradox in itself, as it happens at the same time as logistics has become increasingly important for firms, and industries especially in the industrialized countries are lobbying heavily for improved transport and communication infrastructure. Part of the answer to the apparent paradox is that although relative transport and communication costs have become much cheaper, the spread of production has increased to the extent that transport and communication costs as a percentage of total costs have not gone down (Pedersen, 1994).

3. 'A localised industry gains a great advantage from the fact that it offers a constant market for skills. Employers are apt to resort to any place where they are likely to find a good choice of workers with the special skills which they require; while men seeking employment naturally go to places where there are many employers who need such skill as theirs and where therefore it is likely to find a good market' (Marshall, 1890).

4. 'Subsidiary trades grow up in the neighbourhood, supplying it with implements and materials, organising its traffic, and in many ways conducing to the economy of its material' (Marshall, 1890).

5. 'The mysteries of the trade become no mystery; but are as it were in the air. Good work is rightly appreciated, inventions and improvements in machinery, processes and the general organisation of the business have their merits promptly discussed: if one man starts a new idea, it is taken up by others and combined with suggestions of their own; and thus it becomes the source of further new ideas' (Marshall, 1890).

6. The term Terza Italia, the Third Italy, distinguishes the area of north-central and north-east Italy from the south of the country and from the area of heavy industry in the north-west. It consists of the regions of Tuscany, Emilia Romagna, Umbria, Marche, Veneto, Friuli-Venezia-Giulia and Trentino-Alto Adige (Pyke, Becattini et al., 1990).

7. The financial data for most of the companies was collected from the database of the National Bank of Belgium. The number of employees for the four companies that did not supply the average number of persons employed for 1994, could be obtained from JETRO.

8. This information was collected from the database of the National Bank of Belgium. The total number of incorporated manufacturing companies in Belgium amounted to 19,238, employing 618,675 employees.

9. Information taken from JETRO's annual 'Survey of European Operations of Japanese Companies in the Manufacturing Sector' for 31 of the 34 companies in the sample.

10. The different options were: Belgium, Belgium and selected countries, the EU, Europe, Europe and selected other parts of the world, Worldwide with specific exclusions, and Worldwide.

11. Four categories of decision-making were identified:

    A. Decided mainly by the parent company or regional headquarters *without* consulting with or seeking the advice of the Belgian operations.
    B. Decided mainly by the parent company or regional headquarters *after* consulting with or seeking the advice of the Belgian operations.
    C. Decided mainly by the Belgian operations *after* consulting with or seeking the advice of the parent company or regional headquarters.
    D. Decided mainly by the Belgian operations *without* consulting with or seeking the advice of the parent company or regional headquarters.

The decision-making index is calculated as the weighted average of the four categories, with A, B, C and D having a weight of 1, 2, 3 and 4, respectively.

REFERENCES

Andersson, T. (1993), 'The Role of Japanese Foreign Direct Investment', in L. Oxelheim, *The Global Race for Foreign Direct Investment: Prospects for the Future,* New York; Heidelberg; London and Tokyo: Springer, pp. 205-31.

Arthur, B. (1990), 'Positive feedbacks in the economy', *Scientific American,* **262**, 92-9.

Baptista, R. (1998), 'Clusters, Innovation, and Growth', in P. Swann, M. Prevezer and D. Stout (eds), *The Dynamics of Industrial Clustering: International Comparisons in Computing and Biotechnology*, Oxford: Oxford University Press, pp. 13-51.

Bartik, T.J. (1985), 'Business location decisions in the United States: estimates of the effects of unionization, taxes, and other characteristics of states', *Journal of Business and Economic Statistics,* **3** (1), 14-22.

BEA (several years), *Survey of Current Business,* Washington, DC: Bureau of Economic Analysis, US Department of Commerce.

Behrman, J.N. (1972), *The Role of International Companies in Latin America: Autos and Petrochemicals,* Lexington, MA: Lexington Books.

Belgium Japan Association (1997), *Survey on Japanese Investment in Belgium,* Brussels: Belgium Japan Association.

Best, M. (1990), *The New ompetition: Institutions of Industrial Restructuring,* Cambridge: Harvard University Press.

Brainard, S.L. (1993a), *An Empirical Assessment of the Factor Proportions Exploration of Multinational Sales,* Cambridge: National Bureau of Economic Research.

Brainard, S.L. (1993b), *An Empirical Assessment of the Proximity/Concentration Trade-off between Multinational Sales and Trade,* Cambridge: National Bureau of Economic Research.

Braunerhjelm, P. and R. Svensson (1996), 'Host country characteristics and agglomeration in foreign direct investment', *Applied Economics,* **28** (7), 833-40.

Christopherson, S. and M. Storper (1986), 'The city as studio, the world as back lot: The impact of vertical disintegration on the location of the motion picture industry', *Environment and Planning D: Society and Space,* 4, 305-20.

Coughlin, C.C., J.V. Terza, et al. (1991), 'State characteristics and the location of foreign direct investment within the United States', *Review of Economics and Statistics,* **73** (4), 675-83.

Dunning, J.H. (1979), 'Explaining changing patterns of international production: in defence of the eclectic theory', *Oxford Bulletin of Economics and Statistics,* **41** (4), 269-95.

Dunning, J.H. (1986), *Japanese participation in British industry*, Croom Helm Series in International Business, London; Sydney and Dover, NH: Croom Helm.

Dunning, J.H. (1993), *Multinational Enterprises and the Global Economy,* Wokingham: Addison Wesley.

Dunning, J.H. (1994), 'The Strategy of Japanese and US Manufacturing Investment in Europe', in M. Mason and D. Encarnation (eds), *Does Ownership Matter? Japanese Multinationals in Europe*, pp. 59-86.

Dunning, J.H. (1997), *Alliance Capitalism and Global Business*, London and New York: Routledge.

Dunning, J.H. (1998), 'Location and the multinational enterprise: a neglected factor?', *Journal of International Business Studies*, **29** (1), 45-66.

Emmot, B. (1992), *Japan's Global Reach*, London: Random House.

Florida, R. (1995), 'Toward the learning region', *Futures*, **27** (5), 527-36.

Florida, R. and M. Kenney (1994), 'The globalization of Japanese R&D: the economic geography of Japanese R&D investment in the United States', *Economic Geography*, **70** (4), 344-69.

Ford, S. and R. Strange (1999), 'Where do Japanese manufacturing firms invest within Europe, and why?', *Transnational Corporations*, **8** (1), 117-42.

Gittelman, M. and J.H. Dunning (1992), 'Japanese Multinationals in Europe and the United States: Some Comparisons and Contrasts', in M.W. Klein and P.J.J. Welfens (eds), *Multinationals in the New Europe and Global Trade*, Berlin: Springer Verlag.

Glasmeier, A. (1988), 'Factors governing the development of high tech industry agglomerations: a tale of three cities', *Regional Studies*, **22** (4), 287-301.

Goodman, E. and J. Bamford (eds) (1989), *Small Firms and Industrial Districts in Italy*, London and New York: Routledge.

Gray, M., E. Golob, et al. (1996), 'Big firms, long arms, wide shoulders: the "hub-and-spoke" industrial district in the Seattle region', *Regional Studies*, **30** (7), 651-66.

Head, K., J. Ries, et al. (1995), 'Agglomeration benefits and location choice: evidence from Japanese manufacturing investments in the United States', *Journal of International Economics*, **38** (3-4), 223-47.

Hennart, J.F. (1993), 'Greenfield vs. acquisitions: the strategy of Japanese investors in the United States', *Management Science*, **39** (9), 1054-70.

Howes, C. (1993), 'Constructing Comparative Disadvantage: Lessons from the U.S. Auto Industry', in H. Noponen, J. Graham and J.R. Markusen, *Trading Industries Trading Regions: International Trade, American Industry, and Regional Economic Development*, Perspectives on Economic Change series, New York and London: Guilford Press, pp. 45-91.

JETRO (several years), *Summary of White Paper on Foreign Direct Investment*, Tokyo: Jetro International Communication Department.

JETRO (several years), *Survey of European Operations of Japanese Companies in the Manufacturing Sector*, Brussels: Jetro Overseas Research Department, Europe Division.

Kirkland, R.I.J. (1990), 'The big Japanese push in to Europe', *Fortune*, (2), 94-8.

Knickerbocker, F.T. (1973), *Oligopolistic Reaction and the Multinational Enterprise*, Cambridge, MA: Harvard University Press.

Kravis, I.B. and R.E. Lipsey (1982), 'The Location of Overseas Production and Production for Export by U.S. Multinational Firms', *Journal of International Economics*, **12** (3-4), 201-23.

Krugman, P. (1991), *Geography and Trade*, Leuven: Leuven University Press.

Lincoln, E.J. (1993), *Japan's New Global Role*, Washington, DC: Brookings.

Lorriman, J. and T. Kenjo (1994), *Japan's Winning Margin*, New York: Oxford University Press.

Markusen, A. (1994), 'Studying regions by studying firms', *The Professional Geographer,* **46**, 477-90.

Markusen, A. (1996), 'Sticky places in slippery space: a typology of industrial districts', *Economic Geography,* **72** (3), 293-313.

Markusen, J.R. (1990), *First Mover Advantage, Blockaded Entry, and the Economics of Uneven Development,* Cambridge, MA: National Bureau of Economic Research.

Marshall, A. (1890), *Principles of Economic,* London: Macmillan.

Mason, M. and D. Encarnation (eds) (1994), *Does Ownership Matter? Japanese Multinationals in Europe,* Oxford; New York; Toronto and Melbourne: Oxford University Press.

Micossi, S. and G. Viesti (1991), 'Japanese Direct Manufacturing Investment' in L.A. Winters and A.-J. Venables (eds), *European Integration: Trade and Industry,* Cambridge; New York and Melbourne: Cambridge University Press, pp. 200-31.

MITI (several years), *Survey of Overseas Business Activities of Japanese Companies,* Tokyo, Ministry of International Trade and Industry.

NBB (1996), *Numerical Data of Standardized Annual Accounts,* Brussels: Central Balance Sheet Office, National Bank of Belgium.

OECD (1992), *Globalization of Industrial Activities, Four Case Studies: Auto Parts, Chemicals, Construction and Semiconductors,* Paris: OECD.

OECD (1999a), Boosting Innovation: The Cluster Approach, Paris: OECD.

OECD (1999b), Statistical Compendium, Paris: OECD.

Paniccia, I. (1998), 'One, a hundred, thousands of industrial districts, organizational variety in local networks of small and medium-sized enterprises', Organization Studies, **19** (4), 667-700.

Pedersen, P.O. (1994), *Clusters of Enterprises Within Systems of Production and Distribution: Collective Efficiency, Transaction Costs and the Economies of Agglomeration,* Copenhagen: Centre for Development Research.

Piore, M.J. and C.F. Sabel (1984), *The Second Industrial Divide,* New York: Basic Books.

Porter, M.E. (1990), *The Competitive Advantage of Nations,* New York: Free Press.

Porter, M.E. (1998), 'Cluster and the new economics of competition', *Harvard Business Review,* **76** (6), 77-91.

Porter, M.E. and Ö. Sölvell (1997), 'The Role of Geography in the Process of Unnovation and the Sustainable Competitive Advantage of Firms', in A.D. Chandler, Jr., P. Hagström and Ö. Sölvell (eds), *The Dynamic Firm: The Role of Technology, Strategy, Organizations, and Regions,* Oxford: Oxford University Press.

Pyke, F., G. Becattini, et al. (eds) (1990), *Industrial Districts and Inter-Firm Co-operation in Italy,* Geneva: International Institute for Labour Studies.

Sachwald, F. (1994), 'The Chemical Industry', in F. Sachwald, *European Integration and Competitiveness: Acquisitions and Alliances in Industry,* Aldershot, UK: Elgar; distributed in the US by Ashgate, pp. 233-76.

Saxenian, A. (1990), 'Regional networks and the resurgence of Silicon Valley', *California Management Review,* **32**, 89-112.

Saxenian, A. (1991), 'The origins and dynamics of production networks in Silicon Valley', *Research Policy,* **20**, 423-37.

Saxenian, A. (1994), *Regional Networks: Industrial Adaptation in Silicon Valley,* Cambridge: Harvard University Press.

Schmitz, H. (1989), *Flexible Specialization: A New Paradigm of Small-scale Industrialization*, Sussex: Institute of Development Studies.

Scott, A.J. (1986), 'High tech industry and territorial development: The rise of the Orange County complex, 1955-1984', *Urban Geography*, **7**, 3-45.

Scott, A.J. (1988), 'Flexible production systems and regional development: The rise of new industrial space in North America and Western Europe', *International Journal of Urban and Regional Research*, **12**, 171-86.

Scott, A.J. and A. Paul (1990), 'Collective order and economic coordination in industrial agglomerations: The technopoles of Southern California', *Environment and Planning C: Government and Policy*, **8**, 179-93.

Smith, A. (1776), *An Inquiry into the Nature and Causes of the Wealth of Nations*, Oxford: Clarendon Press.

Smith, D.F., Jr. and R. Florida (1994), 'Agglomeration and Industrial Location: An Econometric Analysis of Japanese-Affiliated Manufacturing Establishments in Automotive-Related Industries', *Journal of Urban Economics*, **36** (1), 23-41.

Storper, M. (1989), 'The transition to flexible specialisation in the U.S. film industry: external economies, the division of labour, and the crossing of industrial divides', *Cambridge Journal of Economics*, **13** (2), 273-305.

Strange, R. (1993), *Japanese Manufacturing Investment in Europe: Its Impact on the UK Economy*, London and New York: Routledge.

Tharakan, P.K.M., J. Waelbroeck, et al. (1989), 'Comparative Advantage and Competitiveness in a Small Open Economy', in A. Francis and P.K.M. Tharakan (eds), *The Competitiveness of European Industry*, London and New York: Routledge, pp. 41-63.

Van Den Bulcke, D. and E. Janssen (1988), 'Japanese direct investment in the Belgian manufacturing industry: activities, motives, performance and effects', *Proceedings of the 1st Conference of AIB Japan Region*, Tokyo: Waseda University.

Van Den Bulcke, D. and H. Zhang (1998), *Survey on US Direct Investment in Belgium - 1997/1998: Corporate Restructuring and Business Confidence*, Brussels: American Chamber of Commerce.

Van Wolferen, K. (1993), 'Japan in the age of uncertainty', *New Left Review*, **200**, 15-40.

Vernon, R. (1974), 'The Location of Economic Activity', in J.H. Dunning, *Economic Analysis and the Multinational Enterprise*, London: Allen and Unwin.

Veugelers, R. (1991), 'Locational determinants and ranking of host countries: an empirical assessment', *Kyklos*, **44** (3), 363-82.

von Thünen, J.H. (1826). *Der isolierte Staat in Beziehung auf Landwirtschaft und Nationalökonomie*, Jena: G. Fischer.

Wheeler, D. and A. Mody (1992), 'International investment location decisions: the case of U.S. firms', *Journal of International Economics*, **33** (1-2), 57-76.

Woodward, D.P. (1992), 'Locational determinants of Japanese manufacturing start-ups in the United States', *Southern Economic Journal*, **58** (3), 690-708.

Yamawaki, H. (1994), 'Entry Patterns of Japanese Multinationals in US and European Manufacturing', in M. Mason and D. Encarnation (eds), *Does Ownership Matter? Japanese Multinationals in Europe*, pp. 91-121.

Zhang, H. and D. Van Den Bulcke (1997), 'European Integration, Corporate Globalization and Belgian FDI in Central and Eastern Europe: A Preliminary Analysis', *Proceedings of the Conference on Enterprise in Transition*, Split: University of Split, Faculty of Economics.

PART V

Observations on the Challenge of Managing
Multiple Markets

10. The Multinational Management of Multiple External Networks

Alexandra Campbell and Alain Verbeke

10.1 INTRODUCTION

Decision centers of multinational corporations (MNEs) are often physically dispersed in environmental settings which represent very different economic, social and cultural milieus (Hofstede, 1980; Ghoshal and Bartlett, 1990). Such dispersal and differentiation means that different individual decision centers must be able to respond in an idiosyncratic fashion to their respective environments. To achieve global competitive success, managers of MNEs need to broaden their perspective from dyadic headquarters-subsidiary relationships to the coordination of a network of established foreign sub-units (Kogut, 1989; Ghoshal and Bartlett, 1990).

In addition, attention must be devoted to the competencies needed to manage relationships with multiple external actors. Although the ability to conceive and execute complex strategies is critical to an organization's long-run success (Prahalad and Doz, 1987), to date, most international business research related to co-operation with external actors has focused on the creation and management of individual joint ventures and other types of co-operative arrangements (Millington and Bayliss, 1995; Oviatt and McDougall, 1994; Contractor and Lorange, 1988; Doz, Prahalad and Hamel, 1990), rather than on networks of inter-connected relationships.

However, researchers (for example, Ghoshal and Bartlett, 1990; White and Poynter, 1990; Malnight, 1996 have recently begun to conceptualize the MNE as a network of exchange relationships among different organizational units. These include the relationships between the headquarters and the various subsidiaries as well as the relationships between each subsidiary and the external actors with which it must interact, especially customers, suppliers, competitors and regulators.

In this chapter, it is argued that such an international network conceptualization is critical to understanding the managerial challenges facing MNEs, especially because many MNEs now operate with multiple centers of strategic decision-making (Gupta and Govindarajan, 1991; Roth and Morrison, 1992; Birkinshaw and Morrison, 1995). One aspect of network management is explored: the management of the interface between a firm's intra-organizational network with multiple centers of decision-making and its various external networks. In this context, the question arises whether it is sufficient for managers to focus on establishing an intra-organizational network with appropriate flexibility to reap benefits of both national responsiveness and integration where required, as suggested by the conventional international business literature.

The effective management of multiple external networks has been largely neglected by the dominant conceptual models in the international business literature. These models, which include the eclectic paradigm (Dunning, 1993), the transnational solution framework (Bartlett and Ghoshal, 1989) and the diamond of competitive advantage model (Porter, 1990) fail to acknowledge the major role that multiple external networks fulfil for firms which compete globally, especially firms from small open economies for which the domestic external network may be quite small. Understanding the tensions between the firm's internal and multiple external networks should allow managers to determine the best strategic fit between their firm and its environment.

10.2 A NETWORK APPROACH TO UNDERSTANDING THE BEHAVIOR OF MNEs

In an era of expanding transnational linkages among individuals and organizations, there is increasing conceptual and empirical support (Westney, 1990; Ghoshal and Bartlett, 1990; Kim and Mauborgne, 1993) for conceptualizing MNEs as networks of exchange relationships. The uniqueness of the MNE as an organizational form arises from the fact that its different constituent units which form the intra-organizational network, operate in different environments. The structure of the external networks of customers, suppliers, competitors, and regulatory agencies with which the different units of the MNE must interact therefore also varies.

Although the internal relational structure of MNEs involves some degree of hierarchical decision-making, recent empirical work on multinationals' global strategies (Kim and Mauborgne, 1993) suggests that the interaction between head office and unit top managers is more appropriately viewed as a co-opting mode based on mutually shared and accepted principles than as a hierarchical governance mode. A co-opting approach towards these interactions increases the possibilities to tap the distinctive knowledge, skills and competencies of sub-units. A network approach in which intra-organizational relationships sustain and reinforce each other provides a way to conceptualize this internal coopting pattern of interaction. This view is also compatible with an evolutionary perspective on the growth of the firm (Kogut and Zander, 1993; Malnight, 1996) whereby firms grow on the basis of their ability to create new knowledge and to replicate this knowledge when entering new markets.

In addition to this intra-organizational perspective, institutionalization theory (Dimaggio and Powell, 1983) proposes that the social and institutional environments exert pressure on firms to conform to existing patterns of behavior. This pressure for similarity with outside constituencies (called 'isomorphism' or 'isomorphic pulls') results from a firm's desire to obtain legitimacy in its external environment. Firm behavior is perceived as legitimate when it appears to be in agreement with the prevailing norms, rules, beliefs or expectations of external constituencies (Oliver, 1990). Thus, firms can increase their perceived legitimacy by emulating the types of organizational structures found in their relevant environments. The 'isomorphic' pressure for increased similarity between actors in a network is consistent with transaction cost explanations of inter-firm linkages (Williamson, 1979, 1985) since transactions are less costly in time and effort between organizations that are similar (Westney, 1993).

While the external relationships between the MNE and its institutional environment exert an influence on the structure and behavior of all MNEs (Ghoshal and Bartlett, 1990), their influence can be predicted to be particularly important to MNEs characterized by a substantial service component in their sales. The service component of most MNEs to customers is increasing dramatically across many industries. The boundary between services and goods is becoming increasingly fluid since significant service components are often inherent to the consumption and use of tangible goods such as automobiles or household appliances.

Services are defined as a bundle of benefits delivered to the customer through the experience that is created for that customer. Intangibility, inseparability/simultaneity and variability are generally viewed as the distinguishing characteristics of services versus physical goods (Berry and Parasuraman, 1991). These three characteristics reinforce the usefulness of adopting a network approach to understanding the interactions of MNEs with their external environments. This is because these service characteristics increase the importance of relationships as a source of a firm's competitive differentiation. For example, the likely presence of variability in service quality not only makes it difficult and riskier for customers and other external actors to evaluate the quality of a service, but it also makes the purchasing process more complex (Murray, 1991). Relationships are an important way to enhance a firm's credibility and thereby lower purchase risk.

The uncertainty associated with the quality of a service makes it critical that firms appear legitimate in the eyes of their external network. Service intangibility means that the customer often finds it difficult to isolate service quality from the 'quality' of the service provider. An MNE characterized by a high service component, therefore, needs to legitimize its relationships with the various external networks (Tichy, Tushman and Fombrun, 1979) within which the MNE is embedded. The relationship between the pressures exerted by the firm's multiple external networks and its internal network is discussed next.

10.3 THE INTERFACE BETWEEN INTERNAL AND MULTIPLE EXTERNAL NETWORK RELATIONSHIPS

The external linkages of the various decision centers in an MNE are associated with specific pressures for similarity or isomorphic pulls. The concept of varying isomorphic pulls has been successfully applied to describe the simple case of the integration-national responsiveness dilemma faced by MNEs (Rozenzweig and Singh, 1991). National responsiveness can be viewed as a response to pressures for isomorphism within each national environment at the level of a subsidiary, a business, a function or a task within a function. In contrast, global integration is a response to pressures for consistency within the multinational enterprise as a whole.

The concept of isomorphic pulls, however, goes far beyond requirements for national responsiveness or integration. For example, isomorphic pulls faced by a specific decision-making center of an MNE may be entirely unrelated to the pressure to become more nationally responsive. The Japanese joint venture between McCann-Erikson Advertising and Hakuhodo employed a large number of expatriates in Japan who brought with them a Western way of advertising and marketing in order to serve the needs of their Western clients. Here, the external network in Japan required, paradoxically, Western know-how to deal with Western clients. Issues which at first might seem related to national responsiveness and integration therefore need to be reconsidered given the context of multiple external networks exerting pressures on the MNE, but whereby these pressures cannot be simply dichotomized as requirements for national responsiveness versus integration.

As MNEs move towards a structure with multiple strategic decision-making centers, each center may be confronted with specific isomorphic pulls arising from a particular customer base, the behavior of rival companies, the operation of specific related and supporting firms, differences in legislation or different cost structures. The behavioral patterns viewed as legitimate by organizations in each external environment may be conflicting with, or complementary to, intra-organizational patterns already established within the MNE. They may also be conflicting to each other irrespective of their consistency with intra-organizational patterns as described in Figure 10.1.

Figure 10.1 highlights the importance of the interface between an MNE's internal network structure and the external networks embedded in different businesses, functions and geographic locations. The left part of this figure describes the conventional national responsiveness-integration dilemma. Here, global industry-specific characteristics related to technology, demand patterns and industry competition, determine the external pressures for integration on the MNE as a whole, whereas specific characteristics of national environments determine the external pressures for national responsiveness facing specific subsidiary activities. The administrative heritage of the MNE then leads to a firm-specific response to these pressures. Capabilities of integration and national responsiveness are created. The former allow MNEs to reap benefits of scale, scope and exploitation of national differences (Rugman and Verbeke, 1992). The latter allow MNEs to gain benefits of adaptation to national requirements. The administrative heritage of the MNE determines the mix of capabilities that will be created and the intra-organizational routines associated with developing and utilizing this mix of capabilities (for example the process whereby the locus for new product developments is selected).

The multiple networks management challenge described on the right-hand side of Figure 10.1 starts from the characteristics of specific external networks (customers, suppliers, competition, related and supporting firms, government regulation, pressure groups). Each external network may consist of a variety of local, national, international, regional and global actors (see also Rugman and Verbeke, 1993) exerting isomorphic pressures on the relevant MNE's decision center. In fact, the very existence of MNEs with a regionalized structure (for example one decision center for each part of the triad) indicates the importance of external forces at a regional level rather than at a national or global level. In addition, strong isomorphic pressures may arise from forces at the sub-national level (Krugman, 1995) or from forces at the international level arising in a single foreign country, as exemplified by the 'double-diamond' literature (Rugman and Verbeke, 1995).

In Figure 10.1, only two decision centers are taken into account to simplify the presentation. The various pulls arising from the multiple external

Figure 10.1 The conventional national responsiveness-integration dilemma versus the multiple networks challenge

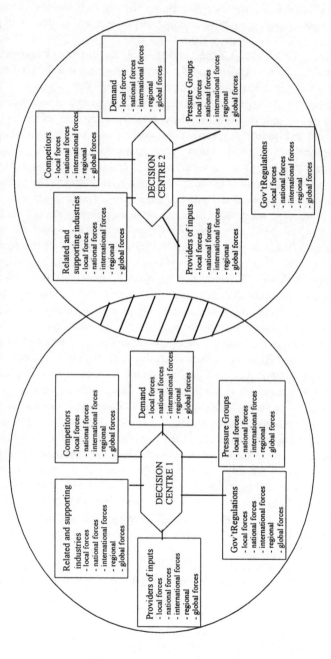

networks may be complementary or conflicting with each other. In addition, isomorphic pulls may have a varying degree of consistency with the firm's existing administrative heritage. Unlike the case of the integration-national responsiveness dilemma (portrayed on the left-hand side of Figure 10.1) whereby environmental forces exert easily identifiable pressures on MNEs, the pressures exerted by the multiple networks (portrayed on the right-hand side of Figure 10.1) are more complex because they span all relevant actors in the firm's networks exerting pressures at multiple geographic levels. The isomorphic pulls on the MNE arising from multiple networks at different geographic levels are illustrated in Figure 10.2.

For simplicity, the external networks of only two decision centers are portrayed in Figure 10.2. While each decision center faces a distinct set of isomorphic pulls, the intersection of the two external networks in Figure 10.2 illustrates that there may be common components in the two decision centers' external networks. For example, to the extent that different decision centers operate in the same or related businesses, they may be faced with identical global forces on the demand side. Likewise, to the extent that two decision centers are located in one trading area (for example NAFTA or the EU), they may be faced with identical regional pressures in the area of government regulation. The isomorphic pulls on the MNE arising from multiple networks at different geographic levels is consistent with the determinants of competitiveness identified by Rugman and Verbeke (1993).

Viewed in this way, the integration-national responsiveness dilemma constitutes only a special (and simple) case of the multiple network management challenge. In that special case, it is assumed that each sub-unit faces primarily national pressures for isomorphism, whereas the MNE as a whole (in most cases this means the corporate headquarters) must take into account global pressures for integration derived from industry characteristics in terms of technological, demand related or competitive parameters (see Ghoshal, 1987 for an overview). In contrast, the multiple network management challenge consists of responding 'appropriately' to pulls exerted by multiple actors at multiple geographic levels on the various decision-making centers within the MNE.

Two possible MNE responses to such isomorphic pulls are to either adapt internal processes to the pressures exerted by various external networks (isomorphic flexibility) or to actively change the external networks to conform to internal processes (institutionalization). These responses are discussed in the next section and illustrated using examples based on the authors' own experiences as consultants with a number of large MNEs.

Figure 10.2 Isomorphic pulls in multiple networks

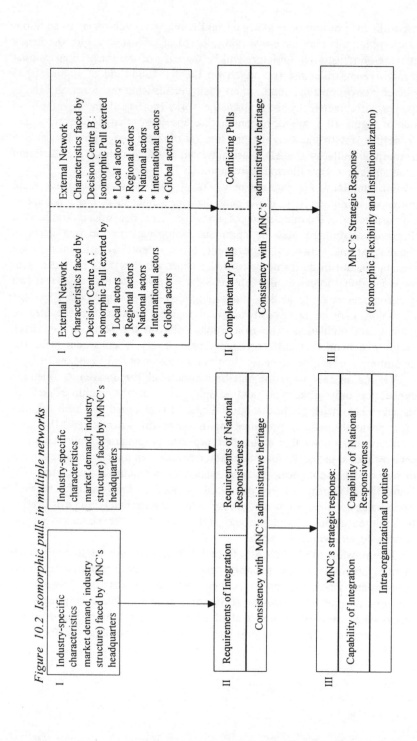

10.4 EXTERNAL NETWORK STRATEGIES OF MNEs

In response to the isomorphic pulls arising from an external network, a decision center may either adapt itself as well as possible to existing network pressures (a strategy of isomorphic flexibility) or attempt to alter the external network in which it operates (a strategy of institutionalization). IBM is a good example of a company that has followed a strategy of isomorphic flexibility. IBM allows all decision centers to accommodate the specific needs of their external networks. These external needs, however, are very complementary across networks. In the absence of a formal division of responsibilities on a global basis, one result is that two groups may be working on providing the same solution simultaneously. This underscores the fact that it is particularly important to diffuse the capabilities developed in different decision centers to other parts of the firm and to the external networks in which the MNE is embedded. For this purpose, IBM allows cross licensing between decision centers in order to facilitate the sharing of know-how on a global basis. When IBM Canada developed a process for determining a project's progress, it was able to sell its know-how to other decision centers. In this way, knowledge is dispersed from one decision center to another without having to be filtered through the US headquarters. There is, however, no obligation to purchase know-how from other decision centers.

Firms adopting a strategy of isomorphic flexibility and characterized by decision centers that face complementary isomorphic pulls, deal with the challenge of diffusing innovations throughout the organization in different ways. The Hotel Group Four Seasons has implemented an employer-incentive program called 'Ideas that Work' which rewards employment for bringing hotel-specific service innovations to the attention of management so that they can be 'syndicated' to other hotels throughout the global organization. Since multiple networks management is reactive, MNEs following this strategy (IBM, Four Seasons Hotels and McCann-Erikson) need to overcome problems of information-sharing throughout the organization through non-coercive incentive programs.

The problems of disseminating knowledge and learning created in various decision centers, characteristic of a strategy of isomorphic flexibility, increase when the MNE faces conflicting isomorphic pulls. Firms pursue a strategy of isomorphic flexibility by adapting the intra-organizational network to conform to the conflicting isomorphic pulls prevailing in the various decision centers. The process of creating and diffusing knowledge throughout the company is difficult since each decision center follows patterns viewed as legitimate by the external constituents on which it depends. Club Med is a firm that fits into this category. Club Med has set up four different geographic strategic centers: North/Central America, Europe/Africa, Pacific/Asia and South America. Each center is responsible for catering to its particular customer base, and as a result the zones are managed quite differently. For example, in Europe, where 65 percent of customers visit Club Med offices to book their vacations, Club Med primarily uses a direct sales approach whereas in North America, 95 percent of sales are done through independent travel agents. The differences between the various zones are reflected in the fact that Club Med staff only rotate positions within their specific geographic zone and not between zones.

Club Med has adopted a regional management structure which facilitates both the gathering of information at the village resort level and the distribution of information to head offices via zone managers. However, the firm's regionalized structure means that the intra-organizational network is split into separate centers, each of which deals with its own external networks. Here the sharing of knowledge among regions is minimal.

In contrast to a strategy of isomorphic flexibility, an institutionalization strategy changes the external network so that it conforms better to the firm's existing intra-organizational patterns (see D'Cruz and Rugman, 1992, 1993, 1994). Federal Express, for example, has acquired European companies and imported American management in order to replicate its Memphis hub and spoke distribution system in Brussels which affects all external network participants. However, an institutionalization approach goes far beyond replicating the conventional intra-organizational behavioral patterns prevailing in the home country as described in the international integration literature on MNEs. It may include recreating external network linkages in the area of labor relations and suppliers according to the 'best global practice' prevailing in any decision center of the MNE (Rugman and Verbeke, 1995).

It is difficult for MNEs to follow a strategy of institutionalization when isomorphic pulls are conflicting. In this case multiple networks management involves an 'institutionalization project' to change the external environment faced by one or a number of decision centers. One reason that it may be difficult for an MNE to sustain such an approach is that the major way to implement this strategy has been to use expatriates to manage decision centers outside the home country. Importing expatriates creates difficulties in maintaining the legitimacy in the eyes of outside actors in each of the decision centers.

In order to adopt a strategy of institutionalization when faced with conflicting isomorphic pulls, MNEs need to have a unique offering and a reputation for 'best practices' which allows them to impose their internal practices on the various external networks in the face of different (and opposing) pressures to conform. One example of a firm in this position is

Arthur Andersen. Accounting practices are very different throughout the world since the financial goals of firms in various countries vary considerably. Despite the fact that many of their customers have very different views about what good bookkeeping and financial management is, Arthur Andersen follows the same procedures in all its decision centers. This is embodied in its philosophy 'One firm, one goal, one vision'. Although each decision center has substantial autonomy as a profit-making unit, the only time decision centers deviate from the established practice is when the practice is in conflict with statutory laws governing them.

When isomorphic pulls are complementary, MNEs may easily institutionalize managerial practices developed in any decision center of the firm faced with a specific external network. Firms impose the 'best proven practice' on external networks. In this way, the whole intra-organizational network benefits from the best proven practice arising from any decision center. Citibank conforms to this pattern. As Malnight (1996) describes, the transition at Citibank from a decentralized to a network-based approach involved the gradual linking and integrating of previously autonomous affiliates by reallocating specialized resources and roles with supporting adjustments in management systems and culture to facilitate operational interdependence.

Citibank's global finance division, for example, delivers a full range of financial services to a select group of corporate and institutional customers whose financial needs are global in nature. The division generally faces complementary isomorphic pulls since clients wordwide demand global, innovative products and consistent quality service. Citibank employs a 'success transfer' process whereby products, marketing strategies and operating expertise that have led to success obtained by a specific decision center are transferred to other markets in the world. Examples of this are the Citibank Advantage Card (rewards customers with frequent flyer miles on American Airlines) and Citigold. Citigold (an integrated way for wealthy customers to manage their banking, borrowing and investment activities) was first pioneered in Singapore and after strong success in the Asia Pacific region was introduced into the US, European and Latin American markets.

As the above discussion illustrates, two parameters can be considered as the main determinants of the multiple external network strategies available to MNEs. The first parameter is the conflicting or complementary nature of the external isomorphic pulls. The second parameter describes the MNE's strategic choice in managing the interface between the firm's internal network and the various isomorphic pulls arising from external networks. This choice may be reactive (isomorphic flexibility) or proactive (institutionalization).

Few MNEs, however, conform exactly to the patterns described above. The reason for this is that strategies of complete isomorphic flexibility or complete institutionalization pose significant problems for MNEs. Adopting a strategy of isomorphic flexibility limits the extent to which know-how can be diffused throughout the intra-organizational network since each center reacts to the specific isomorphic pulls in its environment and operates largely independently in the stages of knowledge development. On the other hand, changing the external environment through an institutionalization strategy requires substantial effort. Kogut (1991) discussed several external and internal constraints which limit the adoption of an institutionalization strategy. With respect to the external environment, there are social barriers to be overcome and there may be insufficient competitive pressure to change existing practices. From an internal perspective, it is difficult to identify what should be learned from the external networks and how it should be learned. In addition, the number of linkages between firms in industrial networks tends to be higher within, for example, national borders than between countries. This relatively higher density of national industrial networks reduces the potential for the diffusion of knowledge from foreign networks, even if the diffusion process occurs through mediation of an MNE.

These difficulties have led some MNEs to choose a 'combination strategy' in which elements of both isomorphic flexibility and institutionalization are incorporated into the firm's strategic posture. Faced with complementary isomorphic pulls, McKinsey & Co, is an example of a firm which has adopted a combination strategy. In the consulting industry, intense competitive rivalry is increasing the importance to firms of isomorphic flexibility to adapt to various external networks on an industry by industry basis (for example consulting work for the steel industry versus the computer software industry). At the same time, however, in order for consulting firms to offer value-added client solutions, new knowledge and learning must continuously be disseminated to external client networks as well as to the MNEs' various decision centers.

In this context, McKinsey is institutionalizing aspects of its consulting through the development of common resource centers such as the one in Brussels to deal with pan-European issues facing pan-European firms. Attempts to change existing external networks include the use of books authored by its consultants which circulate within the business community, industry studies which are published in industry magazines, and keynote speaking engagements at industry conferences. McKinsey is also part of the Industrial Research Institute (IRI) which includes CEOs and other senior managers of 18 IRI companies. In addition to increasing its credibility and legitimacy in the eyes of external networks, all of these forums are also used to present McKinsey's views on how business should be run.

The 'combination' strategy followed by McKinsey helps the firm to ensure that information is effectively diffused internally. While intellectual inputs are concentrated at headquarters and at regional centers, McKinsey also has an elaborate internal network for making discretionary use of the knowledge McKinsey consultants gather on assignments around the world. Employees with common interests are encouraged to participate in competence areas on general subjects (for example change management, integrated logistics, and so on) which helps to improve the firm's knowledge base. A 'Knowledge Resource Directory' provides an on-line guide to each consultant's area of expertise and a special database sorts and stores the knowledge gained by consultants from their projects. This allows the various decision centers to pool knowledge and share innovations.

Clearly there are a number of factors managers of MNEs must consider in choosing how to manage their multiple external networks. Given the diversity of isomorphic pulls arising from diverse external actors, one of the major challenges facing managers is how to aggregate across them to determine whether these pulls are predominantly conflicting or predominantly complementary to the firm's internal network practices. In the next section, hypotheses are developed about the effect of various attributes of both the MNE's environment and its organizational characteristics.

10.5 CONCLUSIONS AND FUTURE RESEARCH DIRECTIONS

The distinction between isomorphic flexibility and institutionalization strategies proposed in this note represents a network-based extension of the national responsiveness-integration framework developed by Bartlett (1986). As argued by Benson (1975), the flow of resources within an inter-organizational network is influenced by the distribution of power within the network. Likewise, the choice of an MNE to conform to or change to behavioral patterns in one of its multiple external networks depends on the balance of power between the MNE and the different organizations within that external network. This leads to the following proposition:

Proposition 1: When the MNE is highly dependent on the resources and contracts stemming from organizations in one of its external networks, the MNE is likely to follow a strategy of 'isomorphic flexibility' whereby the MNE reactively changes its intra-organizational patterns of behavior in order to adapt to this external network.

Conversely, an institutionalization strategy is most likely when different organizations in an external network are highly dependent on the resources of the MNE. The MNE may then attempt to alter its external network so that the process of developing and diffusing knowledge within this network conforms better to the MNE's own internal development and diffusion processes.

Proposition 2: When the organizations in one of the MNE's external networks are highly dependent on the resources and contacts stemming from the MNE, the MNE is likely to follow a strategy of 'institutionalization' whereby the MNE proactively changes the patterns of behavior in this external network to conform to its own intra-organizational patterns.

Our analysis suggests that given the increase of the service component in many firms' sales structures, an MNE's sources of competitive advantage increasingly reside in its ability to effectively manage the interface between both its internal and external networks. Apart from resource dependency, the nature of the MNE's offerings may also influence the propensity to select a strategy of isomorphic flexibility or institutionalization. From the customer's perspective, uncertainty arises when the service attributes of a firm involve a high degree of intangibility, inseparability and variability (Bharadwaj, Varadarajan and Fahy, 1993). In this case, the importance of firm credibility and experience to the customer is likely to prompt an MNE to adopt a strategy of isomorphic flexibility as suggested by the following proposition:

Proposition 3: The greater the intangibility, inseparability and variability of the firm's service offering, the greater the likelihood of an MNE adopting a strategy of isomorphic flexibility.

From the firm's perspective, uncertainty in the competitive or technological environments may also prompt a strategy of isomorphic flexibility. In such environments, the adoption of external behavioral patterns is welcomed because of their uncertainty-reducing properties (Caeldries and Moenaert, 1993).

Proposition 4: The greater the technological and competitive uncertainty, the greater the likelihood of an MNE adopting a strategy of isomorphic flexibility.

In contrast, a strategy of institutionalization is likely when firms achieve a competitive differentiation advantage through the systematization and standardization of the process of delivering products and services (Porter, 1980). Quality control and consistency across borders are paramount for MNEs following this strategy.

Proposition 5: The greater the potential to institute systematization and standardization to achieve a differentiation advantage, the greater the likelihood that MNEs will adopt a strategy of institutionalization.

To achieve global competitive success, an MNE needs to pursue external network strategies in a way that both facilitates organizational learning and maintains legitimacy in the eyes of the organizations in the external networks in which the various decision centers are embedded. This chapter has suggested key parameters to be taken into account by managers contemplating the various options available to MNEs in developing external network strategies. In doing so, the chapter extends previous work on network-based MNE models as in, for example, Ghoshal and Bartlett (1990), Malnight (1996) by arguing that the national responsiveness-integration dilemma is a subset or special case of the broader challenge facing MNEs, namely the management of multiple networks. The analysis is especially relevant for MNEs from small, open economies, faced with the challenge of managing foreign external networks, which may be much larger than the domestic ones.

REFERENCES

Bartlett, C. (1986), 'Building and Managing the Transnational: The New Organizational Challenge', in M.E. Porter (ed.), *Competition in Global Industries*, Boston? MA: Harvard Business School Press, pp. 367-404.

Bartlett, C. and S. Ghoshal (1989*), Managing across Borders: The Transnational Solution*, Boston, MA: Harvard Business School Press.

Benson, J. (1975), 'The interorganizational network as a political economy', *Administrative Science Quarterly*, **20**, 229-49.

Berry, L. and A. Parasuraman (1991), *Marketing Services: Competing through Quality*, New York: The Free Press.

Bharadwaj, S., P. Varadarajan and J. Fahy (1993), 'Sustainable competitive advantage in service industries: A conceptual model and research propositions', *Journal of Marketing*, **57**, 83-99.

Birkinshaw, J. and A. Morrison (1995), 'Configuration of strategy and structure in subsidiaries of multinational corporations', *Journal of International Business Studies*, (4), 729-53.

Caeldries, F. and R. Moenaert (1993), 'International Technology Strategies: The Role of Innovation Uncertainty', in A. Rugman and A. Verbeke (eds), *Research in Global Strategic Management 4: Global Competition: Beyond the Three Generics*, Greenwich, CT: JAI Press, pp. 155-79.

Contractor, F. and P. Lorange (1988), *Cooperative Strategies in International Business*, Lexington, DC: Heath and Company.

D'Cruz, J. and A. Rugman (1992), 'Business networks for international competitiveness', *Business Quarterly*, **56** (4).

D'Cruz, J. and A. Rugman (1993), 'Developing international competitiveness: The 5 partners model', *Business Quarterly*, **58** (2).

D'Cruz, J. and A. Rugman (1994), 'The 5 partners model: France Telecom, Alcatel and the global telecommunications industry', *European Management Journal*, March.

Dimaggio, P. and W. Powell (1983), 'The iron cage revisited: institutional isomorphism and collective rationality in organizational fields', *American Sociological Review*, **48**, 147-60.

Doz, Y., C.K. Prahalad and G. Hamel (1990), 'Control, Change and Flexibility: The Dilemma of Transnational Collaboration', in C. Bartlett, Y. Doz and G. Hedlund (eds), *Managing the Global Firm*, London: Routledge.

Dunning, J. (1993), *The Globalization of Business: The Challenge of the 1990s*, London: Routledge.

Ghoshal, S. (1987), 'Global strategy: an organizing framework', *Strategic Management Journal*, **8**, 425-40.

Ghoshal, S. and C.A. Bartlett (1990), 'The multinational corporation as an interorganizational network', *Academy of Management Review*, **15** (4), 603-25.

Gupta, A.K. and V. Govindarajan (1991), 'Knowledge flows and the structure of control within multinational corporations', *Academy of Management Review*, **16** (4), 768-92.

Hofstede, G. (1980), *Culture's Consequences: International Differences in Work-related Values*, Beverley Hills, CA: Sage.

Kim, W.C. and R. Mauborgne (1993), 'Effectively conceiving and executing multinationals' worldwide strategies', *Journal of International Business Studies*, **24** (3), 419-48.

Kogut, B. (1989), 'A note on global strategies', *Strategic Management Journal*, **10**, 383-9.

Kogut, B. (1991), 'Country capabilities and the permeability of borders', *Strategic Management Journal*, 12 (Special Issue/Summer), 33-47.

Kogut, B. and U. Zander (1993), 'Knowledge of the firm and the evolutionary theory of the multinational corporation', *Journal of International Business Studies*, **24** (4), 625-45.

Krugman, P. (1995), 'Location and Competition: Notes on Economic Geography', in Rumelt, R.P. and D.J. Teece (eds), *Fundamental Issues in Strategy*, Boston, MA: Harvard Business School Press, pp. 463-94.

Malnight, T. (1996), 'The transition from decentralized to network-based MNC structures: An evolutionary perspective', *Journal of International Business Studies*, **27** (1), 43-65.

Millington, A. and B. Bayliss (1995), 'Transnational joint ventures between UK and EU manufacturing companies and the structure of competition', *Journal of International Business Studies*, **26** (2), 239-54.

Murray, K. (1991), 'A test of services marketing theory: Consumer information acquisition activities', *Journal of Marketing*, **55**, 10-25.

Oliver, C. (1990), 'Determinants of interorganizational relationships: integration and future directions', *Academy of Management Review*, **15** (2), 241-65.

Oviatt, B. and P. Phillips McDougall (1994), 'Towards a theory of international new ventures', *Journal of International Business Studies*, **25** (1), 45-64.

Porter, M. (1980), *Competitive Strategy: Techniques for Analyzing industries and Competitors,* New York: Free Press.

Porter, M. (1990), *The Competitive Advantage of Nations*, New York: Free Press.

Prahalad, C.K. and Y. Doz (1987), *The Multinational Mission: Balancing Local Demands and Global Vision*, New York: The Free Press.

Roth, K. and A. Morrison (1992), 'Implementing global strategy: characteristics of global subsidiary mandates', *Journal of International Business Studies*, **23** (4), 715-36.

Rosenzweig, F. and J. Singh (1991), 'Organizational environments and the multinational enterprise', *Academy of Management Review*, **16** (2), 340-361.

Rugman, A. and A. Verbeke (1992), 'Multinational Enterprise and National Economic Policy', in P. Buckley and M. Casson (eds), *Multinational Enterprise in the World Economy*, Aldershot: Edward Elgar, pp. 194-211.

Rugman, A. and A. Verbeke (1993), 'How to operationalize Porter's diamond of international competitiveness', *International Management Executive*, July/August, **35** (4), 283-99.

Rugman, A. and A. Verbeke (1995), 'Transnational Networks and Global Competition: An Organizing Framework', in A. Rugman, J. Van den Broeck and A. Verbeke, (eds), *Beyond the Diamond*, Greenwich, CT: JAI Press, pp. 3-24.

Tichy, N., M. Tushman and C. Fombrun (1979), 'Social analysis for organizations', *Academy of Management Review*, (4), 507-19.

Westney, E. (1990), 'Internal and external linkages in the MNE: The Case of R&D Subsidiaries in Japan, in C.A. Bartlett, Y. Doz and G. Hedlund (eds), *Managing the Global Firm*, New York: Routledge, pp. 279-302.

Westney, E. (1993), 'Institutionalization Theory and the Multinational Corporation', in S. Ghoshal and D. Westney (eds), *Organization Theory and the Multinational Corporation*, New York: St. Martin's Press, pp. 237-52.

White, R. and T. Poynter (1990), 'Organizing for World-Wide Advantage', in C. Bartlett, A. Doz and G. Hedlund (eds), *Managing the Global Firm*, London and New York: Routledge, 95-113.

Williamson, O. (1979), 'Transaction cost economics: the governance of contractual relations', *Journal of Law and Economics*, **22**, 233-61.

Williamson, O. (1985), *The Economic Institutions of Capitalism: Firms, Markets, Relational Contracting*, New York: Free Press.

11. A Resource-based View on Multi-market Competition. A Conceptual Framework for Analyzing the Dynamics of Multi-business Rivalry

Marc van Wegberg and Arjen van Witteloostuijn

11.1 INTRODUCTION

A discussion about multi-market competition should distinguish between statics and dynamics. Static multi-market studies are concerned with the effects of multi-market scope on performance. Because of economies of scope, multi-market penetration improves efficiency and raises profits (Baumol, Panzar and Willig, 1982; Teece, 1980). If the scope of firms overlaps, the firms are said to meet in multiple markets. Strong multi-market contact may enhance collusion between them and raise their performance (Edwards, 1955; Feinberg, 1984; Bernheim and Whinston, 1990).

Firms may learn from these results that they should increase their presence in multiple markets, so as to realize economies of scope or to raise multi-market contact with salient rivals. A change of scope, however, brings us into the realm of dynamic multi-market competition. In the 1990s, some reversed multi-market mergers (such as Matsushita-MCA, Novell-WordPerfect and AT&T-NCR) suggest that failure may occur. What kinds of mistakes and failures can occur when firms change their scope? We are especially interested in failures that go beyond normal business risk. A static approach to strategy may overlook or downplay some disadvantages of a wide scope.

The aim of this chapter is to identify why decisions to change the firm's presence in multiple markets may lead to failure, even when applying an otherwise sound strategy of changing the firm's scope. We begin with discussing the content of a rational strategy with respect to multi-market scope. Next, we identify mistakes that firms can make in changing their scope. We illustrate the argument with a case from the field of information technology: the market for web browsers.

11.2 ALIGNING MULTI-MARKET SCOPE WITH THE RESOURCE BASE

Before identifying the kinds of mistakes that firms can make when they change their scope, we need to know what would be a rational, *ex ante* profit-maximizing course of action.[1] Multi-market competition theory argues that the goals of market power and efficiency benefits drive the optimal choice of a firm's multi-market scope. We will focus in this chapter on efficiency benefits, although market power could play an important role here (Edwards, 1955; Feinberg, 1984; Bernheim and Whinston, 1990). The efficiency benefits are based on economies of scope. Economies of scope arise if it is cheaper to supply two or more products in one process, than to operate separate processes for each product (Baumol, Panzar and Willig, 1982). The reason for this is that the supply of one product makes some resource(s) freely available to another product if both products are jointly supplied.

There are several ways by which a firm can realize economies of scope. It can repackage or combine existing technologies in a new product. It can also use a *shared resource* simultaneously in multiple products. The strategy of umbrella branding is an example, whereby a firm sells a large variety of products, all using the same brand name. Different products may also share some common value activities, such as the development or production of components. As these cases illustrate, a key idea in multi-market competition theory is that the optimal choice of a firm's product scope depends on the resources it uses. Two propositions to be tested in empirical studies link the firm's resource base to its strategic moves.

First, a firm's shared resources lead to efficiency benefits in a new market, if its resources are intensely used in that market. An R&D-intensive firm will likely enter R&D-intensive markets; an advertising-intensive firm will enter an advertising-intensive market. Research in this area (for example, Ramanujam and Varadarajan, 1989, p. 526) suggests:

Proposition 1: Probability of entering new markets: Established-firm entrants tend to come from markets that are related in terms of their resource intensities (capital intensity, R&D intensity, or advertising intensity).

Montgomery and Hariharan (1991) confirm this proposition. They studied entry decisions by 366 major US manufacturing corporations in 258 industries in the period 1973-1977. They found that: 'A firm's selling intensity and research and development intensity are very important indicators of which firms will enter new markets. Further, the breadth of a firm's resource base is a very strong predictor of diversified expansion' (p. 85). Measuring resource requirements in terms of capital, selling, and R&D intensity, 'firms enter industries whose resource requirements are similar to their own resource profiles. This result holds for a firm's relative levels of selling intensity, research and development intensity, and capital intensity, as well as our more specific measure of relatedness' (p. 85). Entry may occur by means of an acquisition. Related resource intensities may not only indicate in which markets a firm will enter, but also which (kinds of) firms it will want to acquire.

Proposition 2: Merger to exploit economies of scope: Mergers inspired by the motive to exploit economies of scope are most likely between firms in markets that are similarly advertising- or R&D-intensive.

Stewart, Harris and Carleton (1984) explored this proposition. They used data of 83 US manufacturing firms acquired during the period 1970-1977, including divisions of other companies before acquisition. Horizontal mergers were omitted. This and other screening conditions reduced the sample to 35 acquired firms. They found that the advertising intensity and R&D intensity of acquiring firms are strongly positively related to those of the acquired firms. Also, if a target firm had a high advertising intensity, this increased the probability of being acquired by a firm in a high advertising industry and lowered the probability of being acquired by a firm in a low advertising industry.

These empirical findings suggest that a firm's shared resources are of prime importance in selecting markets to enter and targeting firms with a view to acquire them. Firms may extend their multi-market scope in order to capture value from their shared resources. A key question then arises if a firm engages in moves consistent with the propositions above: can it still fail?

11.3 FAILURES WHEN CHANGING MULTI-MARKET SCOPE

The business press abounds with cases where a new market entry aimed to gain economies of scope, in fact led to a fall in performance. Mistakes may occur for a variety of reasons: flawed assessments of the resources that drive synergy effects, organizational issues, scope-related feedback effects on the firm's resource base and the effects of changes in scope on product market competition. These various effects are discussed below.

11.3.1 Over-abstraction

We focus on resources that drive the firm's expansion into new markets. Some of these resources consist of relationships. Customer goodwill presupposes a relationship between the firm and its customers. Goodwill represents the accumulation of customers' knowledge of a firm's reliability and product quality. Outside the purview of these customers, no goodwill may exist. The same holds for reputation. Most resources are combinations of inputs. These inputs need to be combined and managed. Their performance depends on this management and on incentives for the individuals involved. Information is at the heart of these resources.

The knowledge embedded in these resources is often tacit. This is usually seen as an advantage, as tacit knowledge is more difficult for rivals to copy or to buy. The tacit nature of knowledge also has a less often noticed disadvantage, however, it makes it more difficult for the firm's own management to assess its knowledge base. Management may suffer from *over-abstraction*, leading to a failure in profitably expanding its multi-market scope. Management may interpret the firm's resources in abstract terms as 'our brand name', 'our technical expertise', and so on. In reality, the resources may represent a highly specific mixture of relationships among individuals, complex combinations of inputs (some bought in open markets, others developed in-house), ways of storing and communicating information and incentives. This highly specific, unique mixture may or may not succeed when put to work in a new environment.

The danger of over-abstraction is to apply resources in a non-appropriate setting. Each market functions within a unique context (of environmental characteristics), such as institutions, routines and relationships. Every market requires a specific kind of expertise. A market, as does a firm, has ways (institutions, routines) to transmit information and to provide incentives. The firm's resources are also associated with a set of institutions, routines and relationships. They may or may not fit in the context of the new market. In the abstract terms of Proposition 1, it would be appropriate for an R&D-intensive firm to enter an R&D-intensive industry. At a concrete level, however, the firm's expertise and the new market's need for expertise may not match at all.

AT&T has a substantial expertise in electronics and such an expertise is surely required in the computer industry, but does this mean it should have acquired NCR? IBM made the same mistake of over-abstraction when it entered into telecommunications by acquiring Rolm. In discussing these two moves, Von Tunzelman and Soete (1987) note that firms usually possess a highly specialized knowledge base. The failure to recognize this point, that is over-abstraction, then leads to misguided attempts to invade new territories.

Firms can try to solve this problem by engaging in a more realistic assessment of their resource base. They can use information technology to aggregate their information-based resources. Groupware software, such as Lotus Notes and Internet-based software, allows firms to create databases that contain the accumulated knowledge of the firm's employees. This software makes the firm's knowledge more visible and allows the firm to assess weaknesses, as well as to identify new opportunities hidden in the data.

Another strategy is to make the firm's resources less abstract. Some resources are more situation- and relation-specific than others. Experience in management and problem solving is more abstract than expertise in LCDs. If employees' skills are highly specialized, the firm has a greater chance of failure in a new environment than if employees developed some general skills.

11.3.2 Organizational Side-effects of Changing Scope

A change in scope has important organizational consequences. These in turn may lead to (unexpected) costs. An important characteristic of a successful multi-market firm is connectedness. A firm's shared resource should be matched to the scope and selection of its product markets, to the other resources, to its employees and their incentives and skills and to its internal organization. The firm achieves an equilibrium when all these components (resources, product markets, human assets, organization) fit together. We label this condition *connectedness*, which is similar to Porter's (1996, p. 70) use of the concept of fit.

Connectedness is a necessary condition to achieve synergy. The existence of scope economies in the production process is, therefore, only one ingredient among many needed to produce synergy. To put it differently, when firms fail to realize synergy, the problem may be their inability to achieve connectedness, rather than a faulty expectation of possible economies of scope.

To create connectedness, a firm should adjust the parts that make up the firm: it may need to invest in or divest in resources, adapt its product portfolio (by entry and exit), its human assets (by promoting learning, through selection and promotion) and the organization (both the organizational structure and the company's culture). Making these adjustments indicates that connectedness is costly. Investing in resources is a case in point.

Designing or adjusting resources so that maximum connectedness is achieved tends to make them unique to the firm, and may reduce their value to other companies. As a result, they become firm-specific. *Firm-specificity is an investment in connectedness.* A firm's investments are firm-specific the more they are tailored to be connected to the (complementary) resources, the workforce and the firm's internal and external organization. The firm increases its effectiveness by designing machinery, training employees, developing products and organizing itself so as to maximize this connectedness. Such moves increase the firm's uniqueness. Some of its characteristics, or a combination thereof, are likely to be unique. By bringing the other resources in line with these features, the firm becomes even more unique. Connectedness, though costly, may thus contribute to competitive advantage.

Figure 11.1 Elements of connectedness

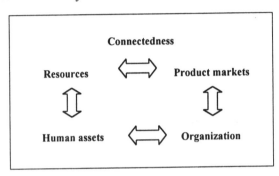

Firm-specificity, however, also represents a form of inertia, which points to another possible cost of connectedness. Durable resources that are difficult to trade are the firm's *inertia factors or commitments* (Ghemawat, 1991). A firm's reputation and goodwill will cause inertia, as do long-term relationships with employees, suppliers and customers. The inertia may be intended, as in the case of reputation, or arise as a side-effect of irreversible investments in immobile production factors.

Connectedness calls for co-ordination, which is costly in several ways (Porter, 1985, p. 259). Multi-market scope leads to synergies only if the multi-market activities are effectively co-ordinated. Co-ordination raises compromise costs, when a compromise between interdependent business units of a firm calls for one unit to take decisions that may run against its own best interest. Co-ordination costs also increase when, due to connectedness, a change in shared resources is accompanied by changes in the other components of Figure 11.1. Finally, if a firm coordinates its decisions across several markets, it becomes difficult to adjust to new information. Each adjustment must be coordinated as well, which is likely to be time consuming. Long communication lines also imply that it may take a while before new information reaches the decision makers. Connectedness thus makes adjustments more costly, which is another way of saying that it reduces flexibility. Porter's analysis therefore points out a trade-off between multi-market spillovers (economies of scope) and flexibility.

Connectedness calls for setting priorities. A firm may have several shared resources which impose inconsistent demands on its connectedness, in terms of the incentives given to employees, the budget to be allocated and the selection of markets that should be served. Once such an inconsistency emerges, top management needs to set priorities and decide upon its core competencies. The opportunities foregone because of such a choice are opportunity costs of the core competence. Philips' shared resources, for example, are its brand name and know how. Its brand name stands for reliable family products, while its know how stands for innovative products. This has led to mismatches, namely when the company failed to attract the customer base it needed. Its compact disk interactive (CD-i) is an example. It should initially have been targeted at the population of 'gadget lovers', but Philips' marketing did not target these people.

Insiders in the company usually understand that new entry will force the firm to change the terms of its connectedness. They may then engage in political activities (Milgrom and Roberts, 1992, p. 192) in order to select entry markets which will have beneficial side-effects for them. The firm's subsequent connectedness may benefit them. More specifically, individuals in a firm may push for entry into the 'wrong' kind of markets in order to protect their existing expertise, relations or career chances.

Firms increasingly understand the need to create connectedness without losing too much flexibility. They are increasingly using alliances and outsourcing as remedies. Alliances can be used to contribute complementary resources to some of the firm's activities, without burdening the firm with the need to create intra-organizational connectedness. If a firm needs specific expertise for one particular new venture, it can turn to an ad hoc alliance, rather than buying or developing that expertise itself.

Whether a firm is flexible or inert also depends on how it organizes its resource base. Some multinational firms keep their core competencies centralized in the country of origin. Most multinational firms are less international in their R&D than in their manufacturing and sourcing activities. This helps to create and ensure connectedness. This strategy can be called centralized or imperialistic, as it imposes resources from one country upon many. US software producers can thereby impose technical standards worldwide (which may very well be efficient). A disadvantage of this approach is that it reduces the firm's adaptability to new markets. An alternative is the 'market of ideas' approach, often adopted by multinational enterprises from small open economies. For example, Dutch companies like Reed Elsevier, Philips and Ahold systematically adopt successful ideas developed in one country in many other nations. The source of the new ideas or products can be located outside the Netherlands. A decentralized resource development approach is flexible, but its disadvantage is the lack of co-ordination and the duplication of efforts.

11.3.3 Market-resource Feedback Effects of Increased Scope

Entry into a new market may have feedback effects on the firm's resource base. Neglecting these may lead to an over-estimation of entry revenues. For example, if the new activity is a failure, it may backfire on the firm's goodwill or reputation: the black-eye effect (Jensen, 1992). The new activity may also strengthen the firm's reputation: the halo effect. In addition to Jensen's unintended feedback effects, there are also intended ones. To make entry a success may call for a change in the firm's connectedness. This in turn may call for further changes in scope, such as exiting from some current markets. A broader scope will usually require a wider pool of resources also to be present and which need to be connected to the rest of the company. With more to co-ordinate, the firm tends to become less flexible.

Feedback effects can be positive or negative. They are positive if they create synergy or if they strengthen the firm's intended inertia factors (its core competencies and its commitment to its home markets). Positive feedback improves the firm's overall competitiveness. Negative feedback occurs if the new activity increases unintended inertia, or if it crowds out existing activities, for example, by creating pollution or negative reputation effects. Feedback effects should be considered part of the entry costs of the new activity (Van Wegberg and Van Witteloostuijn, 1993). They are the most difficult part to assess and the part where management is most likely to err.

It may take a farsighted management to anticipate these feedback effects. A management with a short-term, case-by-case decision-making focus may fail. Compared with a new firm, an established firm that enters a new market faces a complicated situation. On the one hand, the established firm can utilize its existing resources when entering the new market. Its entry costs will thus be lower than for a new firm, which needs to start up production from scratch. On the other hand, the market entered may lead to feedback effects on the established firm's existing markets. The firm's management needs to correctly anticipate such feedback effects.

Table 11.1 The new market entry decision

A new market opportunity		Entry revenue net of direct entry costs		
		Negative	Nil or small	Positive and high
Feedback effects	Negative	Forego	Forego	Exploit and adjust existing market/ Forego
	Positive	Forego?	Exploit	Exploit and raise the stakes

The table shows that management faces two dilemmas. First, the entry opportunity may be attractive per se, but have negative feedback effects on the firm's current products and markets. A solution may be to shield the existing market from the new market by separating them. For example, firms increasingly tend to impose financial targets on each division separately. Treating each division as an independent unit reduces synergies, but also reduces the danger of negative spillovers.

Second, another dilemma occurs if the entry opportunity is not very attractive in itself, but has a positive feedback effect on current activities. If the firm's management is confident about the economic potential of its current activities, it may well enter the new opportunity for the sake of safeguarding these current activities. For instance, consumer electronics companies such as Sony and Matsushita entered the music and movie industries in the 1980s, expecting positive feedback effects on their hardware activities in TV sets, videorecorders and new technologies, such as videogame players and DVD players (the DVD is the successor of the CD-ROM). This strategy aims to maximize the feedback from the new market to the firm's core markets. Integrating and co-ordinating these activities then become of prime importance.

The entry opportunity is non-controversial if it combines positive net revenues with a positive feedback effect.[2] This requires an organizational structure and human resources that allow the new opportunity to strengthen the firm's competitiveness in its current markets. The firm in fact strengthens the specificity of its connectedness in a way that increases the profitability of its current product market scope.

In selecting new opportunities for growth, firms prefer positive/positive opportunities, in terms of the table above: opportunities with positive revenue and positive feedback effects. In this decision process, management is likely to follow a two-stage approach. The first one is to assess the (intended) inertia factors that underly its connectedness. The second stage is to use these to identify new opportunities, their net entry revenues and their feedback effects. The higher the expected value from the firm's current markets, and the more commitment is vital to continued competitiveness in these markets, the more it will be inclined to exclude opportunities with negative feedback effects (even if the entry revenue itself is positive). The feedback effect of an entry opportunity will induce the firm to rethink its current scope. Hence (major) entry decisions need to be assessed in terms of the overall picture: at the level of the corporation, rather than that of a business unit.

11.4 COMPETITOR-DRIVEN FEEDBACK EFFECTS FROM A CHANGE IN SCOPE

The success of a change in scope depends not only on the firm's internal characteristics, but also on the context of competition. A change in scope may change competition both in the market entered and in the entrant's current market. Its current market rivals may react to its move, as do the incumbents in the market entered. If a firm extends its scope, it should anticipate competitor-driven feedback effects on its home market.

If a firm enters a market, it reduces the revenues and perhaps the sales of the incumbents in these markets. These firms may then search themselves for new markets. For example, they may decide to enter the entrant's current market(s). This reciprocal entry may occur for a variety of reasons. The same economic rationale that drives a supplier of product A to supply product B, may drive a supplier of B to enter the market of A. Entry costs from market A to B and from B to A may be low (Brander, 1981). Excess capacity in A may be profitably used for product B, and vice versa (Cairns and Mahabir, 1988; Van Wegberg and Van Witteloostuijn, 1993). An economy of scale or scope may make it efficient to supply both A and B (Baumol, Panzar and Willig, 1982). Strategic reasons may also account for reciprocal entry. A firm may retaliate to incursion into its domain by reciprocal entry (Edwards, 1955). It may try to hurt the entrant in its current market in order to reduce its entry threat. As Watson (1982, p. 40) puts it, 'pursuit of a foreign competitor's domestic markets can help protect the threatened company's own home market share'.

Whatever the reasons for reciprocal entry, it imposes a feedback effect from entry on the entrant's current market. Prospective entrants should take this competitive feedback into account before making their entry move. Entry is not a one-shot activity. The entry changes the market place, the rivals' strategies and the entrant's resource base. These changes are new and often unexpected events that the entrant has to react to. As a consequence, the entry process may evolve in an unpredictable way.

11.4.1 Legitimizing of the Choice of Multi-market Scope

Firms may expand their scope anticipating synergies that may take a long time to emerge. It is a normal business risk that these synergies may not materialize. The real concern is how firms legitimize their belief in these synergies. Social phenomena such as follow-the-leader behavior, imitation and adopting what appears 'fashionable' may be important here. A similar problem occurs if a firm, which wants to expand its scope, must choose from a wide variety of new options. Making the wrong choice can be rationalized *ex post* as the outcome of taking normal business risks. The terms by which decision-makers in a firm legitimize their decisions will affect the decisions themselves. This may lead to a mistaken change of scope. One way to legitimize a new venture is to point to leading rivals who did the same. It may have been sound business practice that in the 1980s and early 1990s, Matushita, Sony and Philips all acquired film companies. It may also be, however, that some element of 'fashion' and imitation crept in. If the new activity fails, at least management did not fail alone. If this motive tends to occur, a firm that enters a market should anticipate that others may follow its move, thus crowding the market entered.

11.4.2 Anticipating Reciprocal Entry

The established firm faces the problem that the market entered differs from its familiar, current market. It may have different players, traditions and institutions. In an international business context, the local firms may interpret foreign entry in a highly personal or cultural way. For instance, they may interpret entry by an American firm in political terms (imperialism), in social terms (a threat to local employment), or in moral terms (a sign of confidence in the locals, an opportunity to learn). As a consequence, they may react to the entry in quite (un)predictable ways. Reciprocal entry can be such a response. If the entrant's management solely focuses on how to efficiently exploit its own resources, it may fail to appreciate the uniqueness of each market entered. The management of a large, multi-market firm may also be 'egocentric'. It may be smart enough to understand what its optimal moves should be, *given* its rivals' current positions. It may, however, fail to realize that rivals may be sophisticated, too, and may come up with unexpected answers to the challenge. It should be able to put itself in the shoes of its rivals to understand their reasoning process.

11.4.3 Raising the Stakes

Dangerous feedback effects may occur when firms compete by raising the stakes. If an entry opportunity promises positive entry profits as well as positive feedback effects, it may induce the firm to expand its resources and their connectedness. Firms which base their large (international) scope on a few core competencies, are likely to invest heavily in them. There are quite a few markets where competitors raise the stakes. Each new generation of memory chips calls for massive investments in R&D and production capacity. The same holds for new cars and civil aircraft. In the software application industry, competition has shifted from separate applications (in word-processing, databases, and so on) to integrated suites comprising all major applications. This move has destroyed all but the most cash rich software suppliers and has reduced the market to three key players (Microsoft, Lotus and Corel). Novell's move into software suites (when it acquired WordPerfect) has been very costly: it was unable to keep up with Microsoft in the suite market and it lost its control over the market of network operating systems.

A firm which raises the stakes, should anticipate two possible problems: loss of flexibility and resource constraints. Investments will become increasingly firm-specific and connectedness will increase. The associated inertia poses dangers if unanticipated events occur. For example, inertia makes dominant suppliers vulnerable to new competitors. Upstarts may have a more narrow scope, but greater flexibility. Then, connectedness of established firms, given the inertia associated with it, creates windows of opportunities for upstarts. Cases abound where upstarts defeated once seemingly invincible rivals such as IBM and General Motors. Their strategies, if successful, force the established multi-market rivals to react, and may ultimately drive them out of the affected markets.

Widening the scope of the firm may weaken the firm's commitment to its current market. Most firms are resource-constrained and entering a new market will force it to forego other developments. A market leader is less at risk when extending its scope than a firm which faces intense competition in its current markets. Under John Sculley, for instance, Apple moved into portable digital assistants with its Newton pen-based hand-held computer. While developing this new operating system, it neglected to update its Macintosh operating system for PCs, thus putting it at a disadvantage relative to the competing Windows operating system.

11.5 A CASE: THE BROWSER MARKET

The dynamic browser market illustrates some of the failures analyzed above. In 1990, an English physicist at CERN, Switzerland, Tim Berners Lee, invented the World Wide Web. He developed standards such as the hypertext protocol, HTTP, and the hypertext language, HTML. He programmed a browser to view and download files stored on distant computers. Berners Lee used a little known computer system for his browser (the Next). A university then wrote the first browser for PCs: Mosaic. The businessman Jim Barksdale enticed the main author of that program, Marc Andreessen, to join him in a new company, namely Netscape. Netscape developed the first 'commercial' browser, the Netscape Navigator. In true Internet fashion, the Navigator was distributed free of charge. From a commercial perspective, however, this approach was an intelligent marketing strategy rather than an

Internet tradition. By distributing Navigator free of charge, the company built marketing power. Most actual revenues came from the server software.

The browser appeared to be a useful tool and numerous companies entered the market with their own browser. The online network companies Compuserve and AOL, for example, decided to enter this market. Quarterdeck, a software company, also entered. As Microsoft realized the market potential of the Internet, it licensed a browser from the Spry company. Synergies were expected between the browser, other applications, online access, and utilities. Competition among these companies led to a 'feature' war. Suppliers introduced new browser varieties at a very rapid pace. The market changed into a 'raising the stakes' contest and by 1996 most suppliers had exited. At present, Microsoft and Netscape basically share a duopoly. Still existing rivals moved into niches. WebTV developed a browser for TV-based Internet. When recognizing that this niche may grow substantially, Microsoft acquired WebTV early in 1997.

The escalation was not simply a matter of Microsoft and Netscape investing increasing quantities of money in their products. Their investments intended to uncover new sources of value. The first source of value is that the browser defines the standards that govern how information should be formatted. Text can be entered in the HTML language; there are also standards for pictures, video, animations and sound. Due to the growing importance of the Internet, these standards will govern all information processing in the future. The distinction between Internet data and the data stored on PCs and mainframes will disappear. Increasingly, users will store their information in formats that are accessible over the Internet. The organizations who control the Internet (standards), will also control the desktop. The competition between browsers seemed to be relatively unimportant. However, the impact of browsers on standards changed this into a much broader battle.

A second reason for the escalation is that the status of the browser product changed over time. At first, it was perceived as a new tool to view and download files. Then it became an application of similar status as word processors and spreadsheets. Finally, Netscape realized that the browser could become an operating system. That is, the user would interact with the PC and all date exclusively via the browser. The underlying operating system, such as Windows, Macintosh, Unix, or OS/2, would become irrelevant. Hence, Netscape developed browsers for all major operating systems. Microsoft realized that it would become irrelevant if Netscape were to win the browser war. In what will surely go down as one of the most controversial maneuvers in business history, Microsoft decided to integrate the browser into its operating system. The analysis above represents a case of an entrant moving from a browser application into the market for operating systems and then facing reciprocal entry by the dominant supplier from the latter market. Netscape surely did not anticipate Microsoft's brilliant move.

Competing by raising the stakes is, therefore, an adventure where each party uses increasing quantities of resources to find new applications and to provide new sources of value to customers. The direction in which the technology develops, determines the ultimate winner. To anticipate how this process will evolve is very difficult. Microsoft's strength is that it can invest its massive software development resources into any new development. Its weakness is that any new product has to be compatible with its previous software releases. Compatibility dominates over other concerns, such as performance and timing. Recently, some security problems in Microsoft's browsers have been attributed to the speed with which Microsoft has to work and the difficulty of combining Internet software with its traditional desktop operating systems and application software. Netscape has no previous commitments to be concerned about. It has pieced together a team of software people totally committed to the one task of Internet software. Its connectedness is completely compatible with the Internet culture. Its weakness is that of any upstart. Microsoft may be able to outperform it merely on the basis of strength of its resources.

In spite of the economic uncertainty, one outcome is clear. Companies that cannot join in the escalation game, drop out. They exit or are acquired. The same holds for companies that cannot justify to themselves, in the light of their other activities, why they should join the escalation game. This explains why Compuserve and AOL gave up, shortly after sinking tens of millions of dollars into the battle.

Raising the stakes may not only lead to exit but also to entry. Raising the stakes increased the economic potential of the Internet. This increased the interaction between the Internet and various industries active in the use, distribution and supply of information. This in turn brings new players into the field. For example, Lotus pioneered the market for groupware. This is software that uses a company's internal computer network to allow employees to exchange information. The Lotus Notes software stores the communication in databases. This development was initially entirely separate from the Internet. However, one outcome of the Microsoft-Netscape battle was the possibility to use browsers and e-mail for giving access to information stored locally within a company. This has forced Lotus to make Notes web-enabled. It now includes a browser. Lotus's response demonstrates that raising the stakes can change the terms of competition. It changes the linkages between an industry and its environment and may draw in new players, with unforeseen effects on the players caught in a raising-the-stake game.

This case study illustrates the extent to which firms can mistakenly change their scope. The online networks and others failed to secure a foothold in the browser market. It shows the importance of feedback that results from learning processes (browsers have made the operating system more user friendly), of reciprocal entry (between browsers and operating systems) and of strategies that raise the stakes (for example by linking browsers to standards). It also shows how unpredictable the process is. As these activities developed the Internet's potential, they drove out some suppliers of browsers, while attracting suppliers into adjacent markets (such as groupware). Existing players such as Microsoft and Lotus can reap economies of scope, but they are less flexible than an upstart such as Netscape.

11.6 CONCLUSIONS AND IMPLICATIONS FOR THE SMALL OPEN ECONOMY FACED WITH GLOBALIZATION PRESSURES

This chapter has argued that firms can derive a competitive advantage from unique, superior resources only through creating linkages among them. Shared resources can only be successfully applied to a new market by connecting them to complementary resources, giving employees suitable incentives and by organizing the new activity appropriately. This requirement of linkages, that is connectedness, creates inertia and may prevent firms from benefiting from new opportunities in the future. In a dynamic world, this constitutes a major problem for multi-market firms, for which there is no easy solution, not even in theory. This is one reason for many firms' failure to successfully extend their scope.

The framework developed in this chapter also has four immediate implications for firms from small open economies faced with globalization pressures. First, the issue of effectively managing connectedness is likely to be much more critical for firms from small open economies, as international markets may be much more important to their survival, profitability and growth than the domestic market, even at an early stage of international expansion. This is also consistent with the double diamond thinking described in Chapter 3 in this book by Moon, Rugman and Verbeke. Second, correctly anticipating feedback effects is again likely to be much more important for firms from small open economies, faced with much larger foreign players, who can rely on their connectedness with their domestic diamond when reacting to foreign entry. Third, firms from small open economies, precisely because of their intrinsically vulnerable position when faced with problems of connectedness and feedback in foreign markets, may be better equipped to effectively anticipate and manage unintended dynamic effects of multi-market competition. In fact, they probably should try to build a firm-specific advantage in this area. Fourth, in this era of global mergers and acquisitions, and the more general tendency towards higher concentration in many industries, the analysis presented in this chapter suggests that there may be 'hope' for small niche players even in the most globalized industries. Large firms, especially diversified global MNEs, are very likely to make mistakes regarding the potential of scope economies when penetrating either foreign markets or new activity sectors, for example, as a result of over-abstraction. Hence, smaller firms should recognize the fact that in this case, mere scale and a high diversification level may constitute weaknesses, rather than strengths, in 'guerilla warfare', where the correct anticipation of the enemy's reactions may be more important than the absolute volume of resources at the firms' disposal.

NOTES

1   Multi-market competion theory continues to be a growing field of research. Analytical models that set out basic ideas of multi-market competition theory include Brander (1981), Bulow, Geanakoplos and Klemperer (1985), Calem (1988), Bernheim and Whinston (1990), and Van Wegberg and Van Witteloostuijn (1993). Cairns and Mahabir (1988) and Van Witteloostuijn and Van Wegberg (1992) contain integrative frameworks. Porter (1980, 1985), Karmani and Wernerfelt (1985) and Yip (1989) derive the implications for strategic management. We will limit our discussion to the core concepts and some key empirical findings.
2   Note that it can be controversial whether feedback effects will be positive at all. Moreover, the feedback effect may be positive for some of the firm's current products and negative for others.

REFERENCES

Baumol, W.J., J.C. Panzar and R.D. Willig (1982), *Contestable Markets and The Theory of Industry Structure*, New York: Harcourt Brace Jovanovich.

Bernheim, B.D. and M.D. Whinston (1990), 'Multimarket contact and collusive behaviour', *Rand Journal of Economics*, **21**, 1-26.

Brander, J.A. (1981), 'Intra-Industry trade in identical commodities', *Journal of International Economics*, **11**, 1-14.

Bulow, J.L., J.D. Geanakoplos and P.D. Klemperer (1985), 'Multimarket oligopoly: strategic substitutes and complements', *Journal of Political Economy*, **93**, 488-511.

Cairns, R.D. and D. Mahabir (1988), 'Contestability: a revisionist view', *Economica*, **55**, 269-76.

Calem, P.S. (1988), 'Entry and entry deterrence in penetrable markets', *Economica*, **55**, 171-83.

Edwards, C.D. (1955), 'Conglomerate Bigness as a Source of Power', in National Bureau of Economic Research Conference Report, *Business Concentration and Price Policy*, Princeton, NJ: Princeton University Press.

Feinberg, R.M. (1984), 'Mutual forebearance as an extension of oligopoly theory', *Journal of Economics and Business*, **36** (2), 243-49.

Ghemawat, P. (1991), *Commitment: The Dynamic of Strategy*, New York: The Free Press.

Jensen, R. (1992), 'Reputational spillovers, innovation, licensing and entry', *International Journal of Industrial Organisation*, **10**, 193-212.

Karmani, A. and B. Wernerfelt (1985), 'Multiple point competition', *Strategic Management Journal*, **6**, 87-96.

Milgrom, P. and J. Roberts (1992), *Economics Organisation and Management*, Englewood Cliffs: Prentice-Hall.

Montgomery, C.A. and S. Hariharan (1991), 'Diversified expansion by large established firms', *Journal of Economic Behaviour and Organisation*, **15**, 71-89.

Porter, M.E. (1980), *Competitive Strategy: Techniques for Analyzing Industries and Competitors*, New York: The Free Press.

Porter, M.E. (1985), *Competitive Advantage: Creating and Sustaining Superior Performance*, New York: The Free Press.

Porter, M.E. (1996), 'What is strategy?', *Harvard Business Review*, Nov-Dec, 61-78.

Ramanujam, V. and P. Varadarajan (1989), 'Research on corporate diversification: a synthesis', *Strategic Management Journal*, **10**, 523-51.

Stewart, J.F., R.S. Harris and W.T. Carleton (1984), 'The role of market structure in merger behaviour', *Journal of Industrial Economics*, March, **32** (3), 293-312.

Teece, D.J. (1980), 'Economies of scope and the scope of the enterprise', *Journal of Economic Behaviour and Organisation*, **1**, 223-47.

Van Wegberg, M. and A. Van Witteloostuijn (1993), 'Credible entry threats into contestable markets: a symmetric multimarket model of contestability', *Economica*, **59**, 437-52.

Van Witteloostuijn A. and M. Van Wegberg (1992), 'Multimarket competition: theory and evidence', *Journal of Economic Behaviour and Organisation*, **18** (2), July, 273-82.

Von Tunzelmann, N. and L. Soete (1987), 'Diffusion and Market Structure with Converging Technologies', *Research Memorandum RM 87-025*, University of Limburg.

Watson, C.M. (1982), 'Counter-competition abroad to protect home markets', *Harvard Business Review*, Jan/Feb 1982, 40-42.

Yip, G.S. (1989), 'Global strategy: in a world of nations?', *Sloan Management Review*, Fall, 29-41.

Index

advanced factors, competitiveness 43
Africa
    Belgian outward investment 153-4
    Belgian platform investors 155
agglomeration economies
    clustering 2, 4, 160
    Japanese firms 161
    types 162-3
agriculture, Belgium 136, 137
alliance capitalism 20, 24, 31, 102
alliances
    connectedness 216
    see also mergers and acquisitions;
        relationships; strategic alliances
AOL 223
Arthur Andersen 203
Asea Brown Boveri 26
Asia
    Belgian outward investment 154
    Belgian platform investors 155
assembly operations, Japanese affiliates,
    Belgium 178
AT&T 213
automotive industry, Belgium
    foreign manufacturers 172
    international competition 156
    Japanese affiliates 166

banking, Belgian trade policy 79, 83
basic conditions, competitiveness 43
Bel-First database 131-2, 156
Belgium
    corporate environment strategy study
        data and methodology 62-5
        results 65-71
    economic performance 93-111
        alliances and networks 102-8
        location-bound and competitive
            advantages 94-5
        RCA measures 95-100
        restructuring 100-102
    Japanese affiliates study 159-84

agglomerations or clusters 162-5
    cluster identification 168-72
    dataset 165-8
    decision-making 180-182
    location motives 172-4, 175
    modes of involvement 175-7
    organizational strategies 177
    research and development 179
    sourcing 177-8
ownership study 129-57
    analytical framework 132-3
    Belgian-based multinationals
        139-49
    data sources 131-2
    inward investment 129, 130, 151-2,
        156
    outward investment 129, 130,
        153-4, 156
    ownership characteristics 133-9,
        140-141
    platform investment 155, 157
trade policy study 75-88
    industries compared 84-7
    managerial approach to political
        economy 77-8
    policy implications 87-8
    results by industry 78-84
benefits, globalization 27-30
Berners Lee, Tim 221
Brandt, Willy 30
browser market 221-4

Carlsson, Ingwar 30
CATI databank 117, 118, 122-4
centralization
    R&D 115
    versus decentralization 23-6
chemical sector, Belgium
    Japanese affiliates 166-8, 170
        joint ventures 176
        location motives 172
China, Belgian outward investment 154

227